CRITICAL CULTURAL STUDIES OF CHILDHOOD

Series Editors:
Marianne N. Bloch and Beth Blue Swadener

This series focuses on reframings of theory, research, policy, and pedagogies in child-hood. A critical cultural study of childhood is one that offers a "prism" of possibilities for writing about power and its relationship to the cultural constructions of child-hood, family, and education in broad societal, local, and global contexts. Books in the series open up new spaces for dialogue and reconceptualization based on critical theoretical and methodological framings, including critical pedagogy; advocacy and social justice perspectives; cultural, historical, and comparative studies of childhood; and post-structural, postcolonial, and/or feminist studies of childhood, family, and education. The intent of the series is to examine the relations between power, lan-guage, and what is taken as normal/abnormal, good, and natural, to understand the construction of the "other," difference and inclusions/exclusions that are embedded in current notions of childhood, family, educational reforms, policies, and the prac-tices of schooling. *Critical Cultural Studies of Childhood* will open up dialogue about new possibilities for action and research.

Single-authored as well as edited volumes focusing on critical studies of childhood from a variety of disciplinary and theoretical perspectives are included in the series. A particular focus is in a reimagining and critical reflection on policy and practice in early childhood, primary, and elementary education. The series intends to open up new spaces for reconceptualizing theories and traditions of research, policies, cul-tural reasonings, and practices at all of these levels, in the United States, as well as comparatively.

The Child in the World/The World in the Child: Education and the Configuration of a Universal, Modern, and Globalized Childhood
Edited by Marianne N. Bloch, Devorah Kennedy, Theodora Lightfoot, and Dar Weyenberg; Foreword by Thomas S. Popkewitz

Beyond Pedagogies of Exclusion in Diverse Childhood Contexts: Transnational Challenges
Edited by Soula Mitakidou, Evangelia Tressou, Beth Blue Swadener, and Carl A. Grant

"Race" and Early Childhood Education: An International Approach to Identity, Politics, and Pedagogy
Edited by Glenda Mac Naughton and Karina Davis

Governing Childhood into the 21st Century: Biopolitical Technologies of Childhood Management and Education
By Majia Holmer Nadesan

Developmentalism in Early Childhood and Middle Grades Education: Critical Conversations on Readiness and Responsiveness
Edited by Kyunghwa Lee and Mark D. Vagle

New Approaches to Early Child Development: Rules, Rituals, and Realities
Edited by Hillel Goelman, Jayne Pivik, and Martin Guhn

Comparative Early Childhood Education Services: International Perspectives
Edited by Judith Duncan and Sarah Te One

Early Childhood Education in Aotearoa New Zealand: History, Pedagogy, and Liberation
By Jenny Ritchie and Mere Skerrett

Early Childhood in Postcolonial Australia: Children's Contested Identities
By Prasanna Srinivasan

Rethinking Readiness in Early Childhood Education: Implications for Policy and Practice
Edited by Jeanne Marie Iorio and William A. Parnell

Global Perspectives on Human Capital in Early Childhood Education: Reconceptualizing Theory, Policy, and Practice
Edited by Theodora Lightfoot-Rueda and Ruth Lynn Peach

Youth Work, Early Education, and Psychology: Liminal Encounters
Edited by Hans Skott-Myhre, Veronica Pacini-Ketchabaw, and Kathleen S. G. Skott-Myhre

Childhood and Nation: Interdisciplinary Engagements
Edited by Zsuzsa Millei and Robert Imre

CHILDHOOD AND NATION

Interdisciplinary Engagements

Edited by

Zsuzsa Millei and Robert Imre

First published 2016 by
PALGRAVE MACMILLAN

The authors have asserted their rights to be identified as the authors of this work in accordance with the Copyright, Designs and Patents Act 1988.

Palgrave Macmillan in the UK is an imprint of Macmillan Publishers Limited, registered in England, company number 785998, of Houndmills, Basingstoke, Hampshire, RG21 6XS.

Palgrave Macmillan in the US is a division of Nature America, Inc., One New York Plaza, Suite 4500, New York, NY 10004-1562.

Palgrave Macmillan is the global academic imprint of the above companies and has companies and representatives throughout the world.

Hardback ISBN: 978–1–137–47782–8
E-PUB ISBN: 978–1–137–47784–2
E-PDF ISBN: 978–1–137–47783–5
DOI: 10.1057/9781137477835

Distribution in the UK, Europe and the rest of the world is by Palgrave Macmillan®, a division of Macmillan Publishers Limited, registered in England, company number 785998, of Houndmills, Basingstoke, Hampshire RG21 6XS.

Library of Congress Cataloging-in-Publication Data

Childhood and nation : interdisciplinary engagements / edited by Zsuzsa Millei and Robert Imre.
    pages cm
Includes index.
ISBN 978–1–137–47782–8 (hardcover : alk. paper)
    1. Children. 2. Nationalism. I. Millei, Zsuzsa, editor. II. Imre, Robert, editor.

HQ767.9.C44557 2015
320.54083—dc23   2015021527

A catalogue record for the book is available from the British Library.

For Bibi and Rezi—
When we met, your lives began.
Soon after, our content ended.
(Inspired by our friend, Lemony.)

CONTENTS

ILLUSTRATIONS

FIGURE

TABLES

Acknowledgment

Zsuzsa Millei acknowledges the funding received from the Relational and Territorial Politics of Bordering, Identities, and Transnationalization Academy of Finland Centre of Excellence grant CoE (grant SA 272168).

CHAPTER 1

Introduction: Childhood and Nation

Zsuzsa Millei and Robert Imre

At the various intersections of academic disciplines, a rich body of work has been produced about the manifold ways that the notions of childhood and nation interweave. Nation and childhood provide frames of reference for societies, subject formation, actions, and particular morals and ethics. Representations, ideals, and futures associated with nation and childhood intensively shape the everyday realities of people. This fertile theme earned its first concerted exploration with Sharon Stephen's book titled *Children and the Politics of Culture*, published in 1995, and the special issue she edited in the journal of *Childhood* (1997) that examined the relationship between conceptualizations of childhood and projects of nation. Stephen's project was one of the first that theorized childhood as cultural and political constructions and focused on the dynamisms between these two modern inventions: childhood and nation. Her book published 20 years ago provided the initial inspiration for this project.

This book offers multiple entry points to investigate the historical entanglements of nation and childhood in their continuous co-construction and representations, and in the lives of those who make up their associated social categories. Each construct is part hope and part history, is about what we choose to remember or forget, and "as an idea, as a social boundary, or as a social institution—[it] is constantly in flux, requiring continual tending and care" (Shanahan 2007, 418). Another specific aspect of this book is that it delivers multidisciplinary engagements with the use of various methodologies that range from literary studies to postcolonial ethnographies, and from childhood studies to critical pedagogy. The chapter selection brings together an international group of scholars from 10 countries to address many pressing questions of today through their studies in 20 different countries: How do national agendas related to economic, social, and political problems exploit children and tighten their regulation? How do representations of nations take advantage of ideals of childhood? Why do nations look to children and search for those characteristics of childhood that help them solve environmental and humanitarian issues? In a transnational world, why are children still considered, socialized, and learn to become national citizens foremost? In what ways are national belonging and exclusions related to racial and gendered notions of national ideals?

The broad aim of the book is to engage with these questions and to provide insightful analyses about our complex social reality marked out by the intersections of childhood and nation. It is hoped that the collected studies provide new perspectives and generate astute understandings that challenge taken-for-granted views, routine actions, and rusty imaginations and point to those newly emerging subjectivities and generative sites for actions "that should not be isolated within a narrowly defined field of 'child research'" (Stephens 1995, 21).

NATION AND ITS RELEVANCE TO THE PROJECT OF "CHILDHOOD AND NATION"

Over the years, the editors have had many discussions with colleagues from a large variety of academic disciplines as well as practitioners in a number of different fields including education and public policy. One major point that continued to be raised was that people around the world were always somehow socialized into a national identity. Effectively, one cannot not be a citizen of a contemporary nation-state, and still have some form of legitimate identity. To be stateless is to be without political power of any kind. For us, this implied that there was prime fodder for a critical examination of what this might mean and what we might be able to do with such an analysis. One way to "start from the beginning" is to examine how the idea of the nation interacts with a lived experience of nationhood, how childhood interacts with the idea of the child and experiences of children, and how these various ideas and experiences interweave each other. In putting together this book, we see the importance of questioning a fundamental assumption: that the "nation" is a cornerstone of the lived experiences of children. It is also important to note that this book is not about nationalism per se, and if people seek to pursue this aspect further, a number of key works are cited in the bibliography to point them in the direction of nationalism studies. Here we are concerned with a very particular aspect of critical childhood studies, that of the nation-state, ideas of nation and their interactions with childhood, and the lived experiences of children.

If we take for granted the idea that nationalism is an instrumental force, designed to deliver cohesiveness of identity, while still embedding diversity, then we are left with a number of problems about children and childhood. The "ethnic"/"civic" divide, and/or the primordialist versus modern debate in nationalism studies (Armstrong 1982; Breuilly 1996), has been surpassed and superseded by other, more nuanced, debates around power and belonging in a national context. While these debates occur in nationalism studies, even progressive social sciences and humanities are often bound by national discourses and frames of some kind.

On one hand, this is an understandable problem, since the bureaucratic arms of states control our physical movements and dictate policies of all kinds, including the types of foods we eat, what our children must read in schools, and how we can access various forms of media electronically. Such a frame is an inescapable part of the daily lives and activities of people around the world. Policies of governments and political parties establish the rules governing what we can and cannot do universally. As such, being critical of the interaction between the lived realities of childhood and the modern nation-state, we have not "chosen sides" among the numerous dichotomous analyses that present themselves in the social science literature about nationalism: cosmopolitanism versus patriotism, ethnic ties versus civic ties, primordialism versus modernism, nationalism versus universalism, and so on (Connor 1993; Brubaker 1996, 2012). Our purpose here was to gather those analyses that could present a series of views on what nationalist discourse could mean for critical childhood studies.

On the other hand, it is also important to acknowledge the importance of the nation-state as the prime organizing political and social force in the industrial age (Gans 2003). Debates about the role of the state, and the importance of nationalism itself in the breakup of various empires and dynastic political rule, are also about modernizing and delivering materially better lives for citizens (Smith 1986). As such, this book is situated in the midst of these debates and the various analyses in the chapters are a way to further the analyses that began in previous decades.

This can then bring us to questions of legitimacy of national discourses, levels of inclusiveness for children in society and how responses to these national discourses can and do occur, and how debates about "inter-" or "multiculturalism" and different forms of pluralism take shape. The authors of this book have addressed portions of the debate about childhood and nation.

THE BIRTH OF NATION AND CHILDHOOD

With the consolidation of modern nation-states and a modern form of nationalism during the nineteenth century, a concomitant modern conception of "the child" and "childhood" emerged associated with notions of freedom from work and duty to learn (Thernborn 1996; Hendrick 1997). The newly formed "social sciences," such as sociology, also delivered conceptualizations of the nation as a living organism "whose physical and mental health was linked to that of the children, who themselves in a state of flux, were its most crucial components" (Kociumbas 1997, 131). The scientific focus on the national organism's "inefficiencies" increased concerns regarding children worldwide. The developing nation-states, extension of suffrage to all males and then to females, the universal applicability of law, and the creation of a citizenry that can bear political responsibilities required a population prepared for rights and responsibilities. The founding of the secular government school system and enlisting mothers for the moralization of children had major relevance in this environment since it provided a platform for the formation of future citizenry from children (Hunter 1994). Nikolas Rose (1989) further elaborates:

> The educational apparatus would be the means of inculcating the aspirations of citizenship in children—the will, as well as the means, to organise their lives within a project of self-betterment through diligence, application and commitment to work, family and society. (187–188)

These discourses constituted "the child" in relation to citizenship, as a key to national efficiency and facilitated an increased focus on developing the institutional grounds and scientific knowledge for children's education, welfare, and health during these decades. Scientific disciplines underpinned by Enlightenment notions of progress and reason, such as medicine, biology, child study and emerging developmental psychology, psychoanalysis, and educational sciences, all contributed to meanings of "the child" and the management of childhood to help national progress (Rose 1989; Steedman 1995; Bloch and Popkewitz 2000; Burman 2008, 2013).

By these sciences the prototypical "child" subject from a "Minority World" perspective was depicted as having an interiority filled with an "essence" of who he or she is (national or otherwise) and who progresses through "advancements." This notion made the development of children parallel with the development of nations (Burman 2008) as less or more advanced or less or more "primitive" (see also Hopkins in this book). Various problems about how to regulate citizens were also made parallel with how to raise the next generation of citizens (Meredyth and Tyler 1993; Millei 2008). The resulting imaginaries—childhood and nation intertwined—produced normative notions, relations, and images that underlie expectations about the present and future of nations, and characteristics, actions, and ethics for its citizens. Being taken for granted and existing deeply seated, the intertwined ideas of childhood and nation are hard to unravel and critique (see exemptions in postcolonial works of Castañeda 2002; Cannella and Viruru 2004; Burman 2008; Hopkins this volume).

More specifically, particular notions of childhood help in reproducing certain views about nations, for example, that they are democratic. In the Danish and Norwegian contexts, Anne Trine Kjørholt (2007) studied children's participatory projects and concluded that by facilitating such projects these nations helped to reinforce a view about themselves as democratic by enabling children's civic participation. In another example, Christopher Drew (2011) examined the discursive constitution of Australian childhoods in Qantas advertising. Drew (2011, 321) explored notions of "freedom," "race," "youth," and "adventure" that typify and (re)affirm "the public consciousness towards Australian childhood identity"; childhood in these advertisements also perform the nation and homeland and re/produce a kind of Australian national identity.

As part of this project on "Childhood and Nation," Affrica Taylor (2014) explored how discourses and symbols of the young Australian nation were strongly intertwined with images of children and childhood. Taylor (2014) in her analysis of an iconic Australian children's book, *Dot and the Kangaroo*, examined the ways in which settler children and kangaroos were enlisted into the cultural politics of colonialist nation-building to trouble notions of the Indigenous population as "backward" or "primitive." "Child as nation" is also at the center of Lucy Hopkins's chapter in this book. By examining the simultaneous growth and deliberate conflation of concepts of "the child" and the "nation" in Salman Rushdie's *Midnight's Children*, Hopkins highlights how Rushdie troubles and rewrites not only colonialist views of societies as "primitive" or "childish" but also manages to problematize the dominant views of childhood that informs this thinking.

In another chapter in this book, Miaowei Weng, through her analysis of children's narratives in the novel and film *The South*, outlines memories of nation that the generations of Franco's children recall. These memories not only create historical perspectives of the nation but also emotionally charge the democratic elements of current imaginaries. These explorations and critiques continue the agenda Sharon Stephens proposed in her special issue in the *Childhood* journal in 1997, to consider the place of "the child" and "childhood" in the national imaginary.

Mikko Joronen takes the treatment of children under occupied territories as his case to help characterize and test the limits of historical and current forms of government. Joronen's analysis of the regulation, control, and abuse of children and childhood in contemporary Palestine outlines certain attributes and statuses of children and soldiers representing the governmental apparatus at work. Joronen provides a sobering insight into how ingrained institutional racism and violence lead to denying children's status as children and open various and legitimated ways to ill-treat children. His case study not only takes the parallel between the regulation of the child and adult citizen to new, extreme levels but also questions the very nature of society that is taking shape in front of the international community's eyes.

In their relationality, childhood and nation lend and borrow meanings from one another as they dynamically co-construct each other. In this complex relationship some aspects of childhood and endowments of children are highlighted and at the same time occluded. In a similar manner some imaginaries of nation are strengthened and some are forgotten when used in relation to childhood. Trish Lunt, in this book, analyses the ways in which selected books on asylum seekers position children readers as the originators of a more humanitarian approach. She helps us question what aspects of the human that is still present in childhood a hostile Australian national approach misses. Her analysis points to a particular relation between childhood and nation, when adults "look to children to educate us" (Burman 2013, 229). To contrast, Lunt highlights the imaginaries of the "white nation" and its hostile orientations toward the arriving children based on skin color. Erica Burman's (2013) critical appraisal of the standpoint of children as educators helps to think further about "the traces of duplication or replication in . . . transposition[s]" of childhood and nation. It helps to highlight "the suppressions, the clashes, conflicts and indeed contradictions" these constructions hold for each other (Burman 2013, 238).

Nation, Childhood, and the Present

Stephen's (1997) second agenda in her special issues was to understand the consequences of nationalist discourses and projects for children. Historically, the state's interest in children has always been about a nation's future (Jenks, 1996); however, through these projections children's present is more intensively regulated and managed. For the state, as Harry Hendrick (1997) argues, children represent "investments in future parenthood, economic competitiveness, and a stable democratic order" (46). In debates about the future, childhood stands in the crosscurrent of various competing cultural and political projects that shape children's present realities and experiences (James and James, 2004).

Competing cultural and political projects are formed at the intersections of gender, race, citizenship, culture, religion, and nation, and construct individual subjectivities and projects of nations that cannot be theorized and debated as separate phenomena. The closest entanglement of gender and nation is the question of women's right to decide whether to have children or not and related to that their responsibility in raising the next generation (Yuval-Davis 1998). Three agendas are related to this right: first, maintaining or increasing the population as part of national interest; second, controlling the population to avoid future disaster; and third, controlling the "quality" of next generations informed by eugenicist discourses and based on race and class. Antonia Darder (2006), in her paper titled "Colonized Wombs? Reproduction Rights and Puerto Rican Women," discusses how mother's wombs served as sites of intervention for the government of United States after the Second World War to tackle Puerto Rico's independence attempts. As part of a complex intervention strategy, a Puerto Rican mother's right to give birth was taken away with the forced use of contraceptives and surgical sterilization. In the name of "development" the birth of a new generation of biologically "un-pure" offspring was prevented as part of the suppression of an entire population of Puerto Ricans. In this book and with a heartbreaking account of the killings of Palestinian children, Mikko Joronen similarly argues that the ethno-national backgrounds of the victims provide justification for their differential treatment to Israeli youth and for taking away their status as children.

Various other national projects sought to control the purity of populations by forcefully intervening in children's lives in many parts of the world. Margaret Somerville (2014) recounts the history of the Stolen Generation, the removal of Indigenous children born from "mixed race" couples in Australia, with a contemporary story of the traditional possum skin cloak and its power to provide a means for reconciliation. As a legacy of Australian colonial history and subsequent white nation policies, the construction of the Australian nation as white remains powerful. Prasanna Srinivasan explores how this legacy and culture regulate children's everyday life in Australian preschools where being Australian is constructed from a taken-for-granted "white" and "cultureless" position. Srinivasan demonstrates that the fact that children can recognize differences of many kinds does not mean anything outside of a particular context that explains how to categorize that perceived difference. As children use "race" and "color" set against the taken-for-granted construction of being Australian in the preschool, they easily classify each other as "Australian" and "not Australian," the outsider.

Culture is a "dynamic contested resource" (Yuval-Davis 1998, 23) that is used differently by differently positioned members of a national collectivity, such as policy-makers or educators. Esther Miedema's chapter in this book explores how different stakeholders construct particular notions of desirable male and female citizenship related to different understandings of the cultural project of nation-building in Mozambique. Miedema accomplishes this task by teasing apart a complex cultural project to show how socialist ideology and colonial, traditional, modernist, familial, and gendered discourses are entwined and performed at multiple scales in the nation to construct gendered citizenship and education's role in enculturating youth. She argues that Mozambican nation-building marks out the responsibility for a young man to "take care of himself" by being an enterprising individual in the knowledge economy. For a young woman, responsibility falls differently. Girls must take care of the nation by being the "mothers of the nation" and by educating the young with good morals, coupled with only a secondary role to be entrepreneurs and that is only in small-scale and informal markets.

Cultural resources are also used differently in the Irish context, as shown by Marguerita Magennis. Magennis critically evaluates the Irish educational system and associated culture that it is divided on religious grounds. As culture intersects with religion, it produces notions of being Irish. Schools and other spheres where children participate re/produce these ideals through everyday forms of nationalism (Billig 1995). In the context of the two Irelands and to cater for non-Irish migrants and the Roma population, multicultural education aims toward a harmonious future, but this project's attempts often fall short when they meet the everyday practices of inclusion and exclusion based on religion and a repeatedly reaffirmed "traditional" national culture.

NATION AND SPACE

Jouni Häkli (2008) succinctly summarizes the modern idea of nationalism as "rooted in space, concretely and mythically." Nationalism is a specific form of territoriality that incorporates a struggle over land and a socio-spatial consciousness that links "territory with culture, language, history and memory" (Paasi 1999, 5). Space is, in itself, a socially constructed view of the world that both "reads" and "read through" cultural and historical knowledge (Murdoch 2006). The national space therefore is filled with hegemonic social-spatial relations that produced them through historical struggles and homogenization (Bauman 1992). Discourses of the "nation" draw upon and reinscribe perceptions of social continuity and cohesion to the spatiality of the bordered country. Disrupting this continuity are, for instance, the Indigenous or migrant communities, whose existence patterns the homogeneity of the nation in particular ways to account for differences (Bauman 1992). Homogeneous national spaces are also crisscrossed with geopolitical trajectories and are overlaid with emotional geographies.

Trish Lunt, in her exploration of children's books that depict the arrival and experiences of "colored" asylum seekers, adds current geopolitical trajectories to the examination of childhood and nation that work against sedimented historical understandings of Australia as a "white nation." The same way as asylum seeker children are denied entry to the geographical area of Australia and kept in dire circumstances in offshore detention centers, their imaginary of a "new life" emotionally attached to imaginary spaces of Australian land are also broken. In another chapter Bree Akesson explores children's developing national identities that are inextricably linked to the divided land of Palestine and how, through their familial relations, they learn to love a land where they have never lived and only heard memories of.

Nationalism is underpinned by a view and an acceptance that nations are the inevitable organizers of "our" world (Paasi 1999), that everyone belongs to a nation, and that all have certain beliefs and attachments to these imagined spaces and communities (Billig 1995). The representation of the world as divided into "mutually exclusive spatial entities: the nation-states" is a particular taken-for-granted territorial imagination that has now been challenged by those "views that conceptualize the contemporary world more in terms of flows and connectivity" (Häkli 2008, 6). Reflecting this view, current studies trouble the assumptions that children develop a homogeneous national imagination, especially those children whose loyalties also fall outside the borders of a nation-state.

For example, Jason Hart (2002, 36) describes, through his field-work in a Palestinian refugee camp in Jordan, how children's imaginary expresses belonging "with wider, transnational processes as well as with notions of [a] more localized and clearly bounded community." Being the grandchildren of originally dispossessed people living in this camp, children are influenced by three main, institutional sources of nationalism: "Palestinian nationalist movement, the Jordanian state and the Islamist movement" (Hart 2002, 37). Hart's study demonstrates the ways in which children take up, resist, and reshape imaginaries of the nation and form dynamic subjectivities in the complex cultural politics of their daily lives. Adding further complexity to examinations of children's national identity formation through flows and connectivities, Bree Akesson (2015) and Stine Bruland (2012) insert the importance of generational relationships in transnational families that Paula Pustulka, Magdalena Ślusarczyk, and Stella Strzemecka also explore in this book. These studies highlight the complex territorial, spatial, relational, and generational nature of children's learning as continuously becoming trans/national subjects.

Re/producing the Nation

Representations, images, and myths of the nation construct an imagined space of the "homeland" that has a subjective and "felt and cared for center of meaning" (Cresswell, 2004, 38). They describe what is familiar or common sense, the "here," "at home" that forms a part of "our psychology of national attachments . . . our common sense in its historical context, 'our' beliefs about nationhood, and about the naturalness of belonging to a nation" (Billig 1995, 16). This type of feeling is often divided by social scientists as "patriotism"— love of one's nation—and "nationalism"—an aggressive feeling and cause of war (Snyder 1976; Janowitz 1983). Established nation states routinely reproduce themselves through symbolic resources and forms of nationalism (Billig 1995; Benwell and Dodds 2011). Everyday forms of nationalism include not only those actions and objects that symbolize the nation (Billig 1995) but also everything that "we do" as national subjects under the influence of the state. These actions are particular because they could turn any minute into opportunities for resistance, such as the campaign in favor of bilingual road signs in Wales between 1967 and 1975 (John and Merriman 2009).

Mapping nationalist discourses in children's experiences more broadly, research demonstrates that children (even young as a couple of years old) mobilize particular representations of nation and land for their identifications and use them for the inclusion and exclusion of others (e.g., Coles 1986; Stephens 1995; MacNaughton 2001; Scourfield et al. 2006; Cheney 2007; Woronov, 2007; Beneï 2008; Habashi 2008; Zembylas 2010; Srinivasan, 2014). As discussed before, in these identifications the context is given to recognized difference by constructs of "nation" and "nationality," and their intersections with race, class, gender, religion, language, land, and other cultural markers.

The largest body of work with regard to how children relate to the nation is located in the cognitive developmental paradigm (Scourfield et al. 2006). Martyn Barrett (2007/2013) in his book titled *Children's Knowledge, Beliefs and Feelings about Nations and National Groups* provides a comprehensive review of the existing research in psychology and offers particular child development theories to explain how children grow in the domain of national identification and acquisition of attitudes toward their nation. Barrett conceptualizes national identity as a structural part of a person's identity that is variably "filled with an essence" depending on individual differences and "cross-national variation" that hinge upon "the specific sociohistorical contexts within which children develop" (Oppenheimer and Barrett 2011, 3). In other words, Barrett links the development of national identity *in* children to acquisition of knowledge of and attitudes to the state and to sociohistorical factors that are present in their particular contexts.

While some scholars suggest that we know little about school-aged and younger children's relation to the nation (such as Scourfield et al. 2006), a growing body of work in the social sciences explores the intersections of various dimensions of identity, national subject formation, and spatial and temporal dimensions of nationality in regard to children. The two special issues of the journal of *Global Studies of Childhood* (2014 and 2015) and this book continue this work by providing forums for concerted investigations. Among these studies are those that examine the formation of national subjects from the perspective of the state. This field of research accounts for heterogeneous institutions and elements, such as social policies, the law, institutional arrangements, and discourses. They consider these elements as irreducible to the state and also differentiated from civil society. Different social institutions, such as the family, pre/schools, and media provide important sites for these studies that delineate the complex regulation and re/production of childhood as part of national projects.

Other studies consider the perspective of children as they partake in or learn about national projects that often ascribe to them homogeneous or unified national identities. Through their participation, children re/produce and/or resist these prescribed ways of being. Prasanna Srinivasan discusses the complex and often silenced ways in which young children re/produce the imaginary of the Australian "white nation" and participate in processes of exclusion and inclusion. Her work demonstrates children's skillful and changing self-positioning as national subjects that often troubles homogeneous notions of what nationality in a context entails. Bree Akesson shows how discourses that produce the nation of Palestine, as attached both to a territory and to symbolical spaces of the "homeland" formed in memories of the past, are handed down to children in families. She also brings examples from interviews with children and family members about how children encounter various signs, objects, symbols, and actions in their everyday lives and how these re/make the nation and divisions associated with them in various, and emotionally charged, ways. Paula Pustulka, Magdalena Ślusarczyk, and Stella Strzemecka provide an insight into the many ways Polish children who live in Norway construct themselves through national, transnational, and global discourses that they encounter through their personal and object relations. Family, peer groups, and cultural constructions all play important parts in their feelings of belonging and the formation of their fluid identities.

In relation to nations, children are frequently labeled as citizens. Notions of children as citizens are rooted in Enlightenment rationality (Wallace 1995). Together with notions that constitute children as "social actors and holders of rights"(Tisdall and Punch 2012, 249), citizenship constructs children as part of the imaginary of nations, as citizens, with particular rights, responsibilities, and relations. Citizenship, nation, and nationality are politically powerful ideas and their use in relation to childhood and children produce powerful effects. However, it is now widely accepted that there is a gap between "the child" and "citizen" (Cheney 2007). This is partly due to the hegemonic relationship between childhood and adulthood, to childhood being conceived of as an apprenticeship to adult citizenship (James and Prout 1990), protectionism, and that children are not recognized in laws and mores despite them reaching particular competencies before they reach "official" adulthood (Archard 1993). Children, however, cannot fully exercise their participatory citizenship rights; if they can, they do so in adult constructed political environments and processes (Kallio and Häkli 2011).

The presence of intense globalizing processes and ubiquitous discourses of global citizenship and the cosmopolitan imaginary bring complexity to how children experience their multiple belongings today. With increasing interconnectedness through technology and the media, the presence of travel in a large number of "Minority World" childhoods, and children's personal and object relations that extend to the globe play an important part in the formation of their trans/national subjectivities. Globalization, as Doreen Massey (1999, 23, cited in Aminy, 2002) argues,

> is a thoroughgoing, world-wide, restructuring of...space-times, along particular lines. It is a remaking of those, inherited but always temporary and provisional, spaces, places, cultures which are themselves the hybrid products of previous restructurings.

The context of globalization and mobilities, such as physical, imaginative, and virtual travel, effect transformations in social lives and contribute to the formation of new kinds of transnational or debordered social spaces, identities, and relations, often with respect to contemporary forms of governance (see Vertovec and Cohen 2002).

Globalizing processes associated with new forms of uncertainty or "risk" impact upon social organization more generally (Beck 1999, 2002). Within this altered imagination of "space-time" and "society" new perspectives on the local and the universal emerge (Appadurai 1996; Rizvi 2006). Views, conceptualizations, and experiences are brought into interconnected networks of global communication and imagination that pose several problematics for understanding nation and childhood, and nation-centered analysis of policies, provisions, and experiences of childhood. By engaging with this context, Alistair Ross's empirical investigations offer a glimpse into how youth in various newly joined European Union nations portray their national belonging and how those are being reshaped in everyday circumstances that disregard national borders or gain a global reach.

Some analysts, from philosophical and methodological angles, propose that we have entered a new historical era, a so-called age of cosmopolitanism (Urry 2000, 186). Others argue for the need to overcome "methodological nationalism" (Beck 2002) and for considerations concerning "internal globalization" (Beck 2002, 28) and the emergence of a construction of global publics (Beck 2002; Delanty 2006). Altered socio-spatial relations, mobility and risk, and the emergence of a perception and sense of "world openness" and global publics transform notions of childhood, experiences of children, and children's ways of understanding the world. The growing number of references to global and cosmopolitan childhoods, and the volume of migrant and stateless children and emerging identities, present important challenges for states and for research and theorization.

Tatjana Zimenkova examines what views of the world, subjectivities, and ethics can be found in Russian curriculum and policy documents and what modes of self-perceptions, loyalties, and responsibilities those suggest to children. She calls for conceptualizations of national citizenship that engage with the so-called age of "cosmopolitanism." Joining her quest to reshape children's sense of national belonging and therefore to effect the future, Trish Lunt argues for embracing a form of humanitarian "hospitality" that lies outside the government's exclusionary practice. While their projects' intention is unquestionable, their and others' examinations in this book still hinge upon particular imaginaries of the world as nation-bound and bordered, and notions of childhood that offer respite and hope in our contemporary contexts of environmental degradation, austerity measures, and worries about the future of humanity. Migration and intercultural studies also suffer from forms of methodological nationalism. This goes to show the embeddedness of modern notions of childhood and nation in our contemporary understandings of societies, the difficulty of their critical appraisal, and the methodological contentions these notions pose for researchers. These are challenges that few social scientists can overcome.

An interesting example of a successful attempt involves the work of Rogers Brubaker and colleagues (2006). In particular, they manage to go beyond what we already know to be true: that nations, ethnicities, and groups labeled as such are social constructions. The problem for us goes much further, since there are shifting contexts in which these groups and group affiliations are created and made legitimate or not, and are often imposed and deployed in ways that have more to do with power than any "organic" affiliation. In *Ethnicity without Groups* (2004), Brubaker challenges these embedded ideas and asks analysts to examine social and political practice rather than imposing analytical categories to label identities, and examine how it is that "groupism" remains, or, in other words, when people occupy the same space, it should not be assumed that "natural" (even opposing) groups are formed based on external identification of persons based on nationality or ethnicity. Similarly, literature around migration, transnational flows, refugee and asylum-seeker movements, and the general movement of people around the planet still take the view of "migration as deviance," and identify people within a national border based on this difference, migrants, independent of the examination of social practices. This means that even though analysts seek to support rights of groups and individuals, or seek to uphold national and transnational agreements that categorically better the lives of people moving from place to place, the movements from one political jurisdiction to another is still examined as a case of deviance from a taken-for-granted norm where migrants' lives are examined as a minority (often oppositional) group to the mainstream. Rather than viewing multiplicity and diversity as a "natural" and/or "organic" condition of both nation-states and populations, contemporary discourse around migration places the migratory patterns of groups and individuals into a structure that views them as "problem people" to nations and treats them as such.

In turning a critical eye to the ways that childhood and nation are groupings of people themselves, the intersection of those two categories marks the beginning of the experiences we examine here, and as such we have tried to put together a series of analyses that might help to trouble the fundamental assumptions associated with those. We hope that the chapters in this book help illuminate some of these issues, problems, and contentions, and provide an impetus for further critical work.

THE STRUCTURE OF THE BOOK

We have divided the book into two components. One part addresses the broader idea of the "nation" and how its plural form as various national myths, representations, nation forming projects, and their resistances, for example, function. The other part deals with what we have termed "subject formation." In the first part of the book the chapters analyze various formulations of childhood and nation and how they operate in creating the boundaries for human beings. In the second part of the book we grouped together those chapters that deal more with subject formation in terms of both bordered national territory and forms of de-bordered transnationalisms experienced in the relevant childhoods in question. These are necessarily somewhat artificial divisions, as the chapters all overlap in their concerns. The following summaries of the individual chapters will help readers to develop their own research that takes further the agendas that we have set here, as well as position the overall project of the book in the innovative territory in which it belongs.

Chapter 2 focuses on the resonance of nationalistic language in children's everyday narratives exchanged in early childhood settings. "Children as national subjects" is a concept that is less explored especially within Australian early childhood settings, with a few exceptions. Prasanna Srinivasan uses some of these narratives to introduce "race"-based nationalism in children's voices. Through these narratives, the chapter highlights how the ownership of national identity is not available for all children, and its impact on the identities of those children who are "brown." The chapter draws upon postcolonial and critical race theories to engage with and challenge these discourses, and to outline some of the counter discourses that can be made available for these educators.

Ideas of childhood and the child have long been central to the imagining of the nation: tropes of immaturity, growth, and development that underpin notions of childhood are co-opted into the service of the nation. The third chapter by Lucy Hopkins explores the ways that discourses of nationalism and nationhood make use of the discursive figure of the child in the process of naturalizing and justifying a range of dividing practices through an analysis of Salman Rushdie's novel, *Midnight's Children*. The chapter examines how the child subject in the novel is conflated with the nation in order to parody and therefore problematize the naturalization of linear narratives of progress that underpin both dominant discourses of national development and child development. The use of a specified, localized child *as* the nation enables a reworking of the child figure's place in the conceptualization of the relationships between nation and citizen, colonizer and colonized, and the home and the world.

Miaowei Weng's chapter examines childhood narratives as national allegories of Spain under the Franco regime as well as during the democratic transition. It revisits Adelaida García Morales's 1981 novella *The South* and Víctor Erice's 1983 film by the same title and historicizes them in the contexts of early Francoism as well as the transition period. It explores the political timing of these two productions and the allegorical means by which they render the reflections on the Francoist nation reconfiguration project as well as on the relevance of the historical past to present and future democratic Spain.

Chapter 5 by Trish Lunt considers the ways in which Australian picture books about asylum seekers (2004–2009) situate readers as either distanced from or involved in the action of the text. When readers are invited to become agential subjects within a text, the prompts for ethical and hospitable action are more demanding. Texts for children are instruments of socialization and therefore often mirror public discourse. Tensions of humanitarian hospitality are especially important in relation to the contemporary Australian political terrain in which asylum is denied and national borders are purposely constructed to exclude the displaced. It is evident in the spatial codings of the analyzed picture books that their sympathies lie outside government positions of exclusionary practice. The ways in which cultural consciousness is embedded in texts for children are revealed in these texts in ways that situate child readers as progenitors of a more humanitarian (future) society.

After decades of occupation and military order, a complex set of exceptional practices, regulations, orders, laws, and overlapping/

offsetting clauses has become normalized as a part of the everyday life in the Palestinian territories. In order to understand how this cavalcade of exceptions produces a widespread, systematic, and institutionalized ill-treatment of Palestinian children today, the sixth chapter by Mikko Joronen focuses on three questions in particular. First, the ways that the security apparatus of the state of Israel keeps its strategic functions operative through the culture of impunity and acceptance, which together allow the loose functioning of the security apparatus. Second, the different Israeli security apparatus that frames Palestinian children as part of the wider security threat. Finally, how Palestinian children are governed through the production of the fear of violence and death, which he approaches in terms of thanatopolitical securitization.

The Republic of Ireland and Northern Ireland have become "multicultural nations" over recent years. In chapter 7 Marguerita Magennis examines these changes and the way they have reinvigorated considerations about the significance of national identity especially in terms of relationships to nonnationals. The presence of nonnationals also accentuate the fact that debating about national identity is not so much about discovering the truth regarding the past, but about understanding the future a nation hopes to shape.

Growing up under occupation, Palestinian children are developing identities that are inextricably linked to the territories of the divided land of Israel and Palestine. Drawing from qualitative research with Palestinian children and families living in the West Bank and East Jerusalem, Bree Akesson in chapter 8 explores the relationship between territoriality and the national identities of Palestinian children and families. Chapter 9 focuses on young people's narratives in constructing their sense of identities with their country, and how these are used to distinguish themselves as a generation distinct from their parents and grandparents. Alistair Ross includes a study of 13–19-year-olds in 12 European countries that were formerly in the communist bloc, and have since joined (or are joining) the European Union.

Chapter 10 engages with the question of how current national and global discourses shape perceptions of childhood/youth, young people's lived experiences, and their roles as citizens. Building on a qualitative multi-method study that explored participants' perspectives on the aims of HIV- and AIDS-related education, Esther Miedema draws on feminist scholars' work to analyze how policy-makers and educators perceived moral fragmentation of society due to "modern" phenomena, such as the multicultural character of cities and an aggressive media. In chapter 11 three researchers collaborate as members of the Transfam project *Doing Family in a Transnational Context* (2013–2016) to examine dimensions of self-identification among Polish migrant children in Norway. The arguments are linked to the child-hood/mobility nexus and foreground children's voices and agency in mobility/migration scholarship, as well as take into account the particularities of the Polish framings of family and ethnic identities. The orientation toward global issues emerges as an integral part of educational practices and policies in many countries. Often curricula and educational materials produce a harmonious picture of responsible citizens, easily switching between different loyalties and obligations and profiting from globalization processes. This picture is challenged by questions of nation-state interests, citizens' responsibilities, and loyalties. The final chapter by Tatjana Zimenkova elaborates empirically on the questions of and troubles what modes of self-perceptions, loyalties, and responsibilities the Russian curricula and educational programs suggest to the learner with the depiction of global issues.

BIBLIOGRAPHY

Acemoglu, Daron, and James A. Robinson. 2006. *Economic Origins of Dictatorship and Democracy.* New York: Cambridge University Press.
Akesson, Bree. 2015. "Trees, flowers, prisons, flags: Frustration and hope shaping national identity for Palestinian families." *Global Studies of Childhood* 5 (1): 33–46.
Aminy, Ash. 2002. "Spatialities of globalisation." *Environment and Planning* 34: 385–399.
Anderson, Benedict. 1991. *Imagined Communities.* London and New York: Verso Press.
Appadurai, Arjun. 2001. "Grassroots globalization and the research imagination." In *Globalization,* edited by A. Appadurai, 1–21. Durham, NC: Duke University Press.
Archard, David. 1993. *Children: Rights and Childhood.* London: Routledge.
Armstrong, John A. 1997. "Religious nationalism and collective violence." *Nations and Nationalism* 3 (4): 597–606.
——— 1982. *Nations before Nationalism.* Chapel Hill: University of North Carolina Press.
Barr, Michael. 2010. "Religious nationalism and nation-building in Asia: An introduction." *The Australian Journal of International Affairs* 64 (3): 255–261.
Barrett, Martyn. 2013 *Children's Knowledge, Beliefs and Feelings about Nations and National Groups.* Hoboken: Taylor & Francis.
Bauman, Zygmunt. 1992. *Intimations of Postmodernity.* London and New York: Routledge.
——— 1998. *Globalization: The Human Consequences.* New York: Columbia University Press.
Beck, Ulrich. 1999. *World Risk Society.* Cambridge: Polity Press.
———. 2002. "The cosmopolitan society and its enemies." *Public Culture* 19: 17–40.

Beneï, Véronique. 2008. *Schooling Passions: Nation, History, and Language in Contemporary Western India*. Sanford, CA: Stanford University Press.

Bhabha, Homi. 2004. *The Location of Culture*. New York: Routledge Classics.

Billig, Michael. 2005. *Banal Nationalism*. London: Sage.

Breuilly, John. 1996. "Approaches to nationalism." In *Mapping the Nation*, edited by G. Balikrishnan, 146–174. London: Verso.

———. 1993. *Nationalism and the State*. Chicago, IL: University of Chicago Press.

Brown, David. 2000. *Contemporary Nationalism: Civic, Ethnocultural & Multicultural Politics*. New York: Routledge.

———. 1993. *The State and Ethnic Politics in Southeast Asia*. New York: Routledge.

Brubaker, Rogers. 1992. *Citizenship and Nationhood in France and Germany*. Cambridge: Harvard University Press.

———. 1996. *Nationalism Reframed: Nationhood and the National Question in the New Europe*. Cambridge: Cambridge University Press.

———. 2004. *Ethnicity without Groups*. Harvard University Press.

———. 2012. "Religion and nationalism: Four approaches." *Nations and Nationalism* 28 (1): 2–20.

Brubaker, Rogers, Margit Feischmidt, Jon Fox, and Liana Grancea. 2006. *Nationalist Politics and Everyday Ethnicity in a Transylvanian Town*. Princeton, NJ: Princeton University Press.

Bruland, Stine. 2012. Nationalism as meaningful life projects: identity construction among politically active Tamil families in Norway, *Ethnic and Racial Studies*, 35(12), 2134–2152.

Burman, Erica. 2013. "Conceptual resources for questioning 'child as educator.'" *Studies in the Philosophy of Education* 32: 229–243.

———. 2008. *Developments: Child, Image, Nation*. London: BrunnerRoutledge.

Calhoun, Craig. 1997. *Nationalism*. Minneapolis: University of Minnesota Press.

Cannella, Gail S., and Radhika Viruru. 2004. *Childhood and Postcolonization*. New York and London: RoutledgeFalmer.

Castañeda, Claudia. 2002. *Figurations: Child, Bodies, Worlds*. Durham, NC, and London: Duke University Press.

Chatargee, Partha. 1986. *Nationalist Thought in the Colonial World: A Derivative Discourse*. London: Zed Books.

Cheney, Kristen. E. 2007. *Pillars of the Nation: Child Citizens and Ugandan National Development*. Chicago, IL: University of Chicago Press.

Coles, Robert. 1986. *The Political Life of Children*. Boston, MA: Atlantic Monthly Press.

Connor, William. 1993. *Ethnonationalism: The Quest for Understanding*. Princeton, NJ: Princeton University Press.

Conversi, Daniel (ed.). 2004. *Ethno-nationalism in the Contemporary World: Walker Conner and the Study of Nationalism*. New York: Routledge.

Cresswell, Tim. 2004. *Place: A Short Introduction*. Oxford, UK: Wiley-Blackwell.

Darder, Antonia. 2006. "Colonized wombs? Reproduction rights and Puerto Rican women." *The Public: A Paper of the People*. http://publici. ucimc.org/?p=1006

Delanty, Gerard. 2006. "The cosmopolitan imagination: Critical cosmopolitanism and social theory." *The British Journal of Sociology* 57 (1): 25–47.

Deutsch, Karl. 1953. *Nationalism and Social Communication: An Inquiry into the Foundations of Nationality*. Cambridge: MIT Press.

Drew, Christopher. 2011. "The spirit of Australia: Learning about Australian childhoods in Qantas commercials." *Global Studies of Childhood* 1 (4): 321–330.

Freeden, Michael. 1998. "Is nationalism a distinct ideology?" *Political Studies* 46: 748–765.

Gans, Chaim. 2003. *The Limits of Nationalism*. Cambridge: Cambridge University Press.

Gellner, Ernest. 1983. *Nations and Nationalism*. Ithaca, NY: Cornell University Press.

Giddens, Anthony. 1984. *The Nation-State and Violence: A Critique of Historical Materialism*. Cambridge: Polity Press.

Greenfeld, Liah. 1993. *Nationalism: Five Roads to Modernity*. Cambridge: Harvard University Press.

Habashi, Janette. 2008. "Palestinian children crafting national identity." *Childhood* 15 (1): 12–29.

Hart, Jason. 2002. Children and nationalism in a Palestinian refugee camp in Jordan. *Childhood* 9(1): 35–47.

Hastings, Adrian. 1997. *The Construction of Nationhood: Ethnicity, Religion and Nationalism*. Cambridge: Cambridge University Press.

Hauggard, Mark. 2006. "Nationalism and liberalism." In *The Sage Handbook of Nations and Nationalism*, edited by G. Delanty and K. Kumar, 345–356. London: Sage.

Hearn, Jonathan. 2006. *Re-thinking Nationalism: A Critical Introduction*. Basingstoke: Palgrave Macmillan.

Hendrick, Harry. 1997. *Children, Childhood and English Society, 1880–1990*. Cambridge: Cambridge University Press.

Hobsbawm, Eric. 1992. *Nations and Nationalism since 1780: Programme, Myth, Reality*. Cambridge: Cambridge University Press.

Hobsbawm, Eric, and Terence Ranger (eds.). 1983. *The Invention of Tradition*. Cambridge: Cambridge University Press.

Hutchinson, John. 1994. *Modern Nationalism*. London: Fontana.

Hutchinson, John, and Anthony Smith (eds.). 1994. *Nationalism*. Oxford: Oxford University Press.

Ignatieff, Michael. 1993. *Blood and Belonging: Journeys into the New Nationalism*. New York: Farrar, Straus and Giroux.

James, Allison, and Adrian James. 2004. *Constructing Childhood: Theory, Policy and Social Practice*. Basingstoke and New York: Palgrave Macmillan.

James, Allison, and Alan Prout. 1990. *Constructing and Reconstructing Childhood*. London: Falmer.

Juergensmeyer, Mark. 2010. "The global rise of religious nationalism." *Australian Journal of International Affairs* 64 (3): 262–273.

———. 2009. *Global Rebellion: Religious Challenges to the Secular State, from Christian Militias to al Qaeda.* Berkeley: University of California Press.

———. 2003. *Terror in the Mind of God: The Global Rise of Religious Violence.* Berkeley: University of California Press.

———. 1993. *The New Cold War: Religious Nationalism Confronts the Secular State.* Berkeley: University of California Press.

Kallio, Kirsi Paulliina, and Jouni Häkli. 2011. "Are there politics in childhood?" *Space and Polity* 15 (1): 21–34.

Kedourie, Elie. 1993. *Nationalism.* New York: Wiley-Blackwell.

———. 1971 (ed.). *Nationalism in Asia and Africa.* London: Weidenfeld & Nicolson.

Kjørholt, Anne Trine. 2007. Childhood as a Symbolic Space: Searching for Authentic Voices in the Era of Globalisation. Children's Geographies, 5 (1–2), 29–42.

Kymlicka, William. 2001. *Politics in the Vernacular: Nationalism, Multiculturalism and Citizenship.* Oxford: Oxford University Press.

———. 1999. "Misunderstanding nationalism." In *Theorizing Nationalism*, edited by R. Beiner, 131–140. Albany, NY: SUNY Press.

Laitin, David. 2007. *Nation, States and Violence.* Oxford: Oxford University Press.

MacNaughton, Glenda. 2001. "Silences and subtexts of immigrant and non-immigrant children." *Childhood Education* 78 (1): 30–36.

Mann, Michael. 1995. "A political theory of nationalism and its excesses." In *Notions of Nationalism*, edited by S. Periwal, 44–64. Budapest: Central European University Press.

———. 1993. *The Sources of Social Power, Vol. 2 The Rule of Classes and Nation States, 1760–1914.* Cambridge: Cambridge University Press.

———. 1988. *States, War and Capitalism.* Oxford: Blackwell.

Massey, Doreen. 1999. *Power-geometries and the politics of space and time.* Hettner Lecture 1998, Department of Geography, University of Heidelberg

Meredyth, Denise, and Deborah Tyler. 1993. *Child and Citizen: Genealogies of Schooling and Subjectivity.* Griffith University, Queensland, Australia: Special Publication of the Institute for Cultural Policy Studies, Faculty of Humanities, Griffith University.

Millei, Zsuzsa. 2008. "A genealogical study of 'the child' as the subject of pre-compulsory education in Western Australia." Unpublished PhD thesis, Murdoch University, Australia.

Nairn, Tom. 1997. *Faces of Nationalism: Janus Revisited.* London: Verso.

Nielsen, Kai. 1999. "Cultural nationalism, neither ethnic nor civic." In *Theorizing Nationalism*, edited by R. Beiner, 119–120. Albany, NY: SUNY Press.

Oppenheimer, Louis, and Martyn Barrett. 2011. "National identity and in-group/out-group attitudes in children: The role of sociohistorical settings: An introduction to the special issue." *European Journal of Developmental Psychology* 8 (1): 1–4.

Ozkirimli, Umut. 2010. *Theories of Nationalism: A Critical Introduction.* Basingstoke: Palgrave Macmillan.

Rizvi, Fazal. 2006. "Imagination and the globalization of educational policy research." *Globalization, Societies and Education* 4 (2): 193–205.

Rose, N. 1989. *Governing the soul: The shaping of the private self.* New York: Routledge.

Said, Edward. 1994. *Culture and Imperialism.* London: Vintage Books.

Scourfield, Jonathan, Bella Dicks, Mark Drakeford, and Andrew Davies. 2006. *Children, Place and Identity: Nation and Locality in Middle School.* London and New York: Routledge.

Shanahan, Suzanne. 2007. "Lost and found: The sociological ambivalence toward childhood." *Annual Review of Sociology* 33: 407–428.

Smith, Anthony. 2000. "Theories of nationalism: Alternative models of nation formation." In *Asian Nationalism,* edited by M. Leifer, 1–20. Basingstoke: Routledge.

———. 1986. *The Ethnic Origins of Nations.* Oxford: Blackwell.

———. 1971. *Theories of Nationalism.* London: Duckworth.

Spencer, Philip, and Howard Wollman (eds.). 2005. *Nationalism: A Reader.* New Brunswick: Rutgers University Press.

———. 2002. *Nationalism: A Critical Introduction.* London: Sage.

Srinivasan, Prasanna. 2014. *Early Childhood in Postcolonial Australia: Children's Contested Identities.* New York: Palgrave Macmillan.

Steedman, Carolyn. 1995. *Strange Dislocations: Childhood and Sense of Human Interiority, 1780–1930.* London: Virago.

Stephens, Sharon. 1995. "Children and the politics of culture in 'late capitalism.'" In *Children and the Politics of Culture,* edited by S. Stephens, 3–50. Princeton, NJ: Princeton University Press.

Thernborn, Göran. 1996. "Child politics: Dimensions and perspectives." *Childhood* 3: 29–44.

Tisdall, Kay, and Samantha Punch. 2012. "Not so 'new'? Looking critically at childhood studies." *Children's Geographies* 10 (3): 249–264.

Turner, Bryan. 2011. *Religion and Modern Society: Citizenship, Secularisation and the State.* Cambridge: Cambridge University Press.

Urry, John. 2000. "Mobile sociology." *British Journal of Sociology* 51 (1): 185–203.

Vertovec, Steven, and Robin Cohen. 2002. *Conceiving Cosmopolitanism— Theory, Context, Practice.* Oxford: Oxford University Press.

Wallace, Jo-Ann. 1995. "Technologies of 'the child': Towards a theory of the child subject." *Textual Practice* 9 (2): 285–302.

Woronov, Terry. 2007. "Performing the nation: China's children as little red pioneers." *Anthropological Quarterly* 80 (3): 647–672.

Yuval-Davis, Nira. 1998. *Gender and Nation.* London: Sage.

Zembylas, Michalinos. 2010. "Children's construction and experience of racism and nationalism in Greek-Cypriot primary schools." *Childhood* 17 (3): 312–328.

PART I

Government, Representations, and Resistances

CHAPTER 2

"How Come Australians Are White": Children's Voice and Adults' Silence

Prasanna Srinivasan

That is to say there may be 'knowledge' of the body that is not exactly the science of its functioning. … Of course this technology is diffuse, rarely formulated in continuous, systematic discourse; it is often made up of bits and pieces; it implements a disparate set of tools and methods.… Moreover, it cannot be localized in a particular type of institution or state apparatus. (Foucault, 1977, p. 16)

INTRODUCTION

This chapter focuses on the resonance of nationalistic language in children's everyday narratives exchanged in early childhood settings. Children as national subjects is a concept that is less explored especially within Australian early childhood settings, with a few exceptions (see MacNaughton 2001; MacNaughton and Davis 2001, 2009; Skattebol 2005). These works particularly reveal how young children use "race" and "colour" to classify the national subject as "Australian" and the "not Australian," the outsider. I use some of the narratives from my doctoral thesis to introduce such "race"-based nationalism in children's voices. Through these narratives, I highlight how the ownership of national identity is not available for all children, and its impact on the identities of those children who are "brown." In the second part of the chapter I further the inquiry to the discourses of the early childhood educators (ECE) who supported and covertly fuelled children's "race"-based nationalism. I particularly draw upon postcolonial and critical race theories to engage with and challenge these discourses, and to outline some of the counter discourses that can be made available for these educators.

TAINTED BY "WHITENESS": NATIONAL CONCEPTION

This nation called Australia is a colonial conception borne out of the colonization of indigenous spaces. In Australia, early colonizers not just claimed ownership of the space, but also politically governed the nation with overt political discourses that legitimized its "whitening." By "whitening," I mean the overt imposition of colonial conceptions of cultural and political systems that aimed to subjectify and to subjugate individuals and groups with nation and national identity. Although one can argue that Australia, as a multicultural nation, has come out of the clutches of colonization, the colonial conceptions of nation and national subjects have become meaningful entities that define and influence one's identity behaviors. And, these nationalistic concepts were originally attached to not just nation-building, but also to building a "white nation" (Hage 2000, 18–19). The aim of the "White Australia Policy" (1901) was to create, protect, and maintain the national identity of Australia and Australians with overt policies that kept its borders closed for those who were not from "white Anglo-Saxon" or "white Anglo-Celtic" heritage. Moreover, this overt political "whitening" also resulted in the erasure of "black" presence, the original owners of this land from whom this space was forcefully clenched to create this nation, Australia. As stressed by many authors, national identities have become the daily colloquial realities not just in Australia, but also in many modern-day societies (Taylor 2004, 17–21; Appadurai 2006, 4–8). Hence, with nation and national identity, the colonial conceptions undeniably becoming daily realities, the then conceptualized national subject, the "white Australian," too, has become a part of everyday discourses of many individuals' thinking, being, and belonging within Australia, the nation. The demise of the White Australia Policy in the early 1970s has done very little in erasing the association of Australia's national subject with "whiteness." With the historical images of "white Australian" conceptualized through "whitening," many who are naturally "white" still claim and cling to the ownership of this national identity, and thereby create a hierarchy of being and belonging as "Australian" and "not Australian." This causes specific tensions and poses a threat to social harmony, especially in a society that is becoming more and more heterogeneous culturally, religiously, and most of all "racially."

The political institutions of Australia are very aware of this complexity and have repeatedly strived to aspire for social cohesion, especially with educational policies. Since the advent of multiculturalism in Australia with the political demise of the White Australia Policy, educational policies have been developed to build a society that aspired for national unity along with the maintenance of diversity. Many authors believe that such multicultural educational policies have been about studying the "other," the cultures of Aboriginals and migrants with the "white Anglo-Australian" as the national subject in the middle (Aveling 2002, 120; Leeman and Reid 2006, 62). These policies underline respect and acceptance for diversity, and at the same time come back to epitomizing the identity of the nation and the national subject to extract commitment toward these identities from all Australians. It is this desire for national integration, which seems to stem from the fear of diversity that fuels and maintains strong nationalistic aspirations in national subjects (Srinivasan 2014, 12–14). Thus, the juxtaposed phenomenon that this presents has tested Australia's social and national cohesion time and time again (e.g., racism against Aboriginal Australians, Cronulla riots, violence against international students, and even recent bouts of individual racism against those seen as outsiders). These incidents were repeatedly based on defining "whiteness" as "Australian," the national subject, and "brownness/blackness" as outsiders or "not Australian." Hence, both the "Australian" and "not Australian" subjects in their day-to-day life still conceptualize this Australian identity in a concrete form with specific attributes, and thereby repeatedly compare and contrast individuals and groups against these characteristics.

Young children are not outside this nationalistic discourse, which is tainted with whiteness. Even the current *Early Years Learning Framework* (Commonwealth of Australia 2009) uses nationalistic language, as it highlights the basis of this framework by quoting Goal 2 from the *Melbourne Declaration on Education Goals for Young Australian* (Ministerial Council on Education, Employment, Training and Youth Affairs [MCEETYA] 2008). This goal (MCEETYA 2008, 8–9) specifically outlines what all young Australians, the national subjects, should become, and thus legitimizes the educators' aspirations for developing national subjects within early childhood settings. With educators being and becoming committed to the development of "Australian," they also simultaneously and unconsciously developed the "not Australian" subject, as Stuart Hall (2003, 72–73) contends: the creation of a subject with particular attributes always results in the creation and elimination of an oppositional subject without those designated attributes.

Did I Want to Talk about "Black/White": My National Contemplation

I did not plan to talk about "race" and its role in categorizing "Australian/not Australian" in my thesis, but the narratives "spoke color." I originally aspired to inquire the contradictions of practicing multiculturalism within discourses of nationalism in early childhood settings. Hence, I engaged in participatory action research (Martin, Hunter, and McLaren 2006, 179; MacNaughton and Hughes 2009, 49–54) in two early childhood settings. I conducted my participatory action research in two long daycare settings that educationally cared for children below one to five years of age. The children, families, and educators in these centers were ethnolinguistically and religiously from varied backgrounds, including "white Anglo-Australian." I wanted to explore how and whose cultures were being named and enacted in these spaces, and I especially wanted to engage with the voices of children and families, who shared my ethnolinguistic background. Hence, these centers, with four to five children and families from the Indian subcontinent, seemed highly appropriate to explore my research topic, and I planned to immerse myself with the physical, social, and metaphysical environment two days a week in each of these settings for six to eight months. However, one center withdrew after the first two months and I continued with the other one till the end of my research journey. Due to my postcolonial partialities, my research project was named as "Contesting identities in othered voices," and as I embarked on my project I was critiquing my own postcolonial lens and yet, I could not relinquish the postcolonial in me. As a theoretical and philosophical body of knowledge, postcolonialism identifies and challenges the colonial discourses of "othering" (Said 1978, 45–46) that were used to classify and categorize the colonized in comparison to who the colonizers were. Edward Said (1978, 40, 140–149) meticulously outlines the colonial discourses with which the colonizers created binaries of "us" and "them" to establish the superior "self" (Us, the colonizers) and the inferior "other" (Them, the colonized). When I embarked on this inquiry I was conscious of my postcolonial subjectivity that repeatedly surfaced, analyzed, and categorized interactions that I perceived as colonial acts of "othering." Authors such as Anshuman Prasad (2004, 7) highlight how earlier works on postcolonialism were critiqued for engaging in the use of the very same binary language that these theories challenged, and therefore I quelled the postcolonial in me that had the propensity to classify and categorize our identity exchanges. However, as my inquiry progressed, the binary language with which children and adults classified self and others became central, and they categorized using whiteness to mark who was Australian and not Australian. I gave myself permission to allow my postcolonial self to raise and make meaning of our interactions. I realized that we were all dominated and colonized by whiteness, which dictated our daily subjective realities, our voices, and our silences (Srinivasan 2014, 144–148). Hence, I combined postcolonial and critical race theory (Frankenberg

1993) to speak with this unspoken element that consumes our daily thoughts and actions. In children's and adults' interactions whiteness was "normalized" (Frankenberg 1993, 14–20, 140–149), and, in this case, nationalized to establish this as the primary and yet undefinable attribute of the national subject, Australian.

Throughout my action research inquiry, children's nationalistic interactions or "color speaks" used in classifying the national subject and the outsider kindled and maintained the desire for whiteness in young brown children. My postcolonial subjectivity erupted and prompted me to respond and react to challenge those categorizing voices. Yet, I allowed to be silenced, and I did not share my postcolonial interpretations with the ECE at that time of my action research inquiry. In the following I share a few of those whiteness tainted nationalistic narratives to trouble the nuanced silences and voices of educators with whom I conducted my inquiry.

My first day at these settings began with "brown" children's open "color speaks" that detested their "brownness" to desire "whiteness." Within the first few weeks, "white Anglo-Australian" children categorized "self" as "white" and "Australian," and the "other," "black/brown" children and adults as "not Australian." It is not that those children who were "brown" did not contend this exclusion; they vehemently tried to argue that they were born in Australia and therefore are "Australians." Due to the repeated continued denial of this national identity for them by those children who named "self" as "Australian," they succumbed to identify themselves as "white." So strong was this urge to claim the national identity, that from *being* "brown," they were "whitened" to *become* "white." ECE who were around allowed children's "race"-based categorization to continue with strategic voices and silences. Their nationalistic fervor was expressed strongly and vociferously, supported with discursive strategies that justified their emotional investment in maintaining the identity of the "white Australian." My subjective experiences of the past that I endured due to my "brownness" in Australia surfaced, as I armed myself to "color" that "white Australian" with vociferous children and silencing "white Anglo-Australian" educators. However, my attempts were repeatedly negated very skilfully by those educators. These educators saw themselves as "just Australian" and therefore vehemently rejected my attempts to designate a hyphenated identity for them. I am equally guilty of engaging in silent practices, as I did choose silence to save my study, in which I had invested much of my time, resources, and emotions. I could not risk losing all of these with my postcolonial quest to "color" and taint the nation and its identity.

PICKING UP THE "BITS AND PIECES":
EARLY CHILDHOOD CONVENTION

I now discuss how to equip oneself to pick up those subtle "bits and pieces" that Michel Foucault (1977, 16) talks about in order to fragment the technology of nation-building. For Foucault (1977), "bits and pieces" served as diffused strategies that discursively epitomized particular knowledge attached to institutionalized systems of power. Discourses serve as maps that inform how individuals should be, think, and act particular subjectivities within a given society (Weedon 1987, 35–37; Spears 1997, 6; Gee 2010, 11). Enacting institutionally backed discourses are dominant, as they endow the subject with realizable normality and power (Weedon 1987, 136–137; Blaise 2005, 18–20) that stem from practicing what is "acceptable" and "appropriate." Discourses, after all, are constituted and held together by strategies, and these strategies specifically aim to convey certain ideas that particular subjectivities want to propagate or resist power. I would like to stress here that strategies include verbal language statements, nonverbal actions or practices, and silences, as all of these mobilize particular ideas that those subjects deem as being worthwhile within that context. Hence, I name these strategies as "bits and pieces" that legitimized the continuation of "whitened nation" technology in particular ways. Here, the nation-building endeavor was mobilized through "bits and pieces" attached to the discourse of childhood innocence. However, this becomes evident only when these "bits and pieces" are picked up and contested to surface their connections to the persistent propagation of this "whitened nation." After all, in early childhood settings, the discourse of childhood innocence is still dominant (Grieshaber 2001, 68; Meyer 2007, 87; Reimers and Peters 2011, 89), and as Paul Connolly (2008, 174) contends, this dominant discourse still dictates and silences the voices that aim to disrupt children's gender and "race"-based arbitrations of power. Educationally caring for the "innocent child," a discursive early childhood convention still attached to dominant sites of power, served as a chaste vehicle to mobilize the "whitened nation" technology in early childhood settings.

In what follows, I share one such sequential narrative and fragment the silencing and silent nation-building technology of "white Anglo-Australian" educators and children into "bits and pieces." These now fragmented "bits" and "pieces" that lock together serve as strategies that remain disguised in the conventional discourses of early childhood educational care. The convenient disguise that early childhood convention offers to epitomize national convention ensures the sustained materialization of "white Australian" by "white Anglo-Australian" adults and children. However, as soon as the "bits and pieces" of national convention are picked up by those who want to contest such practices, they are consolidated by educators with early childhood convention that affects the maintenance of "whitened Australia."

"HOW COME AUSTRALIANS ARE WHITE?":[1]
A NATIONAL CONTENTION

I begin with the mat time during which a book, *All the Colours We Are* (Kissinger 1994), on skin color was read with children by Gina. The children in the following narratives chose their pseudonyms. Gina and Katherine were white Anglo-Australian educators in the room, and right from the very start both these educators maintained the "children don't see 'colors' due to their innocence" discourse, even though they repeatedly heard, from afar, children inquisitively questioning my skin color. In order to respond to children's inquisitiveness, I carried picture books that explained and named skin colors. Bikky (a four-year-old Turkish girl), asked about the origins of my skin color and this time Gina was too close to disregard Bikky's quest:

> "Can I ask you something? Why did god give you black skin and gave me white skin?" asked Bikky in a very low voice. "What does she want?" asked Gina, as she chose a book to read for group time. "Bikky is curious to know about how we get our skin colour and she wants me to read a book on it. I have it in my bag", I replied. "I can read that book if you want" (Gina). She read the book, and Gina stopped and kept asking me about the meanings for words like, "melanin, ancestors, pigments" and adding phrases, "mmm... that is surprising, I don't know why they say that in children's book." (Gina)

Gina, as a qualified educator responding to children's impromptu interest, accepted to read the book. However, Gina's reluctance became highly evident as she stopped and paused with much unease right from the beginning, and the "bits and pieces" of averseness to "color speak" flowed one after the other. With the initial "bit" Gina deemed the words melanin, ancestors, and pigments as unsuitable for young children, which should never be present in a children's book. In fact, this was too much even for her, a qualified ECE to comprehend. Hence, it was my responsibility to explain these terms to both adults and children. Although this "color speak" was started by Bikky, the "piece" that accompanied this "bit: highlighted that I had to carry the burden of "color speaks." I was made to feel as if this was my initiation, interest, and intention and therefore I should handle this. Most of all, the first "bits and pieces," guised and guided with the mask of children's naivety, legitimized Gina's distance and silence. The second "bits and pieces" that followed ensured that the "whitened nation" remained undisrupted:

> "It depends on how hot it is where you live. The sun can make you go very dark, see you have to protect yourself from the sun, it is very hot in Australia. Katherine you don't stand a chance, you are stuck with your skin color" (Gina). "But, how come Australians are white, when it is hot here, because sun makes us go brown doesn't it?"(Lisa the zebra, four years old). "Hey, I dare you to read those words at the bottom, go on read it", Katherine interrupted and giggled as Gina tried to read the sentences written in Spanish.

The book then moved to explain the relationship between skin colors. This was simple language, and a concept not too complex for children to understand. In fact, children understood the relationship between hot sun and dark skin color or "brownness" very adeptly. More so, they were also aware of the language of "race" and "color" attached to the identity of "Australian," the national convention. Hence, Lisa the zebra appropriately queried using this political language, which defined and colonized the identity of this aboriginal land and its "brown" inhabitants with "whiteness." Lisa the zebra asked, "How come Australians are white when it is hot here, because sun makes us go brown doesn't it?" Lisa the zebra expressed her awareness of the politically presumed identity of "white Australia" by "white Australians." This could have been the turning point that forced Gina to engage with "color speak," as Lisa the zebra was disrupting the past overt colonial and the covert postcolonial colonization of "Australian" subjects. Swiftly Katherine guarded this political space by coming to Gina's rescue. She introduced the second "bit" that diverted the conversation by challenging Gina to read the sentences below in Spanish. I wanted to double dare Gina to "color speak," as uncomfortable as it may be for her as a "white Australian." I shockingly heard Katherine's giggles at Gina's attempts, as Lisa the zebra's pursuit to figure out the cause of "whitened nation" was completely dismissed. Here, the giggles were the "piece" that accompanied the "bit," to showcase their disinterest or discomfort in acknowledging the loss of "color" and culture of the original owners of this land. This "piece" had the capacity to reduce the tormented histories of the colonized people of this land into giggles. Thus the "bits and pieces" further sealed the lips of the "white Australian," who now continued to strategically evade any cracks that disrupted the "whitened nation":

> "I give up, okay where do you get your skin color from? Say it in one word and you can go to wash your hands" (Gina). "Paint" (Veejay,

4 year old, Asian Australian girl). "I would have said the same thing, Veejay, well done" (Gina). "White" (Leo, white, Anglo-Australian boy). "What, bright or white?" (Katherine). "I mean bright" (Leo). "Mmm...bright, not white interesting" (Katherine). I remained silent and watched this happen. I later apologized to Gina[,] "I am sorry I put you on the spot by making you read that book". "No worries, can you see children didn't still quite get it. I would have been the same when I was four" (Gina).

The above "bits and pieces" silenced any further "color speak", never to surface again with the children. This final nail buried all "color speaks" and ensured that it was laid to rest in peace. So impatient was Gina that she hastily dispersed the children without completing the book. Gina held the scepter of colonial "whiteness" with such a firm grasp, as I bowed down, ashamed of my own silent governance of my safe research space. This final nail, the "bit" that sealed the deal was to say the origin of our skin colors in one word. In the end, Gina felt that children still did not understand because they were only four and she could empathize with those nascent, innocent, and untainted early years. That was the "piece," the discourse of innocence again that strategically laid anymore "color speaks" to be ironed out of early childhood. Maybe it is because Gina is "white" and I am "brown" that I felt the opposite of what she believed about children's ability to grapple with "color" complexities. I heard Lisa the zebra when she asked, "How come Australians are white?", and to me that indicated that she got it. Moreover, the very same four-year-olds were knowledgeable enough to grasp an understanding of Gina's and Katherine's reluctance to "color speak" and they nuanced their replies to suit those reluctant adults' whims and fancies. What followed showcased how these "bits and pieces" allowed children to take charge of maintaining the "whitened nation."

"'CAUSE AUSTRALIANS ARE WHITE": NATION CONSOLIDATION

The "bits and pieces" of early childhood convention that ever so slightly veered toward national convention was discursively pulled back to silence any "color speaks" with young children. Children continued to "speak colors" just with me and requested me to read the book, *The Colors of Us* (Katz 2002), which I also carried in my bag. Yet, none of these books were allowed to be placed on the bookshelf. I read this book nearly every day with small groups of children, and it made skin colors seem highly palatable. Despite repeated reiterations of this book, the silencing discursive strategies, the "bits and pieces" of early childhood convention, now materialized into defining the "Australian" and "not Australian." In what follows I share those nationalistic narratives that flowed on to consolidate the now "whitened nation" and the further silencing "bits and pieces" that reified the educators' reluctance to disrupt children's "race"-based national consolidation. Feeniyan, a four-year-old, white Anglo-Australian girl classified Pookey, another four-year-old Indian Australian girl, and me to consolidate this national identity:

> "I am white, so I am Australian. Pookey is black not Australian. Like you she is Indian." (Feeniyan). "No, I am white, I am Australian" (Pookey). "But Pookey, remember what we read in 'Colours of us', you are like, peanut butter and is it white?," I asked. "Okay, I am Indian like Prasanna and I am from Melbourne. I am both and so I am a bit white" (Pookey). "Bikky is white, she is Australian" (Feeniyan). "Why do you say that?," I asked. "Cause she is white, Australians are white (Feeniyan)."

Children by now understood that the educators in the setting were going to turn a deaf ear to their "color speaks," and therefore very openly engaged in classifying their peers and adults using "race" as the basis of constructing national identities. More than the "bit" that classified "white" as "Australian," it is the "bit" that classified Pookey as "not Australian" that kindled her desire for "whiteness" in her "brown" self. Pookey immediately was ready to "whiten" her "brownness" to have a slice of that national power. She knew being classified as "not Australian" relegated her to the margins, an outsider status, hence she jumped to become "white." Pookey's desire for national power was so strong that she reconciled to claiming this with "bits" of "white." These "bits" now became linked by "pieces" that reinstated the national identity of Australians, more specifically "white as Australian." Here, Feeniyan, a four-year-old child, moved from the establishment of her individual identity, to conceptualizing the nation's collective identity as, "cause…Australians are white." Feeniyan, the child, now took the role of the colonizer and "spoke" to "whiten" the subjects of Australia, by fuelling a sense of inadequacy in those were otherwise. More "white" children engaged in "othering" our "brownness" and nationalizing "whiteness." Gina and Katherine were not very far from this table but they remained very busy and focused in their tasks. Many weeks later, however, Gina came back to justify their silence:

> But it is difficult to talk about color. If a child comes and asks me, why are you white, I wouldn't know what to say. You say pigments and stuff about your skin when children ask you about color, but what can we say, nothing.

The notion that one had to be "white" to be and become "Australian" continued and so did the exclusion of those who were categorized as "black" and "brown" from the national space. After many weeks of hearing such "color speaks" by children, Gina had to come up with a fresh set of "bits and pieces" that could finally enable her to relinquish her responsibilities of challenging such "race"-based conceptions. This "bit" passed all accountabilities of disrupting "whiteness" to me, because I am "brown." The "bit" suggested that I was the one with all the answers, the "pigment and stuff." Hence, this was my problem, my puzzle, that I had to negotiate, as I had the lot. The final liberating "piece" valorized all who were "white" to maintain their silence, as it suggested that they cannot say anything. Thus, once and for all, Gina released "whiteness" from engaging in any conversations that can even remotely trouble the "whitened nation." This "normalizing and neutralizing of whiteness" (Frankenberg 1993, 228), the ultimate "piece," that regarded their "whiteness" as nothing enabled them to clench and maintain their "white power," and its continued survival through children's undisrupted "whitened nation"-building technology. Once these fragmented "bits and pieces" of early childhood convention were picked up, they surfaced in the national consolidation in the form of "white Australian," the colonizer of the past, the present, and the future. I began to wonder why "white Australians" could not disrupt "whiteness," which may be less pigmented in comparison to my "brownness," nevertheless, endowed with an abundance of power.

Was the "white Australian" so distraught about sharing their ownership of this nation that they will not "color speak?" Or, was it because the "white Australian" was reluctant to share the historical and sociopolitical power attached to "whiteness?" Whatever their reason, in postcolonial Australia the faceless colonizer was now sitting back relaxed on his/her throne, while children and adults colonized by "whiteness" were conducting the "whitening" errands for the colonizer.

How Come "White Australians" Will Not "Color Speak": A National (Re)consideration

Discourses and language serve as points of disruption, to reveal both dominance and resistance at an individual level (Weedon 1987, 35–38; Hall 2003, 72–82). Yet, within early childhood settings it was highly problematic to interrupt "race"-based nationalistic discourses. It is not that the "white Anglo-Australian" educators overtly seconded and condoned children's conceptions of "white Australian." It was their reluctance and silence to engage with children's "color speaks," strategically supported by the discourse of childhood innocence, in combination with those that nullified "whiteness" maintained and circulated the power of "white Australian." One would imagine that the field of early childhood in Australia with the centralization of *Rights of the Child* (United Nations 1989) would consciously engage in challenging discourses of childhood innocence. However, it was evidenced that such notions were not only still dominant, but also deliberately used to divert and avoid engaging with the complexities of contesting "whiteness." I now ask as a "brown," "not Australian" subject, when will "white Australians" "speak color?" After all, "color speak" was initiated by "white Australians" historically to grasp and clench the ownership of this nation and its identity, so should they not also take the responsibility of unclenching this power?

I conclude by challenging "white Australians" to (re)consider "speaking color," especially with young children. It is only then that "brown Australian" will be able to own and share this spatial power in the present and in the future. Otherwise, despite the political abolition of the White Australia Policy, the covert images of "whitened nation" will continue to dominate this space and its subjects. Most of all, the "race" ideology will continue to segment this society, as these will be propagated not via overt exclusionary policies, but in the colonizing voices of young, not-so-innocent children, and in the silences of educators. I hence urge every "white Australian" ECE to take responsibility and

(re)consider the *"bits and pieces"* of early childhood in nation building,
(re)consider their reluctance and silence,
(re)consider hiding behind the disguise of nothing,
(re)consider tainting "whiteness" and that "color" that holds power, and
(re)consider the power in clenching the identity "Australian" with their "whiteness."

And most of all, to (re)consider what it feels to be "brown" and desire "bits of whiteness" with feelings of inadequacy in being and becoming in this space.

Until these national (re)considerations are consciously met to disrupt the discursive practices that establish the binaries of "Australian/ not Australian," "whiteness" will time and again colonize the minds of all subjects, children and adults, in Australia for many years to come. Let us together challenge that faceless "white colonizer" within each one of us.

NOTE

1. I quote here a child's voice. This is how the child asked this question, which was left unanswered hastily.

REFERENCES

Appadurai, A. 2006. *Fear of Small Numbers*. London: Duke University Press.
Atkinson, S. 2009. "Adults constructing the young child, 'race' and 'racism.'" In *"Race" and Early Childhood Education: An International Approach to Identity, Politics and Pedagogy*, edited by G. MacNaughton and K. Davis, 139–155. New York: Palgrave Macmillan.
Aveling, N. 2002. "Student teachers' resistance to exploring racism: Reflections on 'doing' border pedagogy." *Asia-Pacific Journal of Teacher Education* 30 (2): 119–130.
Blaise, M. 2005. *Playing It Straight: Uncovering Gender Discourses in an Early Childhood Classroom*. New York: Routledge.
Commonwealth of Australia. 2009. *Belonging, Being & Becoming: The Early Years Learning Framework for Australia*, edited by Employment and Workplace Relations Department of Education. Barton, ACT: Department of Education, Employment and Workplace Relations, Commonwealth of Australia.
Connolly, P. 2008. "Race, gender and critical reflexivity in research with young children." In *Research with Children, Perspectives and Practices*, edited by P. Christensen and A. James, 173–188. New York: Falmer Press.
Foucault, M. 1977. *Discipline and Punish: The Birth of the Prison*, translated by A. Sheridan. New York: Vintage Books.
Frankenberg, R. 1993. *White Women, Race Matters: The Social Construction of Whiteness*. Minneapolis: University of Minnesota Press.
Gee, J. P. 2010. *An Introduction to Discourse Analysis [Electronic Resource] Theory Method*. Hoboken, NJ: Taylor & Francis.
Government of the Commonwealth of Australia. 1901. Immigration Restriction Act. Canberra.
Grieshaber, S. 2001. "Advocacy and early childhood educators: Identity and cultural conflicts." In *Embracing Identities in Early Childhood Education*, edited by S. Grieshaber and G. S. Cannella, 60–72. New York: Teachers College Press.
Hage, G. 2000. *White Nation: Fantasies of White Supremacy in a Multicltural Society*. New York: Routledge.
Hall, S. 2003. "Foucault: Power, knowledge and discourse." In *Discourse Theory and Practice: A Reader*, edited by M. Wetherell, S. Taylor, and S. J. Yates, 72–82. London: Sage.
Katz, K. 1999. *The Colors of Us*. New York: Henry Holt.
Kissinger, K. 1994. *All the Colors We Are: The Story of How We Got Our Skin Color*. New Jersey: Red Leaf Press.
Leeman, Y., and C. Reid. 2006. "Multi/intercultural education in Australia and the Netherlands." *Compare* 36 (1): 57–72.

MacNaughton, G. 2001 "Silences and subtexts of immigrant and non-immigrant children." *Childhood Education* 78 (1): 30–36.

MacNaughton, G., and K. Davis. 2001 "Beyond 'othering' rethinking approaches to teaching young Anglo-Australian children about indigenous Australians." *Contemporary Issues in Early Childhood* 2 (1): 83–93.

———. 2009. "Discourses of 'race' in early childhood: From cognition to power." In *"Race" and Early Childhood Education: An International Approach to Identity, Politics and Pedagogy*, edited by G. MacNaughton and K. Davis, 17–30. New York: Palgrave Macmillan.

MacNaughton, G., and P. Hughes. 2009. *Doing Action Research in Early Childhood Studies: A Step by Step Guide.* New York: Open University Press.

Martin, G., L. Hunter, and P. McLaren. 2006. "Participatory activist research (teams)/action research." In *Doing Educational Research: A Handbook*, edited by K. Tobin and T. Kincheloe, 157–190. Rotterdam: Sense.

Meyer, A. 2007. "The moral rhetoric of childhood." *Childhood* 14 (1): 85–104.

Ministerial Council on Education, Employment, Training and Youth Affairs. 2008. Melbourne Declaration on Educational Goals for Young Australians.

Prasad, A. 2003. "The gaze of the other: Postcolonial theory and organizational analysis." In *Postcolonial Theory and Organizational Analysis: A Critical Engagement*, edited by A. Prasad, 3–46. New York: Palgrave Macmillan.

Reimer, M., and C. Peters. 2011. "Theorizing young people." *Jeunesse: Young People, Texts, Cultures* 3 (2): 88–99.

Said, E. W. 1978. *Orientalism.* New York: Vintage Books.

Skattebol, J. 2005. "Insider/outsider belongings: Traversing the borders of whiteness in early childhood." *Contemporary Issues in Early Childhood* 6 (2): 189–203.

Spears, R. 1997. "Introduction." In *Critical Social Psychology*, edited by T. Ibanez and L. Iniguez, i–xvi. London: Sage.

Srinivasan, P. 2014. *Early Childhood in Postcolonial Australia: Children's Contested Identities*, edited by M. N. Bloch, G. S. Cannella, and B. B. Swadener, *Critical Cultural Studies.* New York: Palgrave Macmillan.

Taylor, P. C. 2004. *Race: A Philosophical Introduction.* Oxford: Blackwell.

United Nations. 1989. Convention on the Rights Of the Child. New York: United Nations.

Weedon, C. 1987. *Feminist Practice and Poststructuralist Theory.* Oxford: Basil Blackwell.

CHAPTER 3

The Child *as* Nation: Embodying the Nation in Salman Rushdie's *Midnight's Children*

Lucy Hopkins

Ideas of childhood and the child have long been central to the imagining of the nation: tropes of immaturity, growth, and development that underpin notions of childhood have long been co-opted into the service of the nation. As critic Jo-Ann Wallace (1995) argues:

> The category of "the child", a foundational product of the modern episteme, remains an unacknowledged and therefore unexamined organising principle... of the modern nation-state in its relations with many of its own citizens and those of the so-called developing world. (286)

Wallace calls for an investigation of the ways in which dominant discourses of childhood—that naturalize the child's development toward a normative, rational adulthood—are put to use in the making of social and political hierarchies of the nation.

In this chapter I respond in part to Wallace's challenge by exploring the inextricable links between notions of the child and the nation in Salman Rushdie's Booker prize-winning novel, *Midnight's Children* (1981). In making use of the novel as a site of investigation, I situate the reading of narrative within the realm of social and cultural critique. In doing so, I draw on poststructuralist feminism's recognition of the powerful ways in which cultural and literary texts work to endorse and/or resist dominant discourses. With Susan Stanford Freidman (1998), I argue that narrative is both generated by and implicated in the generation of culture, and thus in the making of the social and cultural world. Clearly, I understand the analysis of texts to be central in the exploration of social and cultural spaces.

Midnight's Children becomes a significant site through which to challenge the philosophical practice of linking the development of the child and the development of the nation: here I argue that this novel enacts a politicization of the child subject and the space of childhood through its refusal of the notion of the "natural," and in doing so complicates the use of the child as a mobile signifier for nationhood and actively subverts dominant discursive notions of development as frequently applied to childhood, colony, empire, and nation.

CHILD DEVELOPMENT, COLONIAL NARRATIVES, AND THE NATION

The use of the figure of the child in establishing social and political hierarchies has played out through the building of empires and nations. Both colonial uses of the child and later uses of the developmental model of the child rely on the idea of the child as a natural category of ontology, whose use works to normalize and legitimate that to which it is applied (Castañeda 2002; Burman 2008; Nandy 2010).

Developmental modes of thinking about the child rely on the naturalness of the child's body to articulate a model of normative progress. Although purportedly based on the biological growth of the child, such discourses are also embedded within humanist models of the subject in which the child is positioned as an immanent adult, not yet a full, complete, rational subject. The intertwining of the psychosocial with the biological here works to embed and naturalize such an account of the child.

The implications of such a discourse of the child on ideas of nationhood are manifold. Critical psychologist Erica Burman (2008) notes the impact of the conflation of the developmental processes of child and nation: once the child and nation are linked, the assumed inevitability of the child's physical and psychosocial growth that underpins developmental discourses permits and sanctions the imposition of a particular model of progress the nation. She argues that

> notions of progress, improvement, skill and adaptation emerge, words that might migrate or even flow easily between the specific and the general, or from individual to social allocation... Here we begin to see the political load carried by the discourse of development, and by children who are so often positioned as its bearers. Children thus provide

the conceptual and emotional means by which contested social hierarchy can be perpetuated by being mapped onto an apparently natural social category. (Burman 2008, 95)

The very language of child development easily transfers to the broader development project, obscuring the politics of that which it is used to describe: here, the building of the nation.

The use of the child as a metaphor for ideas of progress is not new: conceptual links between the child and the colonized subject have long been established within colonial literature and critiqued within postcolonial rewritings (Ashcroft, Griffiths, and Tiffin 1998; Gandhi 1998). Ashis Nandy (2010) alerts us to the ways in which the colonial system made use of the trope of the child in establishing narratives of salvation and progress:

Colonialism dutifully picked up these ideas of growth and development and drew a new parallel between primitivism and childhood...What was childlikeness of the child and childishness of immature adults now also became the lovable and unlovable savagery of primitives and the primitivism of subject societies. (15–16; see also Nieuwenhuys 2010)

The slippage between the categories of child and colonized peoples worked to justify the process of colonization. As Wallace (1994, 176) asserts, "'the child' is the necessary precondition of imperialism— that is, the West has to invent for itself 'the child' before it could think a specifically colonialist imperialism" (see also Balagopalan 2011).

Making use of the figure of the child as a model for the colonial Other has worked to depoliticize the relationship between Empire and colony, drawing it into the (natural, inevitable, apolitical) familial space of parent-child relations. Nandy argues that in colonial discourse the colonized subject becomes

an inferior version of the adult—as a loveable, spontaneous, delicate being who is also simultaneously dependent, unreliable and wilful, and this, as a being who needs to be guided, protected and educated as a ward. (cited in Jenkins 1998, 13–14)

Olga Nieuwenhuys (2009, 148) underlines the ideological uses of the hierarchical familial relationship in the justification and practice of colonization, suggesting that "Britain was to be like a good father guiding the young, immature and hence primitive Indian society towards adulthood." Such paternalism has informed colonial politics both on the intimate level of individual interaction and on the grand scale of Empire building in colonial domination. Henry Jenkins (1998, 13–14) suggests that this conceptualization of the Other as child "framed the official politics of colonial domination and the unofficial politics of racial bigotry; white domination was presented as a rational (and benign) response to the 'immaturity' of non-white peoples." The project of colonialism, then, relied upon the figure of child as a means to perpetuate and reproduce this apparently depoliticized narrative within the colonized space of India.

The use of such narratives in legitimating and promoting the building of nation and empire is highlighted and challenged in Salman Rushdie's *Midnight's Children* through the overt linking of child and nation. In what follows, I chart the ways in which the novel works to politicize the child subject and draw attention to his role in the projects of nation and empire.

COLONIAL MYTHS OF NATION AND CHILD: *MIDNIGHT'S CHILDREN*

Narrated by the protagonist, Saleem Sinai, who is born at the moment of the Indian nation's inception in 1946, *Midnight's Children* charts the simultaneous growth of the child and the nation. Saleem's momentous birth endows him with a mystical connection with the nation, played out in part through his telepathic ability to inhabit the mind of anyone in India. It is through his excursions into the minds of the powerful and the poor that he discovers the magical, mystical Midnight's Children, children who, like Saleem, were born in the same hour as the nation, and who each possess fabulous abilities. The Midnight's Children Conference that Saleem convenes in his mind to use the children's abilities for good, ultimately fails, as the children—a microcosm of the nation—are unable to agree on how to use their skills.

In *Midnight's Children*, the child, Saleem, comes to stand in— metaphorically and literally—for the nation. From the moment of birth, events in Saleem's life continue to be intimately connected to those in the infancy of the nation. But we quickly understand that this will not be straightforward in temporal or spatial terms. In a playful critique of Western notions of temporality and teleological historicism and with an explicit acknowledgment of ancient spiritual and occult traditions, we read:

> Clock-hands joined palms in respectful greeting as I came...At the precise instant of India's arrival at independence, I tumbled forth into the world...Thanks to the occult tyrannies of those blandly saluting

clocks I had been mysteriously handcuffed to history, my destinies indissolubly chained to those of my country. (Rushdie 1981, 9)

The twinning of Saleem with India underscores the inextricable ties between the two, yet Saleem's relation to the nation is more than a narrative of parallel growth. Although celebrated by the world at large, Saleem's ties to the country are neither voluntary nor escapable as he figures himself as a kind of a prisoner of time, a slave to the history of his nation.

I read Rushdie's novel as being highly subversive in its explicit engagement with questions of child and nation. In creating a metaphorical conflation between Saleem and the nation, Rushdie's novel highlights and enacts a criticism of the ways in which discourses of nationalism and national development make use of the discursive figure of the child (see Nandy 2010). In tying together the narratives of nation and child, the novel alerts the reader to its purported intention to simulate such narratives, by making use of the child as an organizing principle for its investigation of issues of nationalism, history, and colonization. However, the substitution of an embodied, specific child for the symbolic figure on which such discourses rely reveals the novel's conflation of child and nation to be textual mimicry that seeks to contest the use of the child to justify and naturalize narratives of progress and hierarchies of knowledge. Here I draw on Homi Bhabha's conceptualization of mimicry as an imposed repetition of the (colonial) subject, which, he argues, can also be enacted as a mode of strategic resistance. Politicizing his reading of mimicry as an act of anticolonial defiance, Bhabha (1994, 172) suggests that "to the extent to which discourse is a form of defensive warfare, then mimicry marks those moments of civil disobedience within the discipline of civility: signs of spectacular resistance." Through the performative, through parody, through mockery, Saleem's story draws attention to its imperfect repetition of nationalist narratives.

It is important to note here that the twinning of Saleem and the nation does not simply engender a critique of the role of the child in the conceptualizing of the child, but rather in conflating Saleem's story with that of India, the novel undermines the national narrative of progress and modernization. This is not a nationalist novel: rather, it is, as Theresa Heffernan (2000) suggests, suspicious of the modern nation. This ambivalence toward the nation, I argue, is played out through Saleem's relationship with India and his failure to find coherence. His self cannot bear the weight of the nation, and at the end of the novel Saleem is literally disintegrating, as is the idealism of the nation.

The framing of Saleem's narrative as simultaneously his own and the nation's insists on the localization of the narrative of childhood, while acknowledging the multiple narratives of childhood that appear alongside and within his own story:

> I have been a swallower of lives; and to know me, just the one of me, you'll have to swallow the lot as well. Consumed multitudes are jostling and shoving inside me; and guided only by the memory of a large white bedsheet with a roughly circular hole…I must commence the business of remaking my life. (Rushdie 1981, 9–10)

While it seems a cannibalistic metaphor, Saleem's consumption of lives and narratives does not subsume or erase them. Rather, Saleem makes it very clear that his story is necessarily multiple, incomplete, and unrepresentative; his narrative comes with an imperative to accept it as one of many. A specified, localized child, Saleem's metaphorical relationship with the nation enables a reworking of the child figure's place in the conceptualization of the relationships between nation and citizen, colonizer and colonized, and the home and the world.

Flouting the idea of the child as a passive figure that can only be used as a model for the organization of social and political hierarchies, Saleem's relationship to his country is marked by an insistence on a reciprocal agency. Although he appears to be enslaved by his bonds to history, throughout his narrative, he imagines the reverse: that his life is informing that of the nation:

> Life in Bombay was as teeming, as manifold, as multitudinously shapeless as ever…except that I had arrived; I was already beginning to take my place at the centre of the universe; and by the time I had finished, I would give meaning to it all. (Rushdie 1981, 126–127)

Rather than the symbolic child's relationship to the social world providing a naturalized mode of interaction for the state and its citizens, Saleem envisages that it is he himself—in his centrality—who shapes the nation.

However, Saleem's formulation of his national agency is clearly subversive, and the novel illustrates the ways in which such a notion jostles up against hegemonic views of the child as the nation. Although the auspicious circumstances of Saleem's birth are celebrated by the nation, and he receives a letter from the newly appointed prime minister, Nehru, welcoming him as the newest citizen of India, Saleem is positioned in this letter as a cipher for the nation, rather than an active agent in its construction. On some level Nehru's congratulatory letter (inadvertently) works to reproduce within the new space of independent India the colonial use of the child figure to reflect and naturalize the position of the colonized nation. "We shall be watching over your life with the closest attention; it will be, in a sense, the mirror of our own" (Rushdie 1981, 122). In opposition to Saleem's self-construction, Nehru's mirror metaphor infers a complete lack of agency on the part of the child figure who simply reproduces the progress of the nation on a minute scale. Like the imperial positioning of the colonies, Nehru draws on the child figure to position the nation as childish and immanent, growing toward a future adulthood. While I acknowledge and delight in the ways in which this novel decenters a whole range of normative of hegemonic views and reveals their hegemony to be false, here I argue that as the head of state, Nehru's (fictional) views can be seen to represent the mainstream of the political and social imaginary. In allocating this narrative to Nehru, Rushdie demonstrates the marginal status of Saleem's view of his agency. Although, as I argue later, Nehru's letter also critiques the use of the child as a model for the nation, here his investment in ideas of reflection can be seen to uphold a normative view of the relationship between the nation and the figure of the child that reinforces colonialist uses of the child figure.

Saleem's own interpretation of the many layers of his connection to the nation reveals a richer and much more complex relationship. The metaphor, for Saleem, is neither simply a literal transposition (as in a metonym), nor only a symbolic gesture:

> How, in what terms, may the career of a single individual be said to impinge on the fate of the nation? I must answer in adverbs and hyphens: I was linked to history both literally and metaphorically, both actively and passively, in what our (admirably modern) scientists might term "modes of connection" composed of dualistically-combined configurations of the two pairs of opposed adverbs above. This is why hyphens are necessary: actively-literally, passively-metaphorically, actively-metaphorically and passively-literally, I was inextricably entwined with my world. (Rushdie 1981, 238)

Saleem's world is, of course, the world of India, and his "modes of connection" allow for a breadth of correlations between himself and the nation. Saleem's busy prose—filled with interjections, pauses, multiple clauses, and additional explanations, with "adverbs and hyphens" (Rushdie 1981, 238)—gestures toward the intricacy of the relationship. In analyzing and interpreting the multiplicity of ways in which he and India are interlinked, Saleem alerts us to the fact that this relationship does not simply mimic a colonial simile, which appropriates the subject position of the child to bestow it on the Other (nation, person), but rather complicates the positioning—and agency—of both the nation *and* the child.

In throwing together the fate of the child and the nation, *Midnight's Children* draws attention to the discourses of progress that inform the development of both child and nation. Relying on the obvious conflation of Saleem's infancy with that of India, the novel appears to reinscribe the notion of the nation as nascent: innocent, naïve, dependent, the baby nation strives for a coming of age, a slow development into maturity. The simultaneous advent of key moments of development reinforces the analogous growth of Saleem and India, including his departure from childhood. Leaving behind the India of his childhood and the space of childhood itself, Saleem's new life in Karachi plays out an adolescent sense of estrangement—both of Saleem and his environment, and Saleem and his twin, India:

> I arrived at Karachi, and adolescence—understanding, of course, that the subcontinent's new nations and I had all left childhood behind; that growing pains and strange and awkward alterations were in store for us all. (Rushdie 1981, 309)

Yet even without Saleem, the nation continues to develop through its strange teenage years, and the personification of the new countries of India and Pakistan in terms of the growth of the child's body toward adolescence make evident and politicize the imbrication of the nation within a nineteenth-century paradigm of child development. Indeed, the child figure who informs the positioning of the nation as immanent emerges from such a discourse of child development, which works to medicalize, measure, and regulate the physical—and, by extension, mental and emotional—growth of children toward a normative (white, male) adulthood. Crucially, as a scientific truth, the discourse of the developing child could be replicated and transposed onto the other across a range of areas. Childhood theorist Claudia Castañeda (2002, 22) highlights how "as a theory of progressive differentiation, biological development became a model for realizing human social, moral and cultural developments as well." The figure of the child not only provided a model of growth and development, but also underpinned the moral and social fabric of the colonial state.

The enormous growth of baby Saleem, however, works to parody this developmental model of the nation and the child. Following no rules of the developmental stages of childhood, baby Saleem eats and grows at an incredible rate. "From my very first days I embarked on a heroic programme of self-enlargement. (As though I knew that, to carry the burdens of my future life, I'd need to be pretty big)" (Rushdie 1981, 124). Saleem's growth takes on the rhetoric of nation-building, of bureaucratese; imagining the rapidity with which he grows to be heroic, through this language Saleem's development is intrinsically tied with the growth of the nation. Linking physical development with (emotional, social, and economic) capability or capacity by suggesting that his body size is all-important in supporting the metaphorical weight of the nation, Saleem reveals as outrageous and irrelevant the discourses of development and progress that are used to make sense of both the nation's growth and his own.

Saleem's extraordinary growth also ridicules the medical model of children's development. Although, as the narrator, Saleem reconstructs the infant's growth as heroic, the anxiety that it provokes in his mother(s) highlights as problematic the figure of the child whose development is out of (his parents') control. Sucking dry his mother's breast and driving away the wet nurse, Saleem reverses the positioning of the child as disempowered by the adult's control over the body of the developing child:

> For a time Amina and Mary became afraid that the boy was dumb; but, just when they were on the verge of telling his father (from whom they had kept their worries secret—no father wants a damaged child), he burst into sound, and became, in that respect at any rate, utterly normal, "It's as if," Amina whispered to Mary, "he's decided to put our minds at rest." (Rushdie 1981, 124–125)

Clearly it is baby Saleem who decides when and how to grow and develop, and who controls the narratives of what can be considered normative, rendering farcical the notion of nonnormative, or pathologized, development as damage. By claiming that he is in conscious control of his record growth and developmental "delays," Saleem problematizes the naturalization of notions of child development and the inevitability of growing toward a desired maturity.

Indeed in his enacted critique of the regulation of the child body, Saleem invests in the child subject an alternative model of agency, which has important consequences for the nation embodied by this child. The notion of the child that worked as a justification for colonial rule relied upon a passive and immanent model; as Wallace argues, "it was the idea of 'the child'—of the not yet fully evolved or consequential subject—which made thinkable a colonial apparatus officially dedicated to, in Macauley's words, 'the improvement of 'colonised peoples'" (1994, 176). However, Saleem's self-control undermines such a justification, and hints at a new kind of agency, a new kind of nation. As an agentic subject who creates and indulges parental anxiety, Saleem's developmental independence works to subvert the possibility of lingering colonial control over India; in his role as a metaphor for the nation, baby Saleem's expansion suggests that this new nation can no longer be governed by the colonial parent. India, like Saleem, has an autonomous energy; India, like Saleem, will not be confined to a model of development that posits (the adult) Britain as its goal.

Saleem's body is a site of constant contestation in the novel; indeed, though his embodiment works to contest the use of the symbolic child in reinforcing colonial discourses, Saleem's is also overdetermined by his bodiliness. The growing body of the child has long been a site on which racist imperialist discourses of human development and progress have been played out. Carolyn Steedman (1995) explicates the ways in which the child has been used in colonial discourses of evolution, suggesting that

> entire peoples and races might then be seen as part of the childhood of the human race, in need of guidance and protection certainly, but with the potential (however distant in prospect) for achieving the adult state. (82–83)

Such discourses place social evolutionary history within a model of child development, in which the temporal period of the developing child might be seen to represent the childhood of the human race, and concurrently, the "primitive" might be seen as belonging to this childhood (Wallace, 1995). The development of the child was used as evidence for the idea of the development of the human race; a narrative of centuries of human development played out in the growth of the child. In her exploration of the ways in which the child's body has been used as the site in which a compression of historical time can be observed and documented, Claudia Castañeda draws on anthropologist Johannes Fabian's analysis of nineteenth-century development discourses as a form of "temporal distancing," which, in Fabian's words, explains the "placing of the Now of the primitive in the Then of the Western adult" (Fabian 1983, cited in Castañeda 2002, 13). The child's body becomes a metaphorical theater in which the accelerated progress of history can be observed. This metaphor is literalized, and thus subverted, in the representation of Saleem's body in the novel.

From the first, the history of India is projected onto the body of the child; Saleem embodies the anthropomorphized nation. Nehru's letter to Saleem on the occasion of his birth recreates and undermines

this colonial use of the child's body to observe and document historical development. The letter reads:

> Dear Baby Saleem, My belated congratulations on the happy accident
> of your moment of birth! You are the newest bearer of that ancient face
> of India which is also eternally young. (Rushdie 1981, 122)

By confounding oppositions between youth and age (and also the
corresponding associations with wisdom and innocence), Nehru's letter subverts the developmental focus on linear time. In this delicate
maneuver, Nehru's letter highlights the way in which the narrative of
progress is tied to the metaphor of the child as a theater for history
and contests it, creating a new temporal trajectory for the growth of
the nation that focuses on valuing the historical past and the present-
future equally. Thus, in drawing attention to the role of the child's
body in carrying the image of the nation while "stopping" time in
this way, the letter challenges the correlations between the child's
development into adulthood and that of the primitive nation toward
(normative, Western) maturity.[1]

In a doubling of metaphors, the novel also makes use of the trope of
mapping in positioning Saleem as an embodiment of the nation when
Saleem's body becomes a literal site on which the nation is etched. The
nation (or rather, the two-becoming-three nations of the subcontinent)
is mapped upon the face of the baby who is twinned with India; as his
geography teacher later makes explicit, Saleem's face literalizes the meaning of human geography. Guffawing, Zagallo asks the class, "'In the face
of this ugly ape you don't see the whole map of India?'... 'See here—the
Deccan peninsula hanging down!' Again ouchmynose" (Rushdie 1981,
231). Even in describing his arrival into the world, Saleem conceptualizes his own face in terms of a map: "Dark stains spread down my
western hairline, a dark patch coloured my eastern ear" (Rushdie 1981,
124), which *stand in for* West and East Pakistan (later Bangladesh). A
metaphor for the cartography of the nation, the child holds India within
him; emerging from his body as a "cucumberous" nose.

However, while the history of India is marked on the body of the
child, so, too, is its colonial legacy, however hidden. Swapped at birth
with Shiva, the son of the old colonizer, William Methwold, and the
poor musician Wee Willie Winkie's wife, Saleem displays on his face
the ambiguous status of colonial history in the Indian nation. The
nose that is India is also the nose of a biological French grandmother,
and the nose of an allegorical Kashmiri grandfather. Similarly, Saleem's
eyes signal concurrent French and Kashmiri heritage: "The eyes were

too blue: Kashmiri-blue, changeling-blue, blue with the weight of unspilled tears, too blue to blink" (Rushdie 1981, 125). Within the paradigm of the child's embodiment of human history, the doubling of the significance of Saleem's features reinforces the continued presence of the colonial inheritance within the future of the nation. Yet Saleem's refusal to privilege either the biological or the narrative inheritances handed down to him from his two sets of grandparents—one French, British, colonial; the other Kashmiri, Indian, national—create a national history that is neither a return to an originary India, nor a denial of the authenticity of this hybrid history.[2]

Importantly, the marking of nation on the body of the child, though presenting as bodily characteristics, is also an inscription of a narrative inheritance. Saleem's Kashmiri inheritance is a story, rather than a genome, yet its place on his face (signaled not only through its shape *as* India, but also through the links between the stories of Saleem's assumed, but nonbiological grandfather Aadam's nose and his own) is accorded equal—if not greater—significance than his genetic inheritance. Despite the apparent links between the child's body and the history of the nation, Saleem's physiological resemblance to the nation is also verbally inscribed, imagined onto the child's visage. This imaginative-narrative embodiment of a national history disentangles the notion of physiological inheritance from the discourse of the natural.

The practices of surveilling and measuring (children's) development that occur in relation to Saleem's nose—and its subsequent links to the nation—work to parody the notion of the child's body as space in which history is played out:

> Baby-book records were meticulously kept; they reveal that I expanded almost visibly, enlarging day by day; but unfortunately no nasal measurements were taken so I cannot say whether my breathing apparatus grew in strict proportion, or faster than the rest. (Rushdie 1981, 124)

The growth of nose-as-nation is immeasurable, though the body of the child continues to defy normalcy with its exorbitant growth. Sliding between metaphors of the developing child as colonized Other and the child as history, the empirical recording of the body-as-child-as-nation's growth challenges the legitimacy of each paradigm of knowledge.

For Saleem, the weight of the nation—a burden that becomes too much to bear—rests on an understanding of both the nation and his subjectivity in terms of a narrative of coherence and striving toward a rational, adult self. Yet at the end of the novel Saleem is literally disintegrating. His body, filled with fissures, resists on every level the romance of the unified subjectivity and nation. Indeed it is Saleem's failure to represent the whole nation—through either his narration or his embodiment of India—that allows and makes space for the critique of the nationalist project and its underpinnings in discourses of childhood.

Concluding Thoughts

Ultimately, I argue that *Midnight's Children* politicizes the ways in which the figure of the child and the child's body both are used to naturalize a range of dividing practices that underpin the making of the nation. Through my examination of the relationship between Saleem and India, I have highlighted the ways that the overt conflation of child and nation in the novel simultaneously foregrounds and challenges the ways that the progress of the nation is reinforced by the dominance of the discourse of child development and its reliance on the naturalness of children's bodies to articulate a model of normative progress. Further, as my reading of the text has elucidated, the deliberate conflation of the categories of the child and the nation in *Midnight's Children* works not only as a radical rewriting of the colonialist notion of the child as a metaphor for "primitive" societies, and primitive society and culture as childish, but also as a challenge to the dominant discourses of childhood that inform this colonialist myth. *Midnight's Children* insists that we pay close attention to the ways in which both nation and childhood are conceptualized both within this novel and in the world at large: the text challenges the use of the figure child as a signifier for the nation, and insists on placing the multiplicity of children and childhoods within the social and political space of the nation, rather than using them to shape it.

Notes

1. It is important to note that Nehru's use of the concept of time can also be seen as reinforcing a traditionalist Indian view of time as circular, a reading that does not undermine the potential in Nehru's text to destabilize the narrative of progress, but rather draws the politics of nostalgia into the politics of the nation. See Mujeebuddin Syed (*"Midnight's Children* and its Indian con-texts," *The Journal of Commonwealth Literature* 29 (1994)).

2. Clearly, it is not only a tussle between Saleem's biological and narrative inheritances that comes into play here; Saleem's status as Anglo-Indian also calls into question the notion of an authentic Indian narrative of nationalism. For a further discussion of the hybrid status of the Ango-Indian in *Midnight's Children*, see Loretta Mijares ("You are

an Anglo-Indian?': Eurasians and hybridity and cosmopolitanism in Salman Rushdie's Midnight's Children," *The Journal of Commonwealth Literature* 38 (2003)).

REFERENCES

Ashcroft, Bill, Gareth Griffiths, and Helen Tiffin. 1989. *The Empire Writes Back*. London and New York: Routledge.

Balagopalan, Sarada. 2011. "Introduction: Children's lives and the Indian context." *Childhood* 18 (3): 291–297.

Bhabha, Homi. 1994. *The Location of Culture*. Abingdon, Oxon: Routledge.

Burman, Erica. 2008. *Developments: Child, Image, Nation*. Hove, East Sussex: Routledge.

Castañeda, Claudia. 2002. *Figurations: Child, Bodies, Worlds*. Durham, NC, and London: Duke University Press.

Friedman, Susan Stanford. 1998. *Mappings: Feminism and the Cultural Geographies of Encounter*. Princeton, NJ: Princeton University Press.

Gandhi, Leela. 1998. *Postcolonial Theory: A Critical Introduction*. Sydney: Allen & Unwin.

Heffernan, Teresa. 2000. "Apocalyptic narratives: The nation in Salman Rushdie's *Midnight's Children*." *Twentieth Century Literature* 46 (4): 470–491.

Jenkins, Henry (ed.). 1998. *The Children's Culture Reader*. New York and London: New York University Press.

Mijares, Loretta. 2003. "'You are an Anglo-Indian?': Eurasians and hybridity and cosmopolitanism in Salman Rushdie's *Midnight's Children*." *The Journal of Commonwealth Literature* 38: 125–145.

Nandy, Ashis. 2010. *The Intimate Enemy: Loss and Recovery of Self under Colonialism*, 2nd ed. Oxford: Oxford University Press.

Nieuwenhuys, Olga. 2010. "Keep asking: Why childhood? Why children? Why global?" *Childhood* 17: 291–296.

———. 2009."Editorial: Is there an Indian childhood?" *Childhood* 16: 147–153.

Rushdie, Salman. 1981. *Midnight's Children*. London: Jonathan Cape.

Steedman, Carolyn. 1995. *Strange Dislocations: Childhood and the Idea of Human Interiority, 1780–1930*. London: Virago.

Suleri, Sara. 1992. *The Rhetoric of English India*. Chicago, IL, and London: University of Chicago Press.

Syed, Mujeebuddin. 1994."*Midnight's Children* and its Indian con-texts." *The Journal of Commonwealth Literature* 29: 95–108.

Wallace, Jo-Ann. 1995. "Technologies of 'the child': Towards a theory of the child subject." *Textual Practice* 9 (2): 285–302.

———. 1994. "De-scribing *The Water Babies*: 'The child' in post-colonial theory." In *De-Scribing Empire: Postcolonialism and Textuality*, edited by Chris Tiffin and Alan Lawson, 171–183. London: Routlege.

CHAPTER 4

"Franco's Children": Childhood Memory as National Allegory

Miaowei Weng

INTRODUCTION

Since late Francoism of the 1970s, Spanish novelists and filmmakers have continuously reconstructed childhood under the dictatorship.[1] In the new millennium, representations of Franco-era childhood have come into increasing prominence. This subject has recurred in literature, cinema, television, the Internet, exhibitions, and symposia.[2] The boom of Franco-era child images in contemporary Spain draws attention to itself, provoking a series of questions: In what way did the Spanish Civil War and the subsequent dictatorship affect children? What kind of Franco-era childhood stories have Spaniards recounted in the post-Franco epoch? When and how do these storytellers use their narratives to reflect upon the past and lay claim to the future? These are the fundamental questions underlying my exploration of "Franco's children" in Spanish democratic transition. The phrase "Franco's children," on one hand, implies the status of the authors and filmmakers as those who survived the early Franco regime as children and recall their childhood as adults; on the other hand, it refers to the child protagonists who are set in wartime and the post-war period.

My study of Franco's children covers the past—the immediate post-War period—as well as the present—the Spanish democratic transition of the early 1980s. I explore the effects that the war and the harshest years of the dictatorship have had over Franco's children both in the past and in the present. Under Franco's dictatorship when parents were reticent to speak about history and politics, the state took up the dominant role in childhood education in Francoist "New Spain." Thus, to reconstruct Franco-era childhood is to reflect on the national intervention under the Franco regime in children's lives and, by extension, on Francoism in general from the vantage point of the transitional present.

Spanish democratic transition has been extoled to be a model of peaceful transition, but it has also carried the label of an amnestic period. This period is generally seen as lasting from Franco's death in 1975 to the election of the Socialist government of the Spanish Socialist Workers' Party in 1982. It was characterized by most Spaniards' desire to establish democracy and avoid controversy over the war and the dictatorship (Molinero 2010, 33–52). Historian Charles Powell shows the result of a poll conducted in 1979 concerning Spaniards' political tendencies: 77 percent of those polled Spaniards agreed on a definite reconciliation, and only 6.4 percent opposed the reconciliation without discussing the past (2001, 42). In addition, given that neither the Francoist power nor the anti-Francoist power was strong enough to solely control the dynamic domestic situations after Franco's death, both parties had to concede and reach a "consensus."

Under the temporary official and popular consensus, silence over the past predominated in the public sphere at the time. However, scholars, including Rafael Abella, Francisco Alburquerque, and Paul Preston, observe that, since Franco's death of 1975 a large number of historiographies have appeared that document the retaliations in the Civil War and the ensuing Franco dictatorship, particularly in the period of 1939–1951 (Preston 1976, 9–12; Abella 1978, 29; Alburquerque 1981, 430–431). In other words, historiographies did reveal "the wartime reprisals and its follow-up during the Franco dictatorship" but these studies lacked the audience during the Transition (Labanyi 2007, 93–94). While explicit reference to the war and the postwar period, especially those of the defeated Republicans, did not draw people's attention, artistic representations may have attracted an audience. The novella *The South*, completed in 1981, and the film by the same title, shot and released in 1983, are among the earliest artistic works that referred to the defeated Republicans after Franco's death. The value of the novella and the film lies not only in the unforgettable images of childhood they created but also in the reflections they rendered on the past as well as on the relevance of the past to the present.

WARTIME CHILDHOOD AND HISTORICAL MEMORIES

Philippe Ariès's (1962) consideration of childhood as a construction has become the basic premise in childhood studies (Mills 2000, 3–8; James and Prout 2008, 1–7; Kehily 2009, 1–17). At stake in his theory is that childhood is constructed historically and culturally, and that the construction of childhood changes over time and space. Ariès's argument about childhood shares the same constructionist approach with Maurice Halbwachs's view of memory. Halbwachs conceives of memory as a socially constructed representation of the past (1991, 40). The constructionist perspectives on memory as well as on childhood stress the need to contextualize the discussion of the works under analysis.

While Ariès's argument highlights the importance of the context in which childhood has been shaped, Halbwachs's conception of memory connects the past to the present. According to Halbwachs, memory is a process of reconstructing the past and this reconstruction is informed by the present (1991, 49). Constructions of childhood, in my view, thus become a nexus between the past and the present. The relevance of the past to the present is significant in thought and practice in contemporary Spain, because the recuperation of historical memory is still ongoing and victims' pain has not been fully recognized in the public space.[3]

Exploring the past, I am concerned with how the Franco regime used children for its propagandistic purpose and for an ideological socialization of the future generation. Analyzing the present, I examine how Franco's children have reconstructed this exploited childhood in the transitional period. Franco's children, as the future generation, were the chief preoccupation for the government of Franco's New Spain. Some of these children experienced the trauma and displacement of the war, yet the Francoists, aided by the church, couched their experiences in the victors' triumphalist rhetoric and thus camouflaged their suffering. Others, born in the immediate post-War period of the 1940s, were indoctrinated into the authoritarian discourse of Francoist national-Catholic education. The child protagonists of *The South* in the written and visual forms, for example, are portrayed to suffer from the processes that adjoined typical "politicizing of childhood" during the postwar period, living under the shadow of the allegedly "immoral" lives of their pro-Republican fathers.

Reconstructing childhood experiences, Franco's children criticize Francoism while at the same time rewriting the historical past.

According to José Piquer y Jover, in the early 1940s 72 percent of children in Barcelona "disapproved of the immoral lives" of the Republicans (1946, 76). This disapproval could be due to fear or the involuntary internalization of Francoist political indoctrination. In the late twentieth century, however, Spanish historian Ángela Cenarro interviewed children who were institutionalized in the Social Auxilio in the post-War period. Based on the oral testimonies she collected, Cenarro points out: "The narratives of those young-sters institutionalized by Social Auxilio show how they attempted to construct an alternative identity to that promoted by the regime as children" (2008, 53). The testimonies also show that children, especially those of pro-Republican parents, "recognized their strong awareness of their family identity, even if they had not been allowed to express it publicly (under Francoism)" (Cenarro 2008, 54). It is not fair to say that decades later these former Franco's children lied about their political awareness during childhood, yet it is also naïve to take these statements at face value. Obviously, these statements are the interviewees' interpretations from the vantage point of the present. Children's identification with their Republican parents, as recorded by Cenarro in the present, stands in sharp contrast to the youth's neg-ative attitudes toward the Republicans, as showed by Piquer y Jover in the 1940s. This contrast, I argue, demonstrates the present desire of Franco's children to rewrite the past, a past imposed on them by the victors of the war.

Mourning, National Allegory, and Childhood Memories

In his analysis of Argentine writer Tununa Mercado's *In a State of Memory*, Idelber Avelar proposes that "the labor of mourning has much to do with the erection of an *exterior* tomb where the brutal literalization of the internal tomb can be metaphorized" (1999, 9). By "exterior tomb," Avelar refers to dead objects left by the past; having lost their original utility and become spectrally charged, these objects described by Mercado in her novel become the mask for the unrepresentable "past traumatic kernel" (Avelar 1999, 228). Thus, the met-aphorization of the internal content by an exterior deadly disguise results in double meanings of the narrative while at the same time channeling the mourning for the dead. The link between mourning and doubleness proposed by Avelar, in fact, characterizes Adelaida García Morales's reconstruction of a childhood during the early Franco dictatorship in the novella *The South*. The narrative begins with the adult narrator's promise to visit her father's deserted tomb at dawn; then it goes on with a recollection of her repressed childhood and her pro-Republican father's suicide during the early postwar period; and it ends with a description in the narrator's indifferent tone of a ruin left over by her past life. Specifically, while the father's tomb is similar to the exterior tomb described by Avelar, the hidden sociopolitical connotations communicated through the father's death are the objects of my exploration.

Scholarly critics of both the written and visual forms of *The South* have focused on the themes of the child protagonists' *bildung* or coming of age,[4] the mythification of the father,[5] the daughter-father relationship,[6] and the Gothic vision.[7] None of them have approached the aspect that the writer and the director have constructed their works as memories or, more specifically, memories of traumatic childhood in the postwar period. Additionally, despite the fact that critics have examined both works from the psychoanalytic perspective, the whole complex that links psychoanalysis to historical memory, mourning, and national allegory is still virtually unexplored. Exploring this complex in the novella and the film *The South*, I aim to shed light on how the narrators channel the mourning for the dead fathers on the surface, and how the writer and the director use their depressive childhood memories to render their hidden reflections on the politics of a nation-state in an allegorical form.

Angus Fletcher's discussions of allegory inform my reading of double meanings in the novella. Etymologically, *allos* means "other" while *agoreuein* means "speak openly, speak in the assembly or market" (Fletcher 1964, 2). In his now classic book *Allegory: The Theory of a Symbolic Mode*, Fletcher argues that "*agoreuein* connotes public, open, declarative speech. This sense is inverted by the prefix *allos*. Thus allegory is often called 'inversion'" (1964, 2). More specifically, Fletcher's allegory means something other than public, or something secret, concerning veiled meanings behind public discourses. However, I argue that the relationship between the prefix of the word allegory and its root sense can also be complementary; thus "allegory" can also mean a making-public of something that would otherwise remain secret. In other words, the something other [*allos*] can only be made visible and audible in the root sense of being open to the public [*allegoreuein*] by this means. While Fletcher's interpretation of allegory calls attention to what the something other may be, the additional one I propose emphasizes the means of making the other public. Both connotations of allegory concern me in the exploration of *The South*, in the written form and the visual form.

In his controversial article on the alleged third-world literature, Fredric Jameson proposes the notion of "national allegory," asserting that "third-world texts, even those which are seemingly private and invested with a properly libidinal dynamic necessarily project a political dimension in the form of national allegory" (1986, 69). Although I believe his assertion regarding Asian and African literatures is both Eurocentric and oversimplified, his definition of "national allegory" provides a helpful insight into the entanglement of childhood narratives and the imagining of nation. By "national allegory," Jameson argues that "the story of the private individual destiny is always an allegory of the embattled situation of the public... culture and society" (1986, 69). I consider the novella and the film *The South* as national allegories, exploring the links of the personal to the national in the two works. Specifically, I explore how children's mourning becomes an entry point through which the novella *The South* and its cinematographic adaption allegorically render political and historical reflections on national politics at different key historical moments.

In *The Origin of German Tragedy*, when analyzing German poets' allegorical use of the skull or "death's head" as an emblem of history, Walter Benjamin writes that "everything about history that from the very beginning has been untimely, sorrowful and unsuccessful is expressed in a face or rather in a death's face" (1977, 166). This argument describes the case of *The South*: both versions were produced in the early 1980s when reflections on the past, especially on the defeated Republican's past, appeared to be untimely. These reflections were untimely not because Spaniards did not need them at that time but because the official policy did not encourage them and the media did not welcome them. Thus, these untimely discussions needed a mask, behind which they could appear in public. Apparently, the novella and the film are developed around a childhood marked by the death of the father, who commits suicide for mysterious reasons. These childhood narratives, however, would not be properly appreciated without some sense of Spanish national history and politics. The combination of the allegorical and psychoanalytic perspectives actually reveals hidden political reflections behind the public face of the father's death. Those are officially untimely reflections on the early Franco dictatorship as well as the silence regarding the dictatorship in the early 1980s.

Losing a parent during the war or the postwar period scarred a large number of Spanish children of the time. According to the data of historian Michael Richards: "It has been plausibly calculated that some 350,000 Spaniards met an untimely death during the period

1936–1939...In excess of a further 200,000 Spaniards died in the period 1940–42, as a result of hunger, and of hunger-related diseases, political repression and imprisonment" (1998, 116). While many parents died due to the war and the ensuing political persecution, leaving their children orphaned, many children, especially of the defeated, were forcibly taken from their parents and shuffled between families sympathetic to the new regime during the postwar period.[8] Thus, for children of pro-Republican parents, coming to terms with the past requires, first of all, confrontation with the loss of the parent, or, in other words, the completion of mourning for the dead parent.

In the film, the child protagonist Estrella is burdened by her father's death and secret past. In the sequence of the child Estrella's reaction to the father's death, the long duration of the repressive darkness before she opens her eyes to face the cruel reality of her father's absence reveals the extreme pain the protagonist experiences when she realizes her father will not come back anymore. Only at the very end of the film are we informed that the father commits suicide by shooting himself on the mountain. The father's suicide is the traumatic event that Estrella has made efforts to face, while at the same time all other fragmented memories she retains from her childhood both hide and reveal this fact that has been suppressed in her consciousness.

The scene of her initiation into the magic world of the pendulum foretells her responsibility to publicize her father's past in order to unburden herself. When asked to empty the mind and follow the pendulum in the film, Estrella slowly enters into darkness behind her father and does not come out until she exclaims in delight that "it is spinning. It is spinning." The representation of this scene, aided by the lighting, is symbolic: Only when she masters the pendulum, assuming the responsibility required by it, can Estrella leave behind the repression (or psychological burden) represented as the darkness in the film. In other words, in the film the child's task of understanding her childhood is replaced by her exploration and reconstruction of the father's tragic life; from a possessed object showed at the beginning of the film, Estrella gradually grows into an active constructor, recounting her father's past. For her, to recount the family history is also to reconstruct the national past.

In the film, the father, Agustín, ends the repressed life by committing suicide. From behind Agustín's suicide emerges the director's deep sympathy for the defeated Republicans who endured the repressions during the postwar period. John Pym describes Omero Antonutti's role as Agustín by writing:"He bears it all with silent, melancholy fortitude: Omero Antonutti, sad-eyed, grizzled, passive, has, it seems, absorbed the character into his bones" (Pym 2007, 309). Agustín intends to escape from the responsibility assigned by the pendulum to discover and confront the origin of his tragic life, yet he has no refuge to hide in. During the postwar period of the 1940s and 1950s, being a Republican, Agustín's agency was greatly limited by the authoritarianism of the Franco regime. The seagull, located on the roof of the house in the remote northern village where the family lived, can symbolize the father's image: year after year, it is frozen by ice and fettered by the iron stand. Agustín names the dog Sinbad, alluding to Sinbad the sailor, who has fantastic adventures at sea; ironically, however, the camera lingers on a small river in front of his house. The contrast between the dreamt sea and the actual river reflects the reality many Republicans, including Agustín, had to face after losing the war: a yawning gap existed between their political aspirations and the current situations they needed to face.

While Estrella's childhood stories are dominated by her exploration of her father's sufferings and suicide, the child protagonist Adriana of the novella, like many children of Republican parents, experienced childhood as shadowed by the tragic life of the previous generation and as directly repressed by the Franco regime. She experiences vilification by society since she has an atheist father. She receives forcible indoctrination from being subjected to a rigid religious education. Through reflective recollections the narrator aims to understand what was happening to her childhood; and by adopting some connotative words the author exposes and criticizes the repression many children of Republican parents suffered during the postwar period. When analyzing national characteristics of the Soviet Union and Yugoslavia, sociologist Rogers Brubaker observes the sudden and pervasive "nationalization" of public and private life. According to Brubaker, this includes "the silencing and marginalization of alternative political languages, values and beliefs" (1996, 200). This observation is also applicable in the building of New Spain under the Franco regime. One of the most fundamental principles of the regime was centralism. Therefore, the most common slogan in postwar Spain is "Spain, one, great and free" [*España, una, grande y libre*]. "One" refers to one nation, one highest leader, one political ideology and party, one religion, and one language. The founder of Spanish Falange, José Antonio Primo de Rivera, declared in public that "Spain is diverse and plural, but her diverse peoples, with their languages, customs and characteristics, are irrevocably bound in a unity of destiny on a universal plan" (1941, 105).

To reconfigure Spain as a Francoist nation is actually to homogenize all aspects of people's lives. The homogenizing power forcefully pushed Spaniards, children of the future generation in particular, to identify with New Spain. In the narrative, Adriana's first encounter with her little companion Mari-Nieves evokes the Francoist official discourse that being a Republican or a Republican's child is "a disease" [un mal]. After Mari-Nieves turns down her proposal to play the role of Juana de Arc, Adriana furiously takes revenge by pushing her little companion into a fire and the mother and the maid, Josefa, punish her violent act. The mother and Josefa's punishment propels Adriana closer to her father and enables her to identify herself with her father, who was considered to be "monstrous" by other family members and visitors. Adriana's sad story with her playmate allegorically points to the political ploys the Franco regime used to humiliate and persecute its enemies. Francoist psychiatrists, led by Antonio Vallejo-Nágera, used the word "the disease [el mal]" to describe the pro-Republicans and their children; moreover, the Francoists fabricated the crime of arson to denigrate the Republicans (Vinyes 2002, 49). Such denigrating propaganda dominated children's reading materials of the postwar period, aiming at an ideological socialization of school children.

Being one of the most—if not the most—important pillars in postwar Spain, the Catholic church best illustrates the combination of politics and religion in the ideological reconfiguration of what has been the past and what would be the future of a Francoist New Spain. Concerning the Spanish situation, Pope Pío XI delivered the encyclical *Divini Redemptoris* on March 19, 1937, supporting the nationalist rebels and condemning the Republicans. The Pope declared that the Francoists' "proper and social mission is to defend truth, justice and all those eternal values which Communism attacks," considering Franco's rebellion to be "a crusade for the progress of humanity."[9] The Franco regime adopted Pope Pío XI's description of the Spanish Civil War as the official version, portraying the nation as an innocent victim of atheist Republican sinners, and the Civil War, as the Crusade. According to Francoist psychiatrists, to treat those "sick" pro-Republicans, the most effective "psychotherapy," in addition to the crude application of violence, "existed in official exhortations to redemption and consolation through prayer and moral rectitude" (Richards 1998, 66). *The South* provides an analogous experience. In the novella, Josefa diagnoses the father's "sickness," claiming that "the lack of religious faith is what happened. That is why he will always be hopeless" (García Morales 1985, 9). Josefa's conclusion forms an allegory of the Francoist propaganda that the origin of the Republicans' "moral disease" is the lack of faith (Richards 1998, 68). The textual description allegorizes the official insistence on imposing religiosity on the Spanish popular mentality as one of the basic uniting ideologies in the newly reconfigured nation. In addition, the existence of the two distinct worlds Adriana describes in the novella alludes to the Francoist separatist policy of isolating the atheist pro-Republicans and their children from the rest of the Spaniards in order to avoid the contagion of the Leftist "disease" (Richards 1998, 68).

The narrator's recollections of her childhood stories not only help her understand what was happening to her as a child but also could remind those previous children of Republican parents of the past, unfair treatment they received under the Franco regime. From the narrator's confrontation with her traumatic memories emerges the author's allegorical critique of the persecution the Franco regime imposed on the Republicans and their families during the postwar period. While the narrator Adriana breaks the silence in the family by communicating her childhood experiences, the author breaks the silence in society by evoking the traumatic past that many children of Republican parents suffered but has gone unrecognized.

The attempt to understand postwar childhood masks the author's critique of the Francoist repression during the postwar period in the early 1980s when most of the Spaniards, especially those who experienced the war or the early postwar period as children, chose to keep silent about the past. Interestingly enough, according to the result of Powell's survey, the group that experienced the war and the postwar period as children most favored reconciliation without discussing the past in the early 1980s (Powell 2001, 42–43). García Morales and Víctor Erice belong to this generation yet, unlike their contemporaries, both chose to break the silence regarding the past. The reconstruction of Adriana's traumatic childhood experiences becomes a national allegory, through which García Morales expresses her critique of the political repression the Franco regime imposed on children of Republican parents. Through Estrella's reluctance to begin narrating her childhood memories shadowed by her father's stories, Erice emphasizes the overwhelming impact the pain of the previous generation has had on their childhood. The trauma and extreme pain apprehended by the two child protagonists are attributed by the author and filmmaker to "Franco's children" as a whole. If these childhood stories are impressive texts, the national tragedy, as these two works allegorically speak to, is more powerful than its textual levels.

Facing the father's death, the narrator chooses to fill in the empty world, left by the dead father, through reconstructions of the father's past—the cause of the father's death. In other words, the children take the explorations of their fathers' pasts to be the substitutes to which they transfer their "libido"—in Freud's term. Aiming at the same substitutive missions, Adriana and Estrella encounter different situations and thus offer different solutions. More specifically, silence about the past predominates in Adriana's family and thus she has to travel to her father's hometown to find out what happened to him; unlike Adriana, Estrella collects fragmentary information about her father's past from people around her and is able to complete the story through her imagination.

While the father's, Rafael's, past is an allegory of the national past, the silence that predominates in Adriana's family alludes to the silence that predominated in Spanish society during the early 1980s, evoking critics' explanations for the hush of the transitional time. Teresa Vilarós analyzes reticence regarding the war and the postwar period from a psychoanalytic perspective, comparing the reticence to the mechanism of repression of consciousness (1998, 70–73). According to her, a period of latency is necessary before the subject can figure out the trauma s/he suffered. Rafael's silence, though as early as in the 1940s and 1950s, illustrates this argument. According to Adriana's recollection, her father confesses: "Look, the worst suffering is the one without a particular reason. It comes from everywhere and nowhere in particular" (García Morales 1985, 37). Rafael is not patient enough to wait for his trauma to be resolved. Suffering the repressed life during the postwar period, he ends up killing himself. When he is alive, Rafael covers up his own past from the child. In 1939, the end of the Civil War suspended the public rivalry between the Left and the Right. The Leftists were repressed during the postwar period and the winning Rightists reconstructed the nation based on their will. The new government arising from the wreckage of the war endeavored to legitimize itself by creating a glorious past for the country and imposing it on the Spaniards, especially on the children who did not experience the war. Sadly enough, in the novella Rafael not only keeps silent about his past, but also imposes silence on the other members of the family. Analyzing García Morales's *The South* from the feminist perspective, scholar Akiko Tsuchiya also identifies the family secret with paternal prohibition (1999, 92–97). Under the father's patriarchal authority, the mother takes part in concealing the secret from the child. The mother's submission evokes Carmen Moreno-Nuño's analysis of possible reasons for the Spaniards' silence under democratic governments. According to her, one of the possible reasons for silence can be the consequence of the Franco dictatorship: Spaniards were used to keeping silent under the regime and this custom survived the dictator (Moreno-Nuño 2006, 43–58).

In contrast to the previous generation that experienced the repression of the war and the postwar period and chose to cover up the past, Adriana, who experienced an unhappy childhood without understanding what was happening to her, finally takes responsibility for the past. To understand her father's melancholia and to complete her own mourning, Adriana traces the origin of her father's sufferings by traveling to the south—the father's hometown—to uncover his past. In Seville, the mournful Adriana becomes sensitive to old furniture, clothing, utensils, and ruins of former possessions that the dead father left behind. Ruins are significant for Adriana's journey to the south, because they conjure up the father's past life, while at the same time reminding Adriana of the absence/death of their previous owner. Despite the fact that Rafael's old servant, Emilia, recalls the father's life in the south for Adriana, she refuses to unravel the mystery of his tragic love. When discussing the memories of the Transition, Joan Ramón Resina focuses on the politics of memory, arguing that "the current dispute is really over which fragments of the past are being refloated and which are allowed to sink" (2000, 86). Emilia's memory illustrates this politics. Emilia recalls details of Rafael's childhood, adolescence, and youth while at the same time purposefully excluding the crucial figure of Gloria Valle from his past life in the south. Gloria Valle is crucial not only because the story of Rafael's past remains incomplete without her but also because to visit her is Rafael's unfulfilled desire. In front of Gloria Valle's house, Adriana feels that she is visiting her father's ex-lover at his behest (García Morales 1985, 46). Accomplishing the visit her father did not collect enough courage to realize, Adriana believes she has satisfied her father's unfulfilled desire.

Adriana's journey both begins and ends with ruins. When returning to the northern house, the objects that belong to the common life shared by her father and herself can no longer trigger any remembrance of their past. At the end of the story, the narrator describes the ruins of their house in the north in a calm tone. Thus, by acknowledging the fact of the father's death and overcoming the loss by separating her ego from the dead father, Adriana completes mourning for the loss of her father. Searching among the ruins, Adriana aims to find the hidden truth of her father's death. Similarly, examining memories of postwar childhood in an allegorical way, I focus on revealing the author's veiled political reflections on the past and the present. Both activities share the same purpose of dragging the content out of the veiling masks. The adult narrator Adriana understands her childhood and completes mourning for the dead father. From an allegorical perspective, I recognize the author's position as a postwar child: she is in favor of digging up the painful past not to dwell in it but with the goal of coming to terms with it and not letting it affect her current life.

Adriana completes mourning by traveling to her father's birthplace. Unlike Adriana, Estrella overcomes the loss of the father not through an actual journey but an imaginative one. She gains bits and pieces of information about her father's past life from her mother and Milagros—the maid who took care of her father in the south. Departing from the available information, she employs her imagination to complete her father's past life. The mother fires Estrella's imagination with her description of the south and the mysterious air the mother creates around her father's past. After hearing her mother's narration, Estrella becomes nostalgic for the south where she has never been. In her imagination, in contrast to the arid and cold north, the south should be green and warm.

The south that exists in her imagination offers an allegorical vision of the official image of the folkloric south propagated by the Franco regime during the postwar period. After bloodily seizing power, the Francoists extracted concepts and symbols from southern folklore and assigned them new ideological meanings to feed into a new nation founding discourse. In the words of Carmen Ortiz: "Behind this interest in folklore lies the need (of the Franco regime) to claim key symbols of identity or territorial, ethnic, or political unity... the concept of nation and its identity constituted the deepest nucleus of the ideology of the regime" (1999, 487). The south is an exotic place filled with fountains, flamenco, countrymen, poets, and dancing women in regional costumes. Propagating the folkloric south, the regime appropriated southern lyric and epic for legitimizing and sacralizing the Francoist political leaders, including Franco and José Antonio Primo de Rivera (Ortiz 1999, 479–480). The popular dance, songs, and poems, rich in the south, were reinvented to promote Catholic-nationalism of the new nation. In addition, the regime also idealized images of countrymen as the very representation of the essence of nation in order to disguise and conceal class and regional contradictions (Ortiz 1999, 481). The pristine peasantry of the southern rural area, described as obedient and faithful, became the symbol of the Spanish people, representing the uncontaminated and eternal essence of New Spain. The peasants, mostly living in the south, forcibly assumed the role of "the founding-stone of the whole nation," in Hitler's words (Bausinger 1993 [1971], 70).

Ironically, while the regime promoted a deceptive peaceful image of the south in order to legitimize and eternalize the dictatorship after the war, the director Erice contrasts this image with harsh reality during the postwar period to undermine the Francoist propaganda. In the film, Estrella gazes at the beautiful propagandistic pictures while at the same time the camera shows images outside her window: in contrast to the vivid exuberance in the imaged south, the backyard in their northern house is covered by snow and the water fountain is frozen. By combining the information she collects and her imagination based on this information, Estrella visualizes the south. She takes the same approach to reconstructing the father's secret past, by combining real information and her imagination. Through imaginatively reconstructing a childhood dominated by her father's tragic stories, Estrella overcomes her mourning for the father by being able to confront his death with calmness.

CONCLUSION

It is evident that the childhoods of the young protagonists have been shaped by the particular circumstances of the dictatorship. The dictatorship, in fact, has marked the lives of Franco's children not only in the past but also in the present. However, this generation has never been passively repressed by their circumstances; rather, they have been social actors who construct and reconstruct a national-catholic childhood to articulate their political voices.

The written and visual versions of *The South* depict a childhood not as a romanticized paradisiacal site but rather as a status of endless fear, utter helplessness, and constant bewilderment. As national allegories, these two works conjure up propagandistic discourses the Franco regime employed for its postwar reconfiguration of the Spanish nation. Bringing back the Francoist triumphalist inventions of the nation and national identity, the author and the director not only criticize Francoism in the past but also express an officially untimely opinion in the early 1980s: there is a need to confront the national past in order to leave it behind in the future.

In an article about Spanish ex-prime minister Felipe González's administration, the ambassador of Spain in Vietnam Josep Pons Irazazábal writes: "With Felipe González I learned that in politics it is very important to be right at the right moment, neither before nor after. I also learned that being right is not enough—you need people's recognition."[10] After exploring how the novella and the film

The South render their childhood narratives as national allegories in the late period of democratic transition, I would add to the ambassador's political lesson by arguing that while the timing of a statement is undoubtedly important, the means of stating the opinion is no less crucial. Specifically, in both works, the narrators' understanding of childhood and completion of mourning for their dead fathers allegorically mask the otherwise silent *allos*—reflections on the Francoist nation reconfiguration project as well as the relevance of the past to the present and future democratic nation of Spain.

In the future, there remains a need to examine works produced by these children in the stages of their early life. As children in war, they drew pictures representing horrifying wartime scenes;[11] they also wrote diaries and letters to their family members describing their experiences and feelings in wartime and the early post-War period.[12] An examination of these realistic drawings and writings as national allegories will complement the picture of the entanglement between childhood and nation, of and by "Franco's children."

NOTES

1. The best-known examples include Víctor Erice's *El espíritu de la colmena* (1973), Carlos Saura's *Cría Cuervos* (1976), Carmen Martín Gaite's *El cuarto de atrás* (1977), and so forth.

2. One of the most—if not the most—popular television series in the new millennium is *Cuéntame cómo pasó*, broadcast by TVE1 since 2001; the series recounts the experiences of a middle-class family in the 1970s through a child's perspective.

   The Internet has become one of the most important channels through which Spaniards recall and represent Franco-era childhood experiences, search for their lost siblings, and announce large-scale gatherings. Facebook plays a crucial role in the last two functions. See http://www.facebook.com/events/395828383791644/permalink/395831557124660/ and http://www.facebook.com/pages/PLATAFORMA-AFECTADOS-CLINICAS-DE-TODA-ESPA%C3%91A-CAUSA-NI%C3%91OS-ROBADOS/173164369461093.

   The Library of Andalucía, for instance, hosted the exhibition "Memorias de la escuela (1940–1975)" between January 1 and January 29, 2011. Similar exhibitions have been held in Malaga (October 19–November 20, 2007), in Salamanca (March 30–May 16, 2010), in Leon (February 23–March 14, 2010), and so forth.

   The Forum for the Memory of the Madrid Community [*Foro por la memoria de la comunidad de Madrid*] presented the symposium titled "The 'Other' Victims of the Dictatorship [*las 'otras' víctimas de la dictadura*]," in which the first topic was dedicated to "Childhood under the Francoist Repression [*La infancia bajo la represión franquista*]."

3. This is evidenced by the active operation of the Association for the Recovery of Historical Memory in Spain.
4. Isolina Ballesteros, "Las niñas del cine español: La evasión infantil en *El espíritu de la colmena, El sur y Los años oscuros*," *Revista Hispánica Moderna* 49(2) (1996): 232–242; Susan L. Martín-Márquez, *Essays on Hispanic Film and Fiction* (Corvallis: Portland State University Press, 1995); Bárbara Morris, "Father Death and the feminine: The writer's 'subject' in Adelaida García Morales' *El Sur*," *Romance Languages Annual* 1 (1989): 559–564; Akiko Tsuchiya, "Family plots and romances: Discourses of desire in Adelaida García Morales's narrative fiction," *Bulletin of Hispanic Studies* 76 (1): 91–108.
5. Jo Evans, "The myth in time: Víctor Erice's *El sur*," *Journal of Hispanic Research* 4 (1995–1996): 147–157.
6. Cristina Martínez-Carazo, "El sur: De la palabra a la imagen," *Bulletin of Hispanic Studies* 74 (2) (1997): 187–196; Clare Nimmo, "García Morales and Erice's *El sur*: Viewpoint and closure," *Romance Studies* 26 (1) (1995): 41–49; Peter Evans and Robin Fiddian, "*El Sur*: A narrative of star-cross'd lovers," *Bulletin of Hispanic Studies* 64 (2) (1987): 127–135.
7. Elizabeth J. Ordóñez, *Voices of Their Own: Contemporary Spanish Narrative by Women* (Lewisburg: Bucknell University Press, 1991); Kathleen M. Glenn, "Gothic vision in García Morales and Erice's *El Sur*," *Letras Peninsulares* 7 (1) (1994): 239–250; Abigail Lee Six, *The Gothic Fiction of Adelaida García Morales: Haunting Words* (Rochester: Tamesis, 2006).
8. See Montse Armengou and Richard Bellis (directors), *Los niños perdidos del franquismo* (Barcelona: TV3, 2002).
9. Pope Pío XI. *Divini Redemptoris*, March 19, 1937, web April 10, 2012, http://www.vati can.va/holy_father/pius_xi/encyclicals/documents/hf_p-xi_enc_19031937_divini-redemptoris_en.html.
10. Josep Pons Irazazábal, "Aquel 12 de junio de 1985," *El País*, June 21, 2010, http://0-www.elpais.com/diario/2010/06/21/opinion/1277071205_850215.html.
11. See the exhibition "They Still Draw Pictures" for reference.
12. See Blas V. Sierra, *Palabras Huérfanas: Los Niños y La Guerra Civil* (Madrid: Taurus, 2009).

REFERENCES

Abella, Rafael. 1978. *Por el imperio hacia Dios: Crónica de una posguerra (1939–1955)*. Barcelona: Crítica.

Alburquerque, Francisco. 1981. "Métodos de control político de la población civil: El sistema de racionamiento de alimentos y productos básicos impuestos en España tras la última guerra civil." In *Estudios sobre la historia de España*, edited by M. Tuñón de Lara, 427–498. Madrid: Alianza Editorial.

Ariès, Philippe. 1962. *Centuries of Childhood: A Social History of Family Life*, translated by Robert Baldick. New York: Vintage Books.

Armengou, Montse, and Ricard Bellis (directors). 2002. *Los niños perdidos del franquismo*. Barcelona: TV3.

Avelar, Idelber. 1999. *The Untimely Present*. Durham, NC: Duke University Press.

Ballesteros, Isolina. 1996. "Las niñas del cine español: La evasión infantil en *El espíritu de la colmena*, *El sur* y *Los años oscuros*." *Revista Hispánica Moderna* 49 (2): 232–242.

Bausinger, Hermann. 1993 [1971]. *"Volkskundeo"u l'ethnologiael lemande*. Paris: Éditions de la Maison des sciences de l'homme.

Benjamin, Walter. 1977. *The Origin of German Tragic Drama*, translated by John Osborne. London: NLB.

Brubaker, Rogers. 1996. *Nationalism Reframed: Nationhood and the National Question in the New Europe*. New York: Cambridge University Press.

Cenarro, Ángela. 2008. "Memories of repression and resistance: Narratives of children institutionalized by auxilio social in post-war Spain." *History and Memory* 20 (2): 39–59.

Erice, Víctor (director). 1983. *El Sur*. Murcia: Grupo Editorial Mundografic.

Evans, Jo. 1995–1996. "The myth in time: Víctor Erice's *El sur*." *Journal of Hispanic Research* 4: 147–157.

Evans, Peter, and Robin Fiddian. 1987. *"El Sur*: A narrative of star-cross'd lovers." *Bulletin of Hispanic Studies* 64 (2): 127–135.

Fletcher, Angus. 1964. *Allegory: The Theory of a Symbolic Mode*. Ithaca, NY: Cornell University Press.

García Morales, Adelaida. 1985. *El Sur seguido de Bene*. Barcelona: Ediciones Anagrama.

Glenn, Kathleen M. 1994. "Gothic vision in García Morales and Erice's *El Sur*." *Letras Peninsulares* 7 (1): 239–250.

Halbwachs, Maurice. 1991. *On Collective Memory*. Chicago, IL: University of Chicago Press.

Irazazábal, Josep Pons. "Aquel 12 de junio de 1985." *El País*, June 21, 2010. http://0-www.elpais.com/diario/2010/06/21/opinion/1277071205_850215.html.

James, Allison, and Alan Prout. 2008. *Constructing and Reconstructing Childhood: Contemporary Issues in the Sociological Study of Childhood*. London: Routledge Falmer.

Jameson, Fredric. 1986. "Third-world literature in the era of multinational capitalism." *Social Text* 15 (3): 65–88.

Kehily, Mary J. 2009. *An Introduction to Childhood Studies*. Maidenhead: Open University Press.

Labanyi, Jo. 2009. "The languages of silence: Historical memory, generational transmission and witnessing in contemporary Spain." *Journal of Romance Studies* 9 (3): 23–35.

———. 2007. "Memory and modernity in democratic Spain: The difficulty of coming to terms with the Spanish Civil War." *Poetics Today* 28 (1): 89–116.

Ley 5/1979, de 18 de septiembre, sobre reconocimiento de pensiones, asistencia médico-farmacéutica y asistencia social en favor de las viudas, y demás familiares de los españoles fallecidos como consecuencia o con ocasión de la pasada guerra civil. Septiembre 18, 1979.

Ley 35/1980, de 26 de junio, sobre pensiones a los mutilados excombatientes de la zona republicana. June 26, 1980.

Ley 6/1982, de 29 de marzo, de pensiones a los mutilados civiles de guerra. March 29, 1982.

Ley 37/1984, de 22 de octubre, de reconocimiento de derechos y servicios prestados a quienes durante la Guerra Civil formaron parte de las fuerzas armadas, fuerzas de orden público y cuerpo de carabineros de la República. Octobre 22, 1984.

Martín-Márquez, Susan L. 1995. *Essays on Hispanic Film and Fiction.* Corvallis: Portland State University Press.

Martínez-Carazo, Cristina. 1997. "El sur: De la palabra a la imagen." *Bulletin of Hispanic Studies* 74 (2): 187–196.

Mills, Jean, and Richard Mills. 2000. *Childhood Studies: A Reader in Perspectives of Childhood.* London: Routledge.

Molinero, Carme. 2010. "La transición y la 'renuncia' a la recuperación de la 'memoria democrática.'" *Journal of Spanish Cultural Studies* 11 (1): 33–52.

Moreno-Nuño, Carmen. 2006. *Las huellas de la guerra civil: Mito y trauma en la narrativa de la España democrática.* Madrid: Libertarias.

Morris, Bárbara. 1989. "Father Death and the feminine: The writer's 'subject' in Adelaida García Morales' *El Sur.*" *Romance Languages Annual* 1: 559–564.

Nimmo, Clare. 1995. "García Morales's and Erice's *El sur*: Viewpoint and closure." *Romance Studies* 26 (1): 41–49.

Ordóñez, Elizabeth J. 1991. *Voices of Their Own: Contemporary Spanish Narrative by Women.* Lewisburg: Bucknell University Press.

Ortiz, Carmen. 1999. "The use of folklore by the Franco regime." *Journal of America Folklore* 112 (446): 479–496.

Piquer y Jover, José. 1946. *El niño abandonado y delincuente: Consideración etiológica y estadística.* Madrid: Consejo Superior de Investigaciones Científicas.

Pope Pío XI. *Divini Redemptoris.* March 19, 1937. Web. April 10, 2012. http://www.vati can.va/holy_father/pius_xi/encyclicals/documents/ hf_p-xi_enc_19031937_divini-redemptoris_en.html.

Powell, Charles. 2001. *España en democracia, 1975–2000.* Barcelona: Plaza & Janés Editores.

Preston, Paul. 1976. *Spain in Crisis: Evolution and Decline of the Franco Regime.* New York: Barnes & Noble Books.

Primo de Rivera, Jose Antonio. 1941. *Obras completas*, Vol. 1: Discursos fundamentales y otros discursos de propaganda. Speech on the Spanish revolution in the "Madrid" cinema, Madrid, May 19, 1935, pp. 95–114. Madrid: Ediciones Fe.

Pym, John. 2007. "In the world: *El sur* (the South)." In *The Cinema of Víctor Erice: An Open Window*, edited by Linda C. Ehrlich, 309–312. Plymouth, UK: Scarecrow Press.

Resina, Joan Ramón (ed.). 2000. *Disremembering the Dictatorship: The Politics of Memory in the Spanish Transition to Democracy*. Amsterdam: Rodopi.

Richards, Michael. 1998. *A Time of Silence: Civil War and the Culture of Repression in Franco's Spain, 1936–1945*. New York: Cambridge University Press.

Sánchez, Pedro Poyato. 2003. "Del hipotexto literario al hipertexto fílmico: *El sur* (Adelaida García Morales y Víctor Erice)." *Pandora: Revue D'etudes Hispaniques* 3 (1): 145–158.

Santos, Antonio. 2001. "Piedras vivas, almas muertsa. Al otro lado del mapa: El sur." *Trasdós. Revista del Museo de Bellas Artes de Santander* 3: 182–198.

Sierra, Blas V. 2009. *Palabras Huérfanas: Los Niños y La Guerra Civil*. Madrid: Taurus.

Six, Abigail Lee. 2006. *The Gothic Fiction of Adelaida García Morales: Haunting Words*. Rochester: Tamesis.

Tsuchiya, Akiko. 1999. "Family plots and romances: Discourses of desire in Adelaida García Morales's narrative fiction." *Bulletin of Hispanic Studies* 76 (1): 91–108.

Vilarós, Teresa. 1998. *El mono del desencanto: Una crítica cultural de la transición Española (1973–1993)*. Madrid: Siglo XXI.

Vinyes, Ricard. 2002. *Irredentas: Las presas políticas y sus hijos en las cárceles de Franco*. Madrid: Temas de Hoy.

CHAPTER 5

(Dis)Locating Hospitality: Reader Positioning in Australian Picture Books about Asylum Seekers

Trish Lunt

INTRODUCTION

Since the turn of the millennium, the figure of the asylum seeker has been prominent in Australian social and political discourse. In a post-9/11 environment dominated by fear of the Other, particularly the non-Western Muslim Other (see, e.g., Mansouri 2002; Hage 2011), a pronounced ethos of threat is perpetuated (and challenged) in the mass media, in government fora, and in academia (see, e.g., Papastergiadis 2006; Taylor 2011; Bolt 2014). The Australian government is under scrutiny for its exclusionary policies and practices in regard to South Asian and Middle Eastern asylum seekers (Australian Human Rights Commission 2014). While there is significant resistance to current policy by pro-refugee activists (Hintjens and Jarman 2002), there is an inherent assumption in a democratic system that the government represents the "voice of the people" and that government policy epitomizes the dominant perspectives of the Australian public. This study of representations of asylum seekers in Australian picture books interrogates the ways in which child readers are positioned to accept or challenge the dominant social discourse of fear and threat that pervades print and social media.

It is widely acknowledged that texts for children reflect and sometimes contest dominant social perspectives (Hollindale 1988; Stephens 1992; Nodelman and Reimer 2003). Whether overtly didactic or not, all texts represent particular views of the world(s) in which we live, and children's texts, in particular, fit "firmly within the domain of cultural practices which exist for the purpose of socializing their target audience" (Stephens 1992, 8). Zygmunt Bauman (1990) argues that childhood is a significant time for "social lessons" by which one acquires "common knowledge" or "common sense" understandings. With little power to resist socialization, children learn what is "normal" in their world—from those around them, and from repetition and reinforcement of ideas. As Bauman says: "When repeated often enough, things tend to become familiar, and familiar things are self-explanatory; they present no problems and arouse no curiosity. In a way, they remain invisible" (1990, 15).

Bauman describes refugees as "the absolute outsiders, outsiders everywhere and out of place everywhere except in places that are themselves out of place—the 'nowhere places' that appear on the maps used by ordinary humans on their travels" (2004, 80). If children are offered the adverse views of refugees and asylum seekers commonly dispensed by public media and national government, then readers will regard this public perspective of "outsiders incarnate" (Bauman 2004, 80) as self-explanatory and familiar. Alternatively, if child readers are offered opportunities to challenge public discourse through texts that make familiar the unfamiliar, arouse curiosity, and contest the norm, then opportunities for reader agency are concurrently proffered.

This chapter focuses on the spatial relations of textuality to show how picture books mobilize readers to take up diverse views about asylum seekers within an Australian context. The tools of spatial theory (see, for example, Harvey 1990; Massey 1994, 2005; Sassen 2008) offer to the interpretation of picture books a method of deep reading that considers the relational processes inherent in verbal and visual representation. The materiality of the picture book form embeds the relative positioning of characters and objects, modes of distance and closeness, geographies of emplacement, linear and nonlinear progressions, and visual points of view. Furthermore, the ways in which readers are positioned relative to asylum seeker protagonists in terms of distance and proximity, or detachment and alignment, function as conduits of interaction between the reader and the text. Notably, the reader is either situated in a static observational position, or is invited into participatory action within the text/narrative. These positions of readerly disengagement or engagement significantly influence the kinds of messages offered to readers about contemporary political and social perspectives of the acceptance of asylum seekers by and into the Australian community.

BORDER POLITICS

In the 2000s, Australian political rhetoric about asylum seekers, especially those arriving onshore (to whom the idiom "boat people" has been ascribed), has been expressly negative. This differs significantly from policy and practice around the arrival of Vietnamese "boat people" in the 1970s. As Phillips and Spinks (2003) state:

> Opinion poll data show that boat arrivals have always been an issue of concern to the Australian public, and opposition to boat arrivals has increased steadily over the last four decades. While the first wave of "boat people" (1976–81) was initially received by the Australian public with sympathy, continuing arrivals quickly became a matter of increasing concern.

According to Fiona McKay, Samantha Thomas, and Susan Kneebone (2012, 114–115), in 1977 a public poll revealed that 20 percent of Australians wanted "boat people" "stopped from staying here." Since the beginning of this century, however, most of the asylum seekers arriving in Australia originate from the Middle East and South Asia (McKay et al. 2012; Phillips and Spinks 2013), many of whom are Muslim. The shift from viewing refugees as deserving political asylum to viewing them as a threat to national security was heightened by the events of 9/11 in the United States and the increase in numbers of asylum seekers from Islamic countries. As Fethi Mansouri (2002) notes:

> Media and government representations of refugees in Australia often relate to their morality and implied character. Much has been made of the security risk associated with "illegal" asylum seekers arriving from war-torn countries in the Middle East. In the wake of September 11, this rhetoric reached new levels with senior cabinet members in the Australian Federal Government seeking tougher measures against "illegal" asylum seekers who could pose a security threat to Australia. (3)

Following strenuous efforts by successive Liberal and Labor governments to halt the arrival of asylum seekers by boat and impede the operations of "people smugglers" who were deemed responsible for the deaths of asylum seekers at sea (Needham and Allard 2011), the current Abbott government instituted the Operation Sovereign Borders policy (The Coalition's *Operation Sovereign Borders Policy*, July 2013). Since then, asylum seekers who arrive by boat anywhere on the Australian shore have been denied entry and transferred to offshore immigration processing centers established by international agreement with Papua New Guinea and Nauru. Operation Sovereign Borders was established with the aim of deterring "people smugglers" and asylum seekers through military interception, offshore detention, "turnback operations," visa refusal, and information secrecy (ACBPS 2015). At the time of writing, there are more than 4,000 people in immigration detention centers in Nauru and Australia, and a further 3,000 in community detention awaiting residency determination. This includes 138 children in mainland detention, 73 in residential housing or "transit accommodation," and 119 in Nauru. "Illegal Maritime Arrival[s]" comprise 70 percent of people in immigration detention facilities, and the average length of detention is 422 days (ADIPB, January 2015).

According to an address by Minister Morrison, then Immigration and Border Protection, these practices are justified by limits attached to national identity through political sovereignty. He says:

> Our border is not just a line on a map. Our border is a national asset. It holds economic, social and strategic value for our nation.
>
> Our borders define a space within which, as sovereign nation states, we can apply the rule of law, operate our democracy, conduct our commerce, foster free markets, establish property rights, create the space for civil society, enable expression of culture and provide for the freedom and liberties of all of our citizens.
>
> Our border creates the space for us to be who we are and to become everything we can be as a nation. (Morrison 2014)

According to Morrison, then, borders define the space of the "nation state" and "create the space...for the freedom and liberties [of] citizens". In effect, this configures the nation as a space that excludes the political immigré, the not-yet-citizen, the "they" that threatens a nationally homogeneous "we." This rhetoric situates the marker of us/them at the national border. Giorgio Agamben argues that asylum seekers and refugees represent "a disquieting element in the order of the modern nation-state" (1998, 77); they are perceived as a threat to the (illusory) uniformity of nationalism. Ideations of real and imagined borders of a nation influence beliefs about who is "us" and who is "not-us." This contrivance of distinction between us/them or we/

they is explained by Bauman in *Thinking Sociologically* (1990, 39).
"We" and "they." He says:

> Do not stand for just two separate groups of people, but for the dis-
> tinction between two totally different attitudes—between emotional
> attachment and antipathy, trust and suspicion, security and fear, coop-
> erativeness and pugnacity.

This grouping is clearly apparent in Morrison's rhetoric.

Despite the ongoing political concerns for border control, a number of tragic events in 2001 drew a significant amount of sympathy
for asylum seekers. These events involved children. In August 2001,
the Australian government refused to allow the Norwegian freighter,
MV Tampa, carrying 433 asylum seekers rescued from a ferry sinking off Indonesia, from entering Australian waters; after six days, the
refugees were accepted by New Zealand, Nauru, and Papua New
Guinea.

In October 2001, a fallacious report that asylum seekers had
"thrown their children overboard" from a distressed ship recorded
as the Suspected Illegal Entry Vessel (*SIEV*) 4 was taken up by the
Australian government as a case in point that the (mostly Iraqi) asylum seekers were undeserving of Australian aid and exhibited behaviors that were incompatible with ethical practices of Australia. The
prime minister is reported as saying at the time: "I don't want anyone
in Australia who would throw their own children into the sea" (*Four
Corners,* Australian Broadcasting Commission, cited by Leach 2003,
27) and accused the asylum seekers of sinking their own "damn boat,
which put their children in the water" (Megalogenis 2006). By the
time the report was denounced as a misconception, the stigmatiza-
tion of Middle Eastern asylum seekers had gained some currency.
When the *SIEV X* sank in international waters between Indonesia and
Australia in October 2001, it represented Australia's "worst asylum
seeker mass drowning tragedy," with the death of 353 people, including 146 children (Hutton 2013).

The effect of these events on public opinion is divided. According
to Phillips and Spinks (2013, 7), "in September 2001, 77 per cent of
Australians supported the Howard Government's decision to refuse
entry to the Tampa and 71 per cent believed boat arrivals should be
detained for the duration of the processing of their asylum." As this
is noted in a parliamentary report, it is possible that the data is skewed
in favor of Federal policy and practice. Nevertheless, the figures based
on research by Betts (2001) support a strong public denial of asylum

seekers. The parliamentary report also states somewhat vaguely that "those who supported an 'open borders' approach to asylum seekers in 2001 did so mainly for humanitarian reasons, and also claimed that the Howard Government's hardline policies were damaging Australia's reputation overseas" (Phillips and Spinks 2013, 7).

BORDERING (ON) COMPASSION

It appears that the focus on child refugees in these tragic incidents of death and trauma did have an impact, however, in the field of children's literature. There seems an undeniable connection between public sympathies and the appearance of refugee figures in Australian literature for children. Between 2000 and 2007, nine picture books were published in Australia that reproduced the experiences of asylum seekers (AustLit 2015). Of these, four represent asylum seekers as Muslim, one presents a story of the Bosnian War, and four offer metaphorical figures as unidentified nonnational "others." All but the story of Slavic displacement represent refugee journeys by boat; there are no picture books to date that depict refugee arrivals by air or overstay.

This small influx of picture books that focus on asylum seekers implies a sense of acceptance of Bauman's "absolute outsiders" into the social space of Australian experience. In particular, realist picture book[1] texts, such as *Ziba Came on a Boat* (Lofthouse and Ingpen 2007), *Ali the Bold Heart* (Jolly and Hurst 2006), *A True Person* (Marin and Grantford 2007), and *Rainbow Bird* (Cavouras 2007), offer an insight into the ways that the figure of the asylum seeker is configured for Australian readers, mainly through the common depiction of war-torn countries of origin, treacherous journeys by sea, and the deprivations of Australian detention centers.

A True Person (Marin and Grantford 2007) documents the journey of Zallah and her mother from a war-torn "dry and hot and sandy" "first home" across the "huge and strangely blue" ocean. They are met at the Australian shoreline by suited immigration officials and, as undocumented arrivals, transferred to a detention center that, Zallah notes, is "dry and hot and sandy," an overtly ironic parallel with the despairing landscape of their departure. There is a sense of hope proffered by Zallah's friendship with a fellow detainee, and her release to "community detention" at the end of the text.

The titular protagonist of *Ali the Bold Heart* (Jolly and Hurst 2006), who has escaped war and endures mandatory detention, "locked up behind wire as sharp as tiger's [*sic*] teeth," brings joy to the other detainees by performing magic, making small coins and rings appear from within a silk cloth. This entertains the detained children and for adults is a reminder of "the magic from their childhood in and around markets and bazaars." Ali is desperate to escape from the detention center, and it is presumed that when, "in the deepest part of the night, the metal gates creaked and shuddered," he has effected a magical release.

Written by a 14-year-old, and published by Australians Against Racism Inc., *Rainbow Bird* (Cavouras 2007) depicts the isolation and psychosocial displacement of a refugee child in a bare cell in a remote Australian detention center. According to paratextual information, the book was inspired by "conversations with [the author's] grandfather about his trips to Port Augusta." The heartfelt implications of detention are signified by collages of media headlines as window frames of a cell: "Detainees helped," "promise," "freedom," "detention for families…No more," "Families with children will be detained in the community." This is an overt mechanism of politicization and a call to ethical action. The strangeness of this place of asylum as cold, bare, and boring is highlighted, but a colorful parrot signals hope that "fear is gone, freedom is near."

Ziba Came on a Boat (Lofthouse and Ingpen 2007) alternates between a young girl's journey toward asylum on a "soggy old fishing boat that creaked and moaned" and her "thoughts of home": children's laughter, grazing sheep, her mud-brick house, preparing richly spiced meals with her mother, and the comforting strength of her father's embrace. Ziba dreams that "smiling faces welcomed her to a new land." Ziba's thoughts are warm with hope and happiness reflected in the bright yellow color-motif of the illustration of these memories. Reflections on the war that initiates flight from the homeland occur midway through the narrative as the treachery of the ocean builds, and Ziba grows "fearful and sad." This bridges the past and the present, providing the reason for flight and the purpose of the refugee journey.

In general these picture books position readers to understand some of the difficulties of living in a war-torn land and the risks of the journey toward asylum. They signal hope for displaced persons through discursive framing of the Australian nation as compassionate toward and accepting of refugees. Debra Dudek proposes that texts about refugees may appeal "to the reader's conscience" (2011, 17) and invite child readers in particular "to recognize themselves and/or to acknowledge others; to evaluate the ethical and unethical actions of individuals and groups; and to judge whether or not these actions contribute to human and/or creature flourishing" (13).

There appears, then, to be a framing of hospitable action toward refugees. By bringing their stories into the public domain, by giving asylum seekers an identity, these texts personalize the refugee experience. In doing so, they represent a shift toward the kind of familiarity that Bauman (1993, 149) claims as collapsing the distinction between self and other: once "objects become *visible* I can see them as definite objects" (148, original emphasis).

Looking More Closely

It is this objectification of the figure of the refugee that becomes problematic. Bauman goes on to say that the acquisition of knowledge of the other is a function that *creates* distance between self and other. It is this distancing mechanism that objectifies and, in the manner of circular logic, depersonalizes the social relationship between the reader and the asylum seeker. After all, the other is not Other without an observable distance from the self. To "recognize [oneself]" and to "acknowledge others" (Dudek 2011, 13) sustains rather than collapses the us/them binary.

Despite these positive messages about ethical action and sympathetic understanding in these picture books, an unbridgeable binary distinction between insiders and outsiders is perpetuated. In each of these narratives, there is a strong separation between "home" and "Australia." Variously, the protagonist's place of origin is described as "home" (Lofthouse and Ingpen 2007), "my home" (Cavouras 2007), "his own land" (Jolly and Hurst 2006), and "her first home" (Marin and Grantford 2007). While this reference to a "first home" seems promising, once Zallah and her mother arrive in an unnamed place where immigration officers speak "in a language Zallah did not understand," there is no reference to a "second" home, but to a "new life" (Marin and Grantford 2007).

Each of these four picture books also makes specific reference to Islamic homelands. The environments are depicted as arid, with mostly stone buildings and impoverished conditions. While an iconographic city sits in the background, a mosque is repeated in illustrations in *Rainbow Bird*. Most of the female characters in these books wear a hijab while the main female characters are portrayed with a loose scarf covering their head, more in the style of a *dupatta*, and perhaps deemed less threatening[2] or strange to the reader. In *Ziba Came on a Boat*, Ziba's father wears a turban in the style of the Afghan lungee. While it is undoubtedly a feature of Muslim culture, these depictions of dress set up codings of strangeness, especially when compared with other characters in the texts who wear Western outfits.

On the other hand, despite paratextual reference to the Australian social and political situation, none of the books refers to Australia as the country of asylum. While there are visual indicators of remote Australian environments in which detention centers are situated, mostly in terms of yellow, sandy, desert localities, Australia is not named as the receiving country. This suggests that the site of asylum seeker arrivals is a given, common knowledge that need not be relayed to the reader. In effect, this confirms the implied reader as "Australian," someone who does not need to be told of their position in the narrative exchange. Cavouras's illustrations include a rough depiction of the south Pacific, with Australia centered on a two-dimensional yellow globe. This is, however, entirely problematic as the background represents the Indigenous Australian flag, with black and red bands enclosing a yellow circle. The accompanying verbal text—"Am I better off here?"—can be read ironically as a subversive acknowledgment of colonial genocide. Since the figure of the detainee—a first-person narrator—in *Rainbow Bird* is not depicted in the visual text, the asylum seeker is invisible, erased.

The narrative distancing of the reader through a binary formation of unknown/known, them/us, there/here, self/other is intensified when the spatial positioning of the reader is taken into account. Only once in *A True Person* does Zallah fully face the reader: in a dream image of her in a cap and a gown (too large on the small child) standing outside a turreted institutional building holding a certificate of university completion. The key phrase of the book—"to be a true person all you need are eyes that see you and hearts that love you"—is pathetically ironic; Zallah is not fully viewed by the reader except when she has been assimilated into mainstream culture. In *Ziba Came on a Boat*, too, the protagonist faces the reader only once, being depicted mostly in profile. When her mother whispers *"Azadi...*Freedom" (Lofthouse and Ingpen 2007, original emphasis),[3] she and Ziba face perpendicularly to the reader, and Ziba holds a yellow-haired doll. In contrast to the dark faces of the asylum seekers, this visual reference implies that Ziba's freedom is connected to a white (Australian) culture, an idea reinforced in the depiction of a group of children surrounding Ziba (in a dream image) wherein the only child face forward to the reader is a smiling, rosy-cheeked, blonde girl who contrasts with Ziba, who is in shadow, with a shock of unruly dark hair. The magician in *Ali the Bold Heart* is often set at a deep position on the page, as part of the background, or does not appear in the visual narrative. When in close-up, he never looks directly to the front. The readers of these picture books are rarely invited to look directly at the protagonist, to recognize the asylum seeker, to accept the refugee into their social environment. What this means is that they are not offered an opportunity to engage at a social or communicative level with these characters, nor are there any depictions of interactions between Australian children and children seeking asylum. Child readers are thus placed at a distance from asylum and detention, corroborating a cultural coding of insider/outsider in which the figure of the asylum seeker is positioned as the outsider. The reader is positioned outside the realm of suffering persecution, seeking asylum, and enduring mandatory detention. The asylum seeker is distanced, othered. As Bauman would have it: "The evicted others hover in the background of the perceived world and are prompted to stay there—the feature-less, faceless, empty shells of humanity" (1993, 155).

OPERATING OUTSIDE THE BORDER: *MY DOG* AND *THE ISLAND*

However, some picture books offer an alternative to such rhetorical nationalism. While these texts also offer messages of hope and compassion, and provide inconclusive or adverse potential for asylum, they do so in a way that configures readers as active participants in the structure and meaning of the narrative. The books—*My Dog* (Heffernan and McLean 2001) and *The Island* (Greder 2007 [2002])—predate Australia's more recent experience with refugees and asylum seekers. Despite being published in Australia and by Australian authors and illustrators, they offer a temporal and spatial distance from direct association with the politics and public opinions about refugees discussed earlier. In fact, they offer only an intuitive connection to Australian nationhood.

The Island (published in Australia in 2007) and Heffernan and McLean's *My Dog* (2001) do not locate the asylum seeker within a specifically Australian context. They do, however, reference forced migration to Australia. The island is a common metaphor for the Australian nation-state. The significance of the global refugee movement during and following the Bosnian War, on which *My Dog* is based, is reflected by Australian refugee intakes in the 1990s.[4] Furthermore, these texts are directed at Australian readers and promote a global contextualization of asylum. They position readers to engage not only with nationalist concerns but also with theoretical and historical concepts surrounding asylum and asylum seeking.

These picture books involve variations of spatial arrangements whereby they move the reader from the position of observer of tragedy to alignment with the figure of the asylum seeker as a "stranger" or "foreigner," dispossessed of national identity. It is in this liminal space of coproduction of otherness, I propose, that these narratives offer the potential for ethical action, unsettling conservative exclusionary politics.

My Dog (Heffernan and McLean 2001) opens on a bird's-eye view of the village of Liztar, home to a young boy, Alija, and his family. The reader is positioned above the action, observing the goings-on in a rural village somewhat protected from the events of the Croatian-Bosnian war. Notionally situated between the center of the extant sovereign state and the seaside border, Alija explains:

> Liztar is on the back road to the coast. It used to be quiet. No one travelled on the narrow dirt track twisting through the mountains. Too many pot-holes that could swallow a car, my dad said.

This geographical positioning implies a space that is somewhat protected from the war. In this gap between the mountains and the coast, Serbs, Bosnians, Croats, Muslims, and Christians were "all one people" until the war encroaches.

The artistic medium of the book offers some metaphorical insight into the story that is to happen. The pencil drawings, with ink wash, clearly show rough pencil marks or outlinings that signify the potential for change. This visual medium offers traces of coming into being that aligns not only with the notion of the story "coming into being," but also with the subsequent narrative movement into becoming-refugee. Birds are depicted rising high in the air in the first image, moving up and away from the village, noticeably to the left, and facing away from the village. Birds often are employed as a metaphor for peace and freedom, but these are depicted taking flight from the village and moving away from the reader. The fleeing birds parallel the evacuation of many women from the village.

Liztar is initially presented as a closed community, bordered by dwellings on three-and-a-half sides. This spatial rendering of an enclosed space that is open to the reader suggests safety and shared experience. A sense of protective enclosure is accentuated by the presence of the outdoor baking kilns, in which Alija's father, Nurija, bakes bread for distribution in the village. The significance of this activity as a motif of hospitality increases as the narrative continues. It is reinvested in the narrative when Alija shells spring peas at the end of the book with the family that has offered him refuge.

Liztar is inundated by a throng of the dispossessed: in trucks, cars, carts, and "people walking with suitcases, bags and bundles. Children crying, straggling behind like scraps of rubbish in the wind. Thin mad-eyed women . . . fear stuck all over them." This unremitting verbal barrage is accompanied by the visual depiction of a deluge of people, carry or carting their meager belongings, moving in and around the illustration from mid-right around to bottom right, growing in perspective as they pass and drawing the reader's eye around and down, which indicates despair. The reader is at this point positioned above the height of the action of influx and egress, which indicates an elevated social status in this situation. The direction from Nurija that Alija should "help those who can't help themselves" is didactically persuasive to a reader who takes up this observatory position. The reader is situated as a paternalistic sympathetic protector and aide to the anonymous figures in their flight toward the unknown.

The reader is introduced to the idea of hospitality toward the dispossessed when Alija meets an old man with a little dog and offers them bread. In this way, the reader is more closely aligned with the protagonist and is brought into the frame of his actions. However, there is a power imbalance in this hospitable exchange. Despite being a child, Alija has the privilege of citizenship, protected by secure spatial framing of the village and belonging to the Liztar community. The alignment of the reader with Alija in this instance reinforces the privilege of citizenship in the reader as well.

The potential for hospitality elevates when the old man dies. According to Derrida,

> absolute hospitality requires that I open up my home and that I give not only to the foreigner . . . but to the absolute, unknown, anonymous other, and that I *give place* to them, that I let them come, that I let them arrive, and take place in the place I offer them, without asking of them either reciprocity (entering into a pact) or even their names. (2000, 26, original emphasis)

Since the "old man" is never afforded a name in this text, the offer of bread, and then the cemetery plot in which the unnamed man is interred, are indicators of such "absolute hospitality." The significance of hospitable inclusion into community (albeit through death and burial) is established when Alija sets a bouquet on the dead man's grave, putting "the flowers *in place*" (Heffernan and McLean 2001, my italics). The act of honoring the unnamed old man is achieved not only in the floral tribute but also in the permanence of his *emplacement* in the village.

The hospitality offered to the old man is immediately shifted to the "blotchy dog" that has lost her master. Nurija exclaims: "Hey, it's your own little refugee, Alija," and Alija accepts: "She was my dog now." This brings into focus Derrida's claim that hospitality is a complex condition of exchange. While the adoption of the old man's dog is hospitable, it is not unconditional (absolute). Nurija (perhaps facetiously) says that the family needs a "guard dog." Furthermore, Alija takes ownership of the animal: the dog belongs to him. It is in this exchange that Alija takes not the role of host, but of master, which, as Derrida says, invokes the status of sovereignty. Hospitality can be frustratingly paradoxical.

As the story progresses, Liztar becomes occupied by insurgent forces and Alija and his mother depart the village as refugees. On this perilous journey, the mother is dragged away from the group and presumably raped and murdered. Alija continues on with the dispossessed and is depicted with the other asylum seekers huddled against a wall in a village in which they take refuge. This demonstrates a situation of statelessness *within* national borders. Without having crossed any border, this group represents the subject dispossessed of political protection. In this scene, the implied reader is again positioned centrally from a high vantage point, an omniscient and neutral position. This omniscience has the potential to be agential, but operates as a mechanism for a sympathetic relationship rather than an empathetic relationship with the text. While somewhat psychologically protective, the distancing of the implied reader from the protagonist manufactures a social distinction between the reader and the inhabitants of the text.

Following this view of utter desolation, the reader becomes a more distant observer of the remaining journey to the coast, but becomes a close observer and participant in the action of the final two scenes. When Alija is offered refuge by yet another old man's daughter in her house at the coast, he sits on the lap of the young woman and shells peas. Spatially, the reader is positioned, standing, at the front end of the kitchen table, included in the tableau. While the verbal narrative indicates further dispossession—the aunt to whom Alija was travelling cannot be located—this transitional adoption of Alija reflects his own adoption of the old man's dog.

Alija is represented here as the figure of resettlement in the safe domestic space of a new family home. The splash of pink across the illustration and the ladder that leads to the high branches of the blossoming trees out the window indicate that there is still some way to go, but this is configured as a safe place, from which flight is unnecessary. The act of inviting into their home the young boy who has perceptibly lost his entire family constitutes an act of hospitality.

As the narrative concludes, the reader is positioned on the final spread behind Alija as he sits on the road from Liztar "so that when my dad comes he'll see me and we'll be together again. Then we can find my mum and my little sister and Granny Mirsa." Despite the sense of hope that is implied by this, the positioning of Alija and his nameless dog in the breadth and width of the page positions him in much empty space. He has reached the limit of the sovereign state, the seaside border. Before him lays uncertainty. The road to/ from Liztar curves away to the horizon. The empathic reader, looking down on the curved back of the boy and his dog, will sense the ironic juxtaposition of hope and despair. The shadows behind these figures gesture toward the latter.

The depiction of Alija and the resettled dog at the end of the book (repeated on the final page of the narrative, and in the paratext), situates the pair at the end of a long, winding road that extends from the mountains, and with views to the top right of the bay. It is apparent, however, that this is an ironic situation because Alija's father is yet to emerge from the war-torn country (and it is indeterminable as to whether he will). While Alija sits closest to the bottom right of the recto, nearest the reader, and in a position that signifies completion and arrival—the end of his journey—he looks toward the mountains, looking back to the war that still ravages his country and his people. The slightly hunched back curves in front of a spatially situated reader who looks at and over the child, across the poppied fields and specious bucolic serenity. In effect, this relationship mirrors the way in which the implied reader has been led on a journey toward an ethics of responsibility, in that Alija becomes representative of the reader, and the adopted dog becomes, in kind, representative of the resettled displaced person.

There is no simple conclusion to this text. Alija remains dispossessed of family and from place. The positioning of the reader, behind Alija and his dog, also facing Liztar, initiates a sense of open potential. When the reader joins Alija on his journey (or at least in his waiting), the reader is drawn into the space of the narrative, and takes up the position of the also-dispossessed. This positioning of the reader initiates the momentum for agency. Since the reader is configured as part of the text, aligned with the young asylum seeker, and taking up the space of narrative potential, the reader draws Liztar, and the asylum seekers who travel from the distant mountains and beyond, toward him or her. The reader is not a static element of extra-textuality, but an embedded subject of the text.

Shifts in reader positioning configure mobile reading subjects, and when the reader takes up a position of alignment with the figure of the asylum seeker, the reader becomes an agential product of the text, configured as also-stateless, an outsider within the ephemeral borders of nation. Readerly compassion is replaced by empathic understanding. It is in this space that the "they" becomes "us," the binary formation of self/other is displaced, and the potential for ethical action is made available to the composite figures of protagonist and reader through the sense of displacement of the self.

Greder's *The Island* (2007) opens on a scene of utter destitution: a naked man has arrived at an island by a raft carried by "fate and ocean currents." In comparison to the characters in *My Dog* who seek to escape the violence of war, this man arrives at what is perceptibly a democratic State, governed by "the people." Until named "the foreigner," the asylum seeker in his nakedness represents absolute dispossession. He has been stripped of outward identifiers, reduced to apparent nothingness but the body itself. It is not known from where he has come, so there is no indication of him having a political identity. He is therefore excluded from the political status by which belonging in the contemporary world is made possible.

However, it is noted early in the text that the naked man is "not like" "the people of the island." His difference to the islanders is manufactured by size (he is smaller than them), by manner (he appears humble; they are aggressive), and by the notion of belonging (they belong; he does not). As the hefty people of the island approach him with rakes and pitchforks, an unseen fisherman says: "If we send him back, it will be the death of him and I don't want that on my conscience...we have to take him in." It is only after the people of the island accept him that he becomes identified as "the foreigner." His entry to the nation-state ironically situates him as othered. Once the stranger is invited to cross the national threshhold, absolute hospitality becomes impossible as the conditions of host and guest are established.

The reader is situated in a complex relation to the (in)hospitable action in this text. As in *My Dog*, the reader is variously positioned in relation to the narrative. The reader is distanced by the linguistic separation of I/them: the phrasing of "they took him in" does not include the reading subject. The reader is not involved in this action, but is positioned as a compassionate onlooker (much like the fisherman—invisible, yet present in the narrative structure). Most of the time, the reader is spatially situated as a sympathetic observer. For example, the reader is positioned to the side when the disparately large, menacing men push their weapons across the double spread to drive the stranger forwards across the narrative—to a goat pen[5] on an "uninhabited part of the island"; this is an act of observation, not inclusion in the action. The reader is also situated at a distance when vignettes depict the everyday business of the islanders and the dreamscapes in which their fears are manifested, removing the reader not only from the events, but also from the intentions of the islanders. The framing of vignettes further denotes observation rather than inclusion, positioning the reader at a "safe" distance from the merciless actions of the islanders. While the images are certainly emotive, and the reader is fundamentally aligned with understandings of inequality, trauma, and compassion, their psychological affect is restricted by narrative nonparticipation.

As the story progresses, however, the spatial positioning of the implied reader shifts to bring the reader into the text as an active participant. As fear grows in the community, the angry islanders surge not only toward the stranger with their farming tools raised in threat, but also directly toward the reader. This alignment of the reader with/as the foreigner positions the reading subject as acted upon, as copresent, and in receipt of the violence arising from fear of the outsider. Derrida's conception of "hospitality" recognizes the inherence of violence associated with the risk of hospitality (2002b). As Nyers explains: "Hospitality…involves something much more complicated than merely offering a welcome or an open embrace. It is a question not just of embracing but also of accepting animosity, hostility, and antagonism as an unavoidable component of hospitality" (2006, 73). In *The Island*, violence arises from *fear* of these risks. A mother warns her children that "he will come and eat you up if you don't finish your soup!" The police officer says: "I am sure that he would murder us all if he could." The newspaper reports: "Foreigner Spreads Fear in Town." These accounts blame fear on the foreigner, not on the islanders. As the fear grows, the islanders announce:

> He is not one of us. He isn't our problem.
> He is a stranger. He doesn't belong.
> He has to go.

Under the threat of the potential violence encoded in hospitable action, the islanders "marched him to his raft and pushed him out to sea...And then they set fire to the fisherman's boat, because he had made them help the man...And they build a great wall all around the island."

The copresence of the reader with the foreigner is heightened in the closure of the narrative when the reading subject is positioned with the evicted foreigner *outside* this "great wall." The perspective indicates that the reader, too, is dwarfed by the enormous wall and looking up toward the imposing surveillance towers. In terms of constructions of national borders, this image is formidable; sovereign protection exists only within the heavily bordered and guarded state. The reader is rejected, ejected from the nation-state, situated in the space of the once again dispossessed stranger. With the revocation of hospitality and the principles of humanitarianism, the reading subject can no longer exist in the same physical, emotional, and nationalized state as when entering the narrative. The subjectivity of the reader is shifted by the text. The reader has become the stranger, the foreigner, and, in the case of *The Island*, is utterly dispossessed, stripped of sovereign protection, and becomes the outsider.

These shifting configurations of reader and text unsettle reader positioning. The spatialized movement of the implied reader from an observer to a participant in the narrative creates a shift in self-concept. It is an experiential configuration of placement and displacement that effects alignment with the asylum seeker. In the coming together of the reader and the protagonist, the reader is positioned to *feel* the experience of the asylum seeker, to respond in a way that goes beyond compassion to empathy.

CONCLUSION

When the reader becomes the also-excluded, alignment with the nation-state is disrupted. Reader positioning in *My Dog* and *The Island* works to construct *affec*tive relations with the narrative that stimulate empathetic understandings of hospitality toward asylum seekers. It is in this space of concomitant sociopolitical exclusion that humanitarian agency is tendered. This shifting configuration of the reader within the text operates as an interruption to reader subjectivity. The reader is changed by the text, is relocated outside the sovereign state, and is therefore positioned in opposition to the national consciousness.

If the reader is now situated outside of the nation-state, expelled to an open, inferred space of the narrative and separate from the notional sovereign state, then that reader is freed from the rhetoric of nationalist discourse and cultural consciousness. The disenfranchised body of the reader (aligned with the protagonist) is implicitly reconstituted. This is the space of political potential. It is the space that opens itself to ethical action.

NOTES

1. For metaphorical picture books published at around the same time, see David Miller, *Refugees* (South Melbourne: Lothian, 2003); John Heffernan and Peter Sheehan, *The Island The Island* (Gosford, NSW: Scholastic, 2005); Narelle Oliver, *Dancing the Boom-Cha-Cha Boogie* (Norwood, SA: Omnibus Books, 2005).
2. Recently in Australia, the government made a failed attempt to introduce a policy for women in burqa to sit within an enclosed room in Parliament House. For more information, see James Massola's article "Burqa crackdown: 'Facial coverings' restricted in Parliament House public galleries," *The Sydney Morning Herald*, October 2, 2014, http://www.smh.com.au/federal-politics/political-news/burqa-crackdown-facial-coverings-restricted-in-parliament-house-public-galleries-20141002-10p8pl.html
3. *Azadi* is an Iranic, Pashto, or Kurdish term that translates as "freedom" or "liberty" in English. It was chanted by Hazaras in Australian protests against detention policies and is the title of a short documentary film about these events (see John Stephens, "Schemas and scripts: Cognitive instruments and the representation of cultural diversity in children's literature," in *Contemporary Children's Literature and Film*, ed. C. Bradford and K. Mallan [New York: Palgrave, 2011], 34).
4. According to James Jupp (*From White Australia to Woomera: The Story of Australian Immigration* [Cambridge: Cambridge University Press, 2002]), forced migration from Bosnia-Herzegovina contributed the largest number of humanitarian refugees to Australia in the 1990s.
5. For a discussion of associations between refugees/asylum seekers and animals, see Peter Nyers, *Rethinking Refugees: Beyond States of Emergency* (New York: Routledge, 2006) and Jacques Derrida "The animal that therefore I am," trans. D Wills, *Critical Enquiry* 28(2) (2002a): 369–418.

REFERENCES

Agamben, Giorgio. 1998. *Homo Sacer: Sovereign Power and Bare Life*, translated by D. Heller-Roazen. Stanford, CA: Stanford University Press.
Australian Customs and Border Protection Service (ACBPS). 2015. "Operation Sovereign Borders." http://www.customs.gov.au/site/operation-sovereign-borders.asp, viewed February 15, 2015.

Australian Department of Immigration and Border Protection (ADIBP). 2015. "Immigration Detention and Community Statistics Summary, 31 January 2015." http://www.immi.gov.au/About/Documents/detention/immigration-detention-statistics-jan2015.pdf, viewed February 20, 2015.

Australian Human Rights Commission. 2014. "Commission again raises serious concerns about Migration Act Amendment." May 16. https://www.humanrights.gov.au/news/stories/commission-again-raises-serious-concerns-about-migration-act-amendment, viewed February 17, 2015.

Bauman, Zygmunt. 2004. *Wasted Lives: Modernity and Its Outcasts*. Oxford: Polity Press.

———. 1993. *Postmodern Ethics*. Oxford and Cambridge: Blackwell.

———. 1990. *Thinking Sociologically*. Oxford and Cambridge: Blackwell.

Betts, Katharine. 2001. "Boatpeople and public opinion in Australia." *People and Place* 9 (4): 34–48.

Bolt, Andrew. 2014. "Pictures of illegal immigrants worth a thousand words." *Herald Sun*, March 19. http://www.heraldsun.com.au/news/opinion/pictures-of-illegal-immigrants-worth-a-thousand-words/story-fni0ffxg-1226859493550, viewed February 15, 2015.

Cavouras, Czenya. 2007. *Rainbow Bird*. Kent Town, SA: Wakefield Press.

Derrida, Jacques. 2002a. "The animal that therefore I am," translated by D. Wills. *Critical Enquiry* 28 (2): 369–418.

———. 2002b. *Acts of Religion*. London: Routledge.

———. 2000. *Of Hospitality: Anne Dufourmantelle Invites Jacques Derrida to Respond*, translated by Rachel Bowlby. Stanford, CA: Stanford University Press.

Dudek, Debra. 2011. "Disturbing thoughts: Representations of compassion in two picture books entitled *The Island*." *Jeunesse: Young People, Texts, Cultures* 3 (2): 11–29.

Greder, Armin. 2007. *The Island*. Crows Nest, NSW: Allen & Unwin.

———. 2002. *Die Insel: Eine Tagliche Geschichte*. Frankfurt am Main: Sauerländer.

Hage, Ghassan. 2011. "Multiculturalism and the ungovernable Muslim." In *Essays on Muslims and Multiculturalism*, edited by Raimond Gaita, 155–186. Melbourne: Text Publishing.

Harvey, David. 1990. *The Condition of Postmodernity: An Enquiry into the Origins of Cultural Change*. Oxford and Cambridge: Blackwell.

Heffernan, John, and Andrew McLean. 2001. *My Dog*. Sydney: Margaret Hamilton Books.

Heffernan, John, and Peter Sheehan. 2005. *The Island*. Gosford, NSW: Scholastic.

Hintjens, Helen, and Alison Jarman. 2005. "Acting for asylum: The nexus of pro-refugee activism in Melbourne." In *Critical Perspectives on Refugee Policy in Australia: Proceedings of the Refugee Rights Symposium Hosted by the Institute for Citizenship and Globalisation, Faculty of Arts, Deakin*

University, December 5, 2002, edited by M. Leach and F. Mansouri, 59–87. Burwood, VIC: Institute for Citizenship and Globalisation, Deakin University.

Hollindale, Peter. 1988. *Ideology and the Children's Book*. Stroud: Thimble Press.

Hutton, Marg. 2013. "SIEVX.com: About this site." http://sievx.com/about.shtml, viewed February 15, 2015.

Jolly, Jane, and Elise Hurst. 2006. *Ali the Bold Heart*. Balmain, NSW: Limelight Press.

Jupp, James. 2002. *From White Australia to Woomera: The Story of Australian Immigration*. Cambridge: Cambridge University Press.

Leach, Michael. 2003. "'Disturbing practices': Dehumanizing asylum seekers in the refugee 'crisis' in Australia, 2001–2002." *Refuge* 21 (3): 25–33.

Lofthouse, Liz, and Robert Ingpen. 2007. *Ziba Came on a Boat*. La Jolla: Kane/Miller.

Mansouri, Fethi. 2002. "The legacy of Australia's treatment of onshore asylum seekers." *Mots Pluriels* 21: 1–16. Web. http://motspluriels.arts.uwa.edu.au/MP2102fm.html, viewed February 14, 2015.

Marin, Gabiann, and Jacqui Grantford. 2007. *A True Person*. Frenchs Forest, NSW: New Frontier.

Massey, Doreen. 2005. *For Space*. London: Sage.

———. 1994. *Space, Place, and Gender*. Minnesota: University of Minnesota Press.

Massola, James. 2014. "Burqa crackdown: 'Facial coverings' restricted in Parliament House public galleries." *The Sydney Morning Herald*, October 2. http://www.smh.com.au/federal-politics/political-news/burqa-crackdown-facial-coverings-restricted-in-parliament-house-public-galleries-20141002-10p8pl.html, viewed February 15, 2015.

McKay, Fiona, Samantha Thomas, and Susan Kneebone. 2012. "'It would be okay if they came through the proper channels': Community perceptions and attitudes toward asylum seekers in Australia." *Journal of Refugee Studies* 25 (1): 113–133.

Miller, David. 2003. *Refugees*. South Melbourne: Lothian.

Morrison, Scott, Minister for Immigration and Border Protection. 2014. "A new force protecting Australia's borders: Address to the Lowy Institute for International Policy." Sydney, May 9. http://www.minister.immi.gov.au/media/sm/2014/sm214247.htm, viewed July 20, 2014.

Needham, Kirsty, and Tom Allard. 2011. "People smugglers blamed as 27 feared dead." *Sydney Morning Herald*. November 2. http://www.smh.com.au/national/people-smugglers-blamed-as-27-feared-dead-20111101-1mtzn.html, viewed February 15, 2015.

Nodelman, Perry, and Mavis Reimer. 2003. *The Pleasures of Children's Literature*. Boston, MA: Allyn & Bacon.

Nyers, Peter. 2006. *Rethinking Refugees: Beyond States of Emergency*. New York: Routledge.

Oliver, Narelle. 2005. *Dancing the Boom-Cha-Cha Boogie.* Norwood, SA: Omnibus Books.

Papastergiadis, Nikos. 2006. "The invasion complex: The abject other and spaces of violence." *Geographiska Annaler, Series B, Human Geography* 8 (4): 429–442.

Phillips, Janet, and Harriet Spinks. 2013. "Boat arrivals in Australia since 1976." Research paper, Department of Parliamentary Services, Parliament of Australia. Web. http://www.aph.gov.au/About_Parliament/ Parliamentary_Departments/Parliamentary_Library/pubs/rp/rp1314/ BoatArrivals, viewed February 15, 2015.

Sassen, Saskia. 2008. *Territory, Authority, Rights: From Medieval to Global Assemblages.* Princeton, NJ: Princeton University Press.

Stephens, John. 2011. "Schemas and scripts: Cognitive instruments and the representation of cultural diversity in children's literature." In *Contemporary Children's Literature and Film,* edited by C. Bradford and K. Mallan, 12–35. New York: Palgrave.

———. 1992. *Language and Ideology in Children's Fiction.* New York: Longman.

The Australian Literature Resource (AustLit). 2015. http://www.austlit. edu.au, viewed February 17, 2015.

"The Coalition's *Operation Sovereign Borders Policy,* July 2013." Authorised and printed by Brian Loughlane, Barton, ACT. http://lpaweb-static. s3.amazonaws.com/Policies/OperationSovereignBorders_Policy.pdf, viewed February 10, 2015.

Taylor, Lenore. 2011. "Morrison sees votes in anti-Muslim strategy." *The Sydney Morning Herald,* February 17. http://www.smh.com.au/ national/morrison-sees-votes-in-antimuslim-strategy-20110216-1awmo. html, viewed February 17, 2015.

CHAPTER 6

Minor(s) Matter: Stone-Throwing, Securitization, and the Government of Palestinian Childhood under Israeli Military Rule

Mikko Joronen

INTRODUCTION

Since the Six-Day War in 1967, the year 2014 was the all-time bloodiest for the civilians living in the occupied Palestinian territories. According to the annual report of the UN Office for the Coordination of Humanitarian Affairs (OCHA 2015), during the year 2014 Israeli activities resulted in the death of 2,314 Palestinians, while causing altogether 17,125 injuries. Although the year was overshadowed by the massive corollaries of the 50-day-long Israeli military aggression in Gaza, Operation Protective Edge, which, along with the material destruction, led to the death of at least 2,220 Palestinians, 551 of them children, the significance of the everyday ill-treatment of Palestinians under the military regulation cannot be overlooked. While in the West Bank and East Jerusalem the number of Palestinian fatalities in incidents with Israeli Defence Forces (IDF) was the highest since 2007, the year 2014 also witnessed a sharp increase in the percentage of child casualties caused by the IDF (OCHA 2015, 7). After the decades of occupation, the exceptionalities of Israeli military rule have not only become a status quo in the Palestinian territories, West Bank in particular, but also accumulated into a complex system of government with overlapping clauses, exceptional laws, racist categorizations, and offsetting regulations. Also, notable territorial and ethno-national differences in the government of the occupation have become established during the decades. After the withdrawal of Israel from Gaza in 2005 (which was followed by its still-continuing siege) and Israel's unilateral annexation of the occupied Palestinian capital, East Jerusalem, to its own united capital of Jerusalem (officially declared in 1980), it is West Bank Palestinians alone who are automatically treated under the military law and regulations. Yet, military jurisdiction in the West Bank does not apply to the Israeli settlers living in the colonized part of the area, while East Jerusalem Palestinians with permanent residency in Israel (the so-called Jerusalem ID) can be treated under the military law, if the offense they were accused of was connected to the West Bank in one way or another.

Ethnicity-, territory-, and nationality-based discrimination is thus a visible part of how the military and criminal justice function in the occupied territories. As the number of reports produced by different United Nations organizations and Israeli, Palestinian, and international nongovernmental organizations have highlighted, the ill-treatment of Palestinian minors is deeply embedded in the legal provisions, military regulations, and in situ practices (e.g., DCIP 2009, 2014a; NLF 2011; CAABU 2012; DBL 2012; UNICEF 2013, 1–28; 2015; MCW 2014). Although military legislation itself includes a number of security-related exceptions and overall shortcomings that altogether fail to offer proper protection for Palestinian children, a wide disparity between the institutionalized discrimination and the treatment of Palestinian children in practice does prevail. Despite the recent amendments such as the establishment of the Juvenile Military Court in 2009—a problematic institutional apparatus in itself—the practices and regulations regarding the arrest, interrogation, and transfer, and institutionalized provisions and practices regarding the conviction, imprisonment, and complaints regarding the Palestinian minors are insufficient and discriminatory.

In this chapter, I focus on the widespread ill-treatment of Palestinian children living under the Israeli military rule in the occupied territories, West Bank in particular. In order to scrutinize how the cavalcade of exceptional practices, regulations, orders, laws, and overlapping/offsetting clauses produce a widespread, systematic, and institutionalized ill-treatment of Palestinian children today, I focus on three questions in particular. First, I look at the ways in which the security apparatus of the state of Israel, especially military, police, and juridical institutions, produce Palestinian children as a part of the wider security threat. In particular, I focus on the rationalities, such as those of racist categorization or the denial of the right of a child to be treated as a child, through which children are framed as targets of government. Second, I scrutinize different techniques of government used to implement the military order in practice. Here particular focus is given to the practices on the ground: arrest, transfer, and other cases where different forms of violence and abuse are used. Finally, I examine those governmental rationalities—impunity, acceptance, and flexibility—that support and strengthen the strategic functions of the security apparatus. In many respects, I show that children are not treated as passive targets of power and government, but, quite on the contrary, as an active part of the security threat and, as such, accountable for their acts often in ways similar to adults. All in all, I look at the ways through which Palestinian children are positioned as a part of the broader security threat, not only through the institutional proceedings and provisions, but also via systematic violence and racism embedded in the established practices of Israeli authorities (see also Stephens 1995; Scheper-Hughes and Sargent 1998; Hyndman 2010; Wells 2014a).

CHILD AS A SECURITY THREAT: INSTITUTIONAL PROVISIONS AND PROCEEDINGS

One of the prominent and controversial features of the Israeli military order is without doubt the ethno-national division upon which the two juridical systems, the civilian and the military, function in the West Bank territory. The discriminatory aspect comes forth in several military laws and regulations, which do not allow proper protection for Palestinian minors, but instead make their lives vulnerable through the number of techniques following the purposes of the military rule. Even the Juvenile Military Court, which was established in 2009 to improve the status of Palestinian children under the military law, is embedded in this dual system. It combines the standards of the juvenile court system with the existing military regulations and practices. Despite the recent amendments regarding the role of minors in the military law, there remains ambivalence on what counts as a proper juvenile court. In practice the juvenile military courts use not only the same facilities, court staff (many of the judges do not have juvenile court training or are trained military court judges), and military orders as the adult military courts, but also clear discrimination regarding the standards of how Palestinian children are convicted under the military rule (seeDCIP 2013; UNICEF 2015). Laws, thus, not only contain exceptional clauses, under which Palestinian minors can be legally ill-treated, but also the court verdicts in general are substantially harsher for Palestinian minors than for Israeli ones (MCW 2013, 4).

On many occasions verdicts and legal exceptions, of course, go hand in hand, as the exceptional clauses related to the so-called security offenses highlight. A case in point: although in the court proceedings the age of majority among Palestinians was raised to 18 in 2011, this does not apply to the security offenses for which the maximum penalty is 5 years or more. According to an extensive report published by Defence for Children International, Palestine (DCIP 2012, 120; 2014b), the most common charge children face in military courts is stone-throwing. Stone-throwing is considered as a serious security offense, of which children aged 14 or more can be sentenced for a maximum of 20 years in prison. Even children aged 12 and 13 are potentially sentenced for the maximum of 6 months in prison (IDF 2009, Chapter G). In practice, children are most commonly arrested, accused, and convicted on the basis of this one peculiar security offense. While other security offenses exist, such as the attendance of an unauthorized protest, this carries a maximum penalty of ten years in prison. Despite the amendments in the juvenile military court proceedings, such forms of securitization can be, and have been, used to enable and legitimize the extraordinary means to govern Palestinian children.

In addition to the legal provisions, extreme means for governing Palestinian children also reflect the disparities between the law and the practices. Most of the Palestinian children, for instance, already confess before going to the court, which alone suggests the interrogation has more weight than the court process for their conviction. Even though mechanisms are in place to ensure the confessions were given willingly and without coercion, they have not been able to provide a proper legal cover for the Palestinian minors. The so-called trial-within-trial process, where the testimonies given in the interrogations need to be presented in the court, is rarely used. During the last two years only a small portion of the complaints regarding the abuse, coercion, and torture of Palestinian children have led to a criminal investigation, and even less to the conviction of the detaining body (e.g., Yesh Din 2013b). Due to the lack of "trial-within-trial" processes and success in complaints, ill-treatments are almost solely brought out where they have most effect on the criminal justice process: in the plea bargains (e.g., NLF 2011, 37; DCIP 2012, 41; PCATI 2012). According to different studies approximately 98 percent of cases end in plea bargains (NLF 2011, 7; DBL 2012, 22), which is why neither the discretion of the court nor the actual evidence carry significant weight in the military juvenile court.

Due to exceptional clauses related to security threats and the embedding of juvenile court standards in the existing military rule, amendments in the military law have not had substantial effect on how Palestinian children are treated under the military rule in practice. In fact, the case seems to be almost the opposite: a well-functioning practice is allowed to continue, either by making exceptional clauses that, in practice, are those most often used, or by simply forming practices that diminish the role of court proceedings. Yet, the law does not contain exceptions that can only be used in the security threat cases. If compared to the civilian law under which Israeli minors are treated, the military law in general gives a substantially more insecure and precarious cover for the Palestinian minors. Security of the Israeli citizens is hence established on the grounds of the ethno-national securitization, which makes Palestinians, including minors, prone to the insecurities of the military law and the exceptionalities of the security threat cases.

Considering the above, securitization poses a form of discriminatory politicization of Palestinian childhood that is established not only through the institutional provisions, but also through the bodies that implement the military rule on the ground. Discrimination, hence, not only is part of the harsh juridical measures against Palestinian children, but can also be found within the practices and procedures of other security bodies, such as the military and the police. The absolute number of arrests of Palestinian minors, for instance, is substantially higher than Israeli minors. In addition, it is noteworthy that according to the recent UNICEF report (published in February 2015), the two most common forms of violence and abuse were painful hand-tying upon arrest (in 189 cases) and physical violence during the arrest, interrogation, and/or detention (in 171 cases) (UNICEF 2015, 3).

Taking the long-term normalization of the extraordinary situation in the occupied territories, I feel compelled to approach the treatment of Palestinian children with a setup that grows from the situation in the West Bank. Apparently a number of aspects could be conceptually deepened, the details of which I do not intend to go into here. For instance, an entire "lawfare" is embedded in the strategic aim to make legal provisions fit in for the practical purposes of controlling occupied territories and to reply to the growing international pressure and criticism (Morrissey 2011; Hajjar 2013). There are also studies approaching children's politics with ways open to small-scale politicizations and abrupt becoming(s), which have the power to position Palestinian children in other ways than the governmental apparatuses of the Israelis do (Marshall 2014). As Jouni Häkli and Kirsi Pauliina Kallio (2015) specify, one of the clear-cut dividing lines in the research of children's spatial politics can be found between the inquiries identifying children as victims "of war, oppressive social orders, unfavorable socio-economic situations, and natural disasters" and the approaches that emphasize those active roles children take in the political processes and construction of lifeworlds/environments. Though the divide should not be taken categorically, exceptional conditions of Palestinian children under the military rule might hint why, in some cases, a separation of these two aspects is not particularly helpful.

Accordingly, inasmuch as it would do violence to the everyday life of Palestinian children to turn a blind eye to the ways in which they are positioned as political subjects—that is, how the suffering and ill-treatment of children are made acceptable and institutionalized as a part of the bigger "security concerns"—it would be one-sided to reduce the spatial politics of Palestinian children only to the frame produced by Israel's security concerns. Lives targeted by the security apparatus are never fully penetrated by the governmental forces, as lives of children include daily routines and contain aesthetic beauty, for instance (see Habashi 2013; Marshall 2013). Although the bodies of state apparatus position and reveal children's lives under their governmental logics, these logics never exhaust the lives of children into a political framing done in the name of securitization. In short, subjectification (positioning of subjects) and subjectivation (reception of positioning) can never be completely separated from one another. Hence, a more fundamental question is, *how* their acts *are related to* the governmental apparatuses (Joronen 2011; Agamben 2014). Such a question is less concerned with whether children are seen as victims of governmental order or as capable of ad hoc politicization.

What, then, accrues from within the political situation in the West Bank? In the following I suggest a reading of the securitization, and the discrimination of Palestinian childhood that follows from it, through the "governmental rationality/governmental apparatus" nexus (Foucault 2000, 416–417). Discrimination and exceptionalities of the securitization, I show, are produced through the bodies of the Israeli security apparatus, which position, with all of their connections, institutions, practices, and techniques, Palestinian children via different governmental rationalities. Governmentality, as Michel

Foucault originally formulated it (1979, 20; 1997, 81; 2007, 201, 207–208), can be defined broadly as a government centered on the people. It operates by governing and guiding lives of populations and individual bodies, rather than things and territories, either by framing and positioning human conducts or by encouraging subjects to self-government. While there has been some debate concerning the relation between power as it is imposed upon subjects and power as a means by which subjects relate to themselves (Huxley 2008; Joronen 2013), or, alternatively, of how governmentality is related to the territorial (Elden 2007) and material (Braun 2000) arts of government, herein, as explicated below, I will approach governmental rationality from a somewhat more specific perspective (cf. Wells 2014b).

First, instead of looking at the individuation and isolation of subjects as a form of power relation, wherein the conducts of bodies are guided by encouraging the acts of self-government, I focus on the ways through which the state security apparatus conditions, governs, and frames Palestinian childhood. With the term "apparatus" I refer to what Giorgio Agamben (2009, 12) calls somewhat broadly a set of practices, measures, and institutions "that aim to manage, govern, control and orient—in a way that purports to be useful—the behaviors, gestures, and thoughts of human beings." An apparatus is not only a network, or a collection, of heterogeneous, diverse, and changing elements such as practices, measures, institutions, decisions, laws, and statements, but also something capable of capturing, directing, and determining the layout where these elements operate. Apparatuses thus have dominant strategic functions, as they aim to manipulate, rationalize, and affect the former elements and their relations by blocking and directing them to certain directions, and by stabilizing and utilizing them according to particular strategic purposes (Foucault 1980, 196). In the case of securitization, the framing of childhood thus preoccupies the subject. It constitutes Palestinian children beforehand as responsible actors accountable for the acts no Israeli child is held accountable for. But security apparatuses also operate more loosely and abruptly, when extending the security-based government in response to uncalculated threats (for instance, Braun 2014; Millei and Cliff 2014). In short, the apparatus poses peculiar forms of government through different techniques, institutional provisions, procedures, and tactics—some state-based, others more loosely grounded on the state institutions—which are all pivotal for how the widespread and systematic ill-treatment of Palestinian children is legitimized and implemented in practice. Palestinian children, of course, do face settler violence (DCIP 2014a), while private security companies also have a growing role in the West Bank (Braverman 2011). Yet, the ethno-national violence against Palestinian children is deeply embedded in the state institutions and the practices they have developed during the almost five decades of occupation.

Second, the focus on human conducts does not exclude material and nonhuman entities. To be sure, a stone thrown at the military vehicle is a material object that is embedded in the wide collection of human and nonhuman relations that apparatuses frame and politicize (see Rautio 2013; Nolte and Yacobi 2015). Children carry stones in their pockets, and do throw them toward military vehicles, but none alone tell about the politicization of a stone or the power relations behind the stone-throwing upon which a number of ill-treatments of Palestinian children can be legally justified. Regardless of whether the stone hit the target, caused any damage, or was thrown/existed at all, under the securitization the mere possibility of a security threat poses a legitimate reason for treating children according to the exceptional standards that aim to ensure the safety of the occupying population. Accordingly, rationalities of securitization are inherent, but irreducible, to the relations between human and nonhuman entities, as the strategic functions of the apparatus do contain a preoccupying politicization, which enforces the emerging connections within its power relations. Despite the material embedding, I am more interested in focusing on the rationalities of framing, through which security offenses, such as stone-throwing, are produced (see Butler 2009, xxvii, 3–7).

Third, I look at the treatment of Palestinian children, not so much in terms of positive encouragement and rewarding self-government, but rather as thanatopolitical securitization. In thanatopolitical securitization the production of vulnerability collides with the fear of violence and killing. It refers to the politicization of death rather than to the blunt act of killing, and thus produces government of life and bodies through the tactical presence of violence and death (See Joronen 2015). Killing, to be sure, is a part of the government of Palestinian children, as the annual death rates indicate (OCHA 2015). Yet, death is often delayed and left to populate the atmosphere of government through the moods of fear, threat, and terror. In its subtler forms thanatopolitics thus operates through the everyday visibility of military presence, harsh disciplinary conducts, night arrests, and curfews, all reminders that every Palestinian is considered as a potential security threat, and whose killing can be legitimized, if necessary, as an act of prevention (see Ghanim 2008).

Considering the above, my aim in the chapter is to look at the (ill-)treatments of Palestinian children as they are implemented, framed, and enabled by the Israeli security apparatus. My focus, hence, is on the rationalities implemented within three operational sections of the apparatus: first, on the governmental rationalities of the apparatus that support and enable its strategic functions, including impunity, acceptance, and flexibility; second, on the ways the apparatus frames Palestinian children through security exceptions, racist categorizations, and by denying the role of children as children; and third, on the thanatopolitical securitization, which governs children through the fear of death and violence. Through the three rationalities—the framing of the target, the control of the target via fear, and the rationalities maintaining the inner functions of the apparatus—I look not only at the practical operations of the apparatus, but also at its strategic ways of framing, positioning, and rationalizing the Palestinian children as security threats.

Framing Childhood: Rationalities and Techniques

> Out of nowhere many soldiers jumped out and ambushed Samir. They shot him first in the leg, yet he managed to run away towards the village. But how far can an injured child run? Twenty, maybe 30 meters? They could have easily arrested him, especially when he was injured, but instead they shot him in the back with live ammunition... To me this is premeditated murder.

The words of 16-year-old Malek Murrar, whom Amnesty International (2014, 5) interviewed in 2013 at the site near the West Bank village of Budrus, where he was an eyewitness to the killing of his coeval Samir Awad, manage to capture several aspects relevant to the way Palestinian children are treated under the Israeli military rule. It was only after a petition to the Israeli High Court of Justice and a two-year-long foot-dragging of the case that the State Attorney Office finally decided on March 2015 to charge the responsible IDF soldier for "a reckless and negligent act of using a firearm" (B'Tselem 2015). The soldier was charged with committing a minor offense of reckless behavior, instead of murder or manslaughter, despite the several testimonies and eyewitnesses. Without doubt the decision sent a strong message to the IDF in the occupied territories: a Palestinian, a wounded youth, who poses no threat to the military, can be shot dead without significant consequences. To be sure, such a message contains nothing peculiarly new, as the testimonies of ex-Israeli soldiers (Breaking the Silence 2011, 37) and the diminutive number of seven IDF soldiers that military courts have convicted between 2000 and 2013 for the unlawful killing of Palestinians, highlight (Yesh Din 2013a, 3).

It is thus not the circumstances of the killing, but the ethno-national background of the victim, that seems to be a key factor here. The case of Samir may be an extreme example, a "new low in Israeli authorities['] disregard for the lives of Palestinians in the occupied territories" as the Israeli human rights organization B'Tselem (2015) described the decision, but the institutional impunity and racism it highlights are hardly exceptional. Between 2000 and 2011, over 700 complaints were made to the Israeli attorney general about the torture and other forms of ill-treatment committed by the Israeli Security Agency (ISA, also known as Shin Beth and General Security Services) against Palestinians—none of them led to a criminal investigation, which is not surprising considering the fact that the preliminary inquiries in these cases are carried out by ISA agents (Ballas 2012, 41; PCATI 2012). The state of affairs is similar to the complaints made against the Israeli police and the IDF. During the same ten-year period the percentage of complaints that did not lead to indictment was close to one hundred in both cases (MCW 2014, 21). In the following year (2012), altogether 78 out of the 240 complaints about the crimes committed by the IDF against the Palestinians led to investigations—but not a single one led to an indictment—while in 2013, 6 out of the 199 investigations against the IDF led to indictment; the overall throughput rate for the complaints was 1.4 percent between 2012 and 2013 (PCATI 2012; Yesh Din 2013b, 2014). In short, chances of making Israeli authorities accountable for the ill-treatments barely exist in practice. This systematic impunity is also reflected in a significant drop in the number of complaints made about the ill-treatment of Palestinian children. In 2013, for instance, 76.5 percent of the Palestinian minors detained by Israeli military in the West Bank had faced some form of physical violence or abuse during the arrest, transfer, and/or interrogation (DCIP 2014c, 2), but only less than 3 percent of them made a formal complaint (MCW 2014, 21).

The case of Samir, as the short explication above underscores, brings forth several rationalities of government that are used to support the harsh treatment of Palestinian children in the West Bank. Institutional impunity even regarding the most extreme acts, systematic racism, ethno-national discrimination and the enactment of the government based on fear, violence, and death, are all part of how the Israeli security apparatus frames and governs children through different practices and techniques of government. Yet, the case contains more. Not only was the status of Samir as a child denied, when he became a mere "security threat," a suspect of an "infiltration attempt" (Levy and Zitun 2013), but he could also be killed without committing homicide. Also, the exceptional act of shooting dead from close range a child, who did not pose any threat to the soldiers, was normalized and made an acceptable part of the standard procedure in the occupied West Bank. Consider the comment that military spokesman, Captain Eytan Buchman, gave after the killing of Samir Awad, when he said that troops, which were securing the (illegal) fence Israel had built to separate the villagers from their farmlands in 2003, only "initiated standard rules of engagement, which included live fire" (Khoury 2013). Accordingly, when considered a security threat the child is no more a child who should not be held accountable with ways similar to adults, but rather framed as a part of the broader ethno-national security threat (see Hannah 2006; Hyndman 2010, 252). Such racist exceptionalism preoccupies the situation by enforcing its targets within the power relations, where extreme acts, such as killing, can be legitimized in the name of security. Such exceptionalism, hence, is not exceptional, but a standard procedure that has a widespread institutional acceptance among both military and juridical apparatuses.

The logic of impunity works through various channels, from the court decisions to the interrogations of the police and the arrest of the military. But the way the impunity appears to the soldiers on the ground most probably forms knowledge about the institutional security mechanism always backing their decisions. Eventually the institutional impunity forms a ground for the soldiers' own arbitrary acts through the knowledge that, if a decision to investigate is made afterward, they hardly ever lead to more than a reprimand for "reckless behaviour." As the affidavit of a 14-year-old boy "M. H." from Ash Shuyukh village near Hebron, exemplifies, an arrest can be made on dubious grounds (MCW 2014, 43–45):

> I left the house at around 8:30 a.m. to go to an optician in Hebron to have my glasses repaired. As I walked to catch a bus I saw lots of Israeli soldiers and stones on the ground. At the time I didn't think much of it as soldiers are always in our village, which is situated near the settlement of Kiryat Arba. Three girls walked by the soldiers and were not bothered. When I was about three meters from the soldiers, one of them shouted at me. I was so scared I started to run. I couldn't help it. The soldiers chased me and fired tear gas in my direction. A military Jeep then blocked my way. I fell on the ground and they caught me. About eight soldiers started to kick me and beat me with the butts of their rifles. They beat me all over my body, on my head and my back. A

soldier dragged me by my arms while another kicked me in the stomach...They placed a hood over my head, shackled my feet with metal shackles and tied my hands to the back with metal handcuffs. I was then pushed into the vehicle and made to sit on the metal floor.

The fact that a child was arrested for the mere sake of running is not only troubling, but also telling. It underlines how the security apparatus operates by allowing a space for the discretion of the soldiers. Also, commanders and units are under pressure to make arrests regarding incidents that the ones eventually arrested did not have anything to do with. As M. H. continues in his testimony:

He [interrogator] accused me of throwing stones. He claimed I threw stones sometime ago, but did not say when. I denied the accusation and told the interrogator exactly what I had done that morning. He then told me that if I confessed he would call my father to come and pick me up. He asked me about other children and kept yelling and shouting at me. He interrogated me for about four hours. He kept repeating the same questions and asked me how many stones I had thrown and told me he would release me immediately if I confessed. I wasn't given any food or water and I didn't see a lawyer before I was interrogated.

Under conditions such as these the obvious happens:

Towards the end of the four hours the interrogator and two guards were shouting louder and louder. They were banging on the table and the walls. I was so tired and scared I confessed to throwing three stones. The interrogator made me sign a document written in Hebrew. When I asked him what it said he told me it was my confession. I was then taken to another interrogator...He asked me the same questions. I told him I confessed to throwing three stones. I was then taken to a person in the room next door who took my fingerprints and my photo.

Against the Fourth Geneva Convention (article 76) M. H. was taken to a facility located in Israel—an act that should be considered as a war crime under the Rome Statute (article 8). After two weeks, which included periods of solitary confinement in a cell, where M. H. felt scared as it "was pitch dark," and several court hearings, M. H. was released on bail and ordered to house arrest for one year. "I find it very hard to stay home while all my friends go to places and have fun without me. I cannot stand it," M. H. ends the testimony. Considering the amount of violence, coercion, and intimidation a 14-year-old child needed to face, it is unfortunate to note that the story is not an exception, but contains almost all the common forms of ill-treatment, which Palestinian children face during arrest, transfer, interrogation, and detention. While the numbers depend on the year and the size of sampling, in the 185 affidavits Military Court Watch has collected since the beginning of the year M. H. was arrested (January 2013–April 2015), in 95 percent of cases children's hands were tied, in 96 percent a lawyer was not consulted before the interrogations, in 96 percent parents were not present during the interrogations, 78 percent were not informed of the right to silence, 85 percent were blindfolded, while physical violence was used in 61 percent of cases, and verbal abuse, humiliation, and intimidation in 43 percent of cases. Moreover, 45 percent were arrested at night, 46 percent transferred on a vehicle floor, 68 percent were shown or made to sign a paper in Hebrew, while solitary confinement was used in 13 percent of cases (MCW 2015, 13, 44; see also DCIP 2009; UNICEF 2015).

Although the numbers alone paint quite a clear picture about the regularity of the ill-treatments, apparatuses always contain diverse, even contradictory, techniques and practices (Braun 2014, 50). Such loose ties come out in the flexibility the apparatus has toward new situations. For instance, in September 2014, a Military Order 1745 came into power, which requires that interrogations need to be audio-visually recorded and carried out using the language of the arrested. However, in order to soak up the new requirements within the prevailing logic of the apparatus, a technique of double interrogation can be used (B'Tselem 2013). While the first interrogator makes the child confess by using very harsh methods, after the coerced confession a second interrogator comes up and asks the child to "willingly" repeat the confession on a video. Moreover, the new military order does not apply to security offenses, such as stone-throwing (UNICEF 2015, 2). Security apparatuses can thus connect new requirements into existing standards without actually disturbing their strategic functions.

In addition to flexibility, the loose connections of the apparatus operate by allowing a space for the arbitrary and abrupt decisions of the soldiers. As the IDF sergeant's testimony below shows, a security apparatus does not pose a totalizing scheme from which new practices usher forth. It rather operates by placing more emphasis on the discretionary power of the soldiers, interrogators, and so on, who are positioned to make decisions that are arbitrary in many occasions, but still supported by the institutionalized acceptance, as the following quote exemplifies (Breaking the Silence 2012, 18):

> We took over a school and had to arrest anyone in the village who was between the ages of 17 and 50, something like that. It lasted from

morning until noon the next day. Anyway, all sorts of people arrived, [and were] shackled and blindfolded. What happened was that when these detainees asked to go to the bathroom, and the soldiers took them there, they beat them to a pulp and cursed them for no reason, and there was nothing that would legitimize hitting them. Really terrible things. An Arab was taken to the bathroom to piss, and a soldier slapped him, took him down to the ground while he was shackled and blindfolded. The guy wasn't rude and did nothing to provoke any hatred or nerves. Just like that, because he is an Arab. He was about 15 years old, hadn't done a thing. We arrested many of the people just in order to collect information about them for the Shabak [Hebrew acronym for Israeli Security Agency, ISA], not because they had done anything…In general people at the school were sitting for hours in the sun, they could get water once in a while, but let's say someone asked for water, five times, a soldier could come to him and slap him just like that. Or let's say, I saw many soldiers using their knees to hit them, just out of boredom. Because you're standing around for 10 hours doing nothing, and you're bored, so you hit them. Perhaps that was the only satisfaction they had.

Although the strategic purposes of the military and the ISA may be clear here, even means as arbitrary as boredom can be used to promote them (see also Breaking the Silence 2012, 35). These unreasonable and racist acts are never merely arbitrary, but promoted by their acceptance among the soldiers and their superiors, inasmuch as they are supported by the governmental rationality that is based on the knowledge of institutional impunity. Not all soldiers, of course, accept the ill-treatment, like the existence of organizations like *Breaking the Silence* underline. As an example from Nablus outlines:

Soldier: My company commander caught a 12-year-old kid there [Nablus] once, and made him get down on his knees in the middle of the street. Yelled like a madman—it looked like some Vietnam War movie—so that the other guys come out or else…he'd do something to that kid. I knew it was just a hollow threat, after all the guy's an officer…
Interviewer: What did he yell at the kid?
Soldier: He yelled at him to shut up and the kid cried of course…He also peed in his pants, in front of the whole village. He got him on his knees and began to scream in Hebrew, to swear at him…Regardless if there's shooting or stones, no matter what, he's a kid in the middle of the street. (Breaking the Silence 2012, 7)

Though an adult soldier may see through the threats, it is doubtful whether the case is so with the children. Children have heard stories and experiences from other kids and almost every family has a relative, friend, acquaintance, or neighbor who had been arrested, mistreated, or killed by the IDF. Situations that do not necessarily look scary for the soldiers, for whom Palestinian children are primarily security issues, may be so for a child. On many occasions the military just wants to show off, to make their presence felt, and to show they are there and the ones in power. Such showings, however, are not based on abrupt decisions of the commanders alone, but are, on many occasions, strategic. They are planned beforehand to show that Palestinians are all potential security threats and therefore can be treated in any way, even if they are children. But they are also done for a particular purpose, as the so-called Happy Purim technique exemplifies. Bluntly speaking, "Happy Purim" is about not letting people to sleep—about "coming in the middle of the night, going around the village throwing stun grenades and making noise" (Breaking the Silence 2011, 38). Sometimes it is just about paying back some earlier incident, usually stone-throwing, but it has also been ordered and instructed by the high-ranking military officers, from the battalion, for instance (Breaking the Silence 2012, 7).

Creating an atmosphere of fear is strategic by all standards. It poses a thanatopolitical rationality of government that is based on the strategic promotion of the fear of violence, loss of freedom, and ultimately one's (or loved one's) life. As the 16-year-old boy M. I. from the Al Khard describes his interrogation in October 2013:

> The interrogator kept insisting that I confess to throwing stones at soldiers and claimed that other children had confessed against me and that I had to confess. I told him I didn't see any point in confessing if other children had already confessed against me. Then the interrogator took me outside and showed me other boys who were blindfolded and were sitting on the ground in the distance. He then threatened me saying if I didn't confess he would give me an electric shock. He then brought an electric baton and placed it in front of him, but did not hit me with it. I was scared and then confessed that I threw stones at soldiers. (MCW 2014, 52)

Unfortunately these fears are not just mirror images of the hollow threats of the soldiers. The use of electric shocks, for instance, is one of the harsh methods of torture still used to make Palestinian children confess (e.g., MCW 2015, 47, 56). But more often children are beaten up, or face other forms of physical violence during the interrogations. As the 14-year-old M. S. describes his arrest in September 2013:

> At around 1:00 p.m. I was walking home from school. I was limping because I fell and injured my knee at school. As I walked past the

Israeli military watchtower at the entrance to our village, I looked back and saw four Israeli soldiers approaching me. They stopped me and one of them asked me whether I threw stones on Monday. I told him I didn't. He told me I was a liar and detained me. Somebody told my father I had been detained and he came to the watchtower. My father asked the soldiers why they were holding me. The soldier repeated that they had seen me throwing stones. My father challenged the soldier and his ability to identify me from among hundreds of boys who pass the watchtower each day. Then the Israeli commander came and tried to calm things down. I was very scared. Despite his father's protest, M. S. was moved to the Etzion Facility for further interrogation. He continues:

The interrogator cut the tie off and asked me how many stones I threw in my life. I told him I didn't throw stones. He asked me who throws stones with me but I denied the accusation. Then the interrogator left the room and a big fat man wearing civilian clothes entered. He saw blood on my trousers where I fell and asked me to lift my trousers up. He then kicked me on my injured knee. It was very painful. The interrogator came back and asked me the same questions again. In the end I confessed to throwing stones, I told him I threw 15 stones in my entire life. I was scared that if I didn't confess the fat guy would kick me again. (MCW 2014, 49–50)

The violence and abuse Palestinian minors face during the interrogations, detention, and arrest have far-reaching effects. Arrested children talk about nightmares, phobias, and panic attacks that had come after the harsh experiences. As the 12-year-old Sameer S. describes, after he was kicked, slapped, and threatened to be "thrown out of the window" during the interrogation, he is "still afraid of soldiers" and "can't sleep at night." "I'm anxious and still traumatized because of what happened," he says, and continues: "This was the first time I went through such a horrible experience which terrified me. I'm scared of the darkness. I keep thinking soldiers will come back and arrest me" (DCIP 2012, 107). But the harsh experiences also affect other members of the family. In the interviews collected by *No Legal Frontiers* between 2010 and 2011, Palestinian families told how siblings of the arrested constantly talk about soldiers coming to their houses, a two-year-old, for instance, remembering "even the smallest detail" and being "in constant fear of any knock on the door." Also, a void and a feeling of emptiness are left at home, usually accompanied with yearning and concern, for instance, when a mother cannot stop thinking whether her son "ate," "is sick," or "in cold," or when young siblings keep pointing at the pictures of the arrested child and say how they miss them (NLF 2011, 58–59; see also MCW 2014, 54).

CONCLUSION

Although the situation of Palestinian children under the military law has been widely recognized by the international community (e.g., US Department of State 2013; Amnesty International 2014; UNICEF 2015), recent years have not brought changes that would have significantly affected how Palestinian children in the West Bank are treated in practice. One of the main reasons for this is that amendments, such as the establishment of the Juvenile Military Court, are combined with the existing institutions with established practices and rationalities of government. In this chapter I have touched on some techniques and practices through which the security apparatus of the state of Israel functions in the West Bank, and so brought out several rationalities of government, whose existence and strategic functions make it hard for the single amendments to break through. Many of them have much to do with the exceptions that are allowed under the frame of security threats. The word "exception," however, should be used with caution, as security exceptions, such as stone-throwing for which a child aged 14 or over can be sentenced for a maximum of 20 years in prison, are also the most common reasons for arresting children.

As a child becomes framed as a part of the broader "Palestinian security threat," which requires specific and resolute military handling, it is his/her humanity, and childhood, that become politicized and contested for the sake of particular security purposes. In many cases children are treated in ways similar to adults; regarding stone-throwing, for instance, the military law applied to Palestinian children is even stricter than the civilian law applied to Israeli adults. Children, hence, are not framed merely as passive targets of the apparatus, but as a responsible and active part of the security threat and should be held accountable for. Such rationality of framing blurs the line between childhood and adulthood in one ethno-national group (Palestinian minors), while protecting it in the other (Israeli minors). The ethno-national segregation of Palestinian and Israeli children operates in many ways. Children are treated under different juridical systems, even in the case when they both live in the same territory, which produces discriminatory security politics that are racist at the level of its institutional constitution. But the discrimination of Palestinian children is also embedded in the ways the security apparatus operates in practice, for instance, Palestinian children are arrested and interrogated at night, but Israeli children are not (MCW 2015, 25).Despite the seemingly democratic legal system, which contains channels for making complaints about the unjust treatments, the harsh treatment of

Palestinian children cannot take place without the wide support given by the institutional bodies of the security apparatus. Whether we look at the military procedures or court proceedings, quiet support for the violence against Palestinian children comes forth through the several forms of impunity and acceptance. The proceedings and verdicts of the military court, for instance, include conspicuous impunity, which allows not only the military to move in the gray area, but also for soldiers to make violations without a fear of being held accountable. Impunity thus ensures that the strategic functions of the apparatuses can be maintained, as it supports the diverse and arbitrary acts of soldiers and commanders. The impunity, however, goes hand in hand with the institutionalized acceptance. Whether allowing a systematic torture of Palestinian children or unnecessary violence that soldiers arbitrarily use against them, institutional acceptance is needed for such techniques to emerge. Accordingly, the security apparatus is never a totalizing system of strategic functions, from which different practices and networks of government merely pop out. The apparatus allows loose connections, abrupt decisions, and flexible use of various techniques as long as they serve the occupying functions of the apparatus. Such flexibilities allow the apparatus to respond to the changing situation, to adapt them within its own power relations. Moreover, loose connections enable the context-specific conducts of soldiers and units, and thus the adaptation of the innovations regarding the success of government. The apparatus, hence, is not only about being systematic, calculated, and controlled, but also about government that is loose enough to be able to react to the uncertain, sudden, and unexpected. Yet, inasmuch as the apparatus remains tuned to face the potential—the sudden and the unknown—it aims to control these potential security threats by making Palestinian children more afraid of its disciplinary reactions—the violence, the abuse, and death.

The way the Israeli security apparatus, with all its institutional, disciplinary, juridical, and military power, treats Palestinian minors seems suffocating, especially regarding its capabilities to affect the everyday lives of children living in the occupied West Bank. Different operational parts of the apparatus— (1) those maintaining its inner functions, (2) those framing its targets, and (3) those constituting a thanatopolitical atmosphere of self-governing fear—all mobilize different sets of rationalities: (1) institutional acceptance, impunity, and flexibility; (2) exceptionalism, racist categorization, and the denial of child as a child; and (3) the fear of violence and death. In his essay *Recovering Childhood: Children in South African National Construction* Njabulo Ndebele (1995, 327) approaches such a state of affairs with a rhetorical question. After describing how the violence against children has worked in South African poems, literature, and history as a metaphor for measuring societal degeneration, he asks: What if the metaphor loses its shock effect? What if children are abused and killed in real life? What if such acts are normalized and stripped off their metaphoric power? What is there left in the metaphor to show societal degeneration? Sometimes reality answers in strange ways. The apparatuses may have a power to frame and position children, to rip away their status as a child, and to scare them and treat them as dehumanized security threats; yet, for a child the conflict situation may well be all about play, an invitation to a game that has all the excitement. "We're the attraction and they come out to play," an ex-Israeli soldier frames it in an anecdotic way (Breaking the Silence 2012, 10), while continuing:

At first you use some rubber ammo and then realize, it's silly. Once…there's this PA system we have, so we put on music from a cell phone and everyone started dancing. Yes, it was huge. We put on music and suddenly they all stopped throwing stones and began to dance. It was eastern music so they were dancing with their hands. Then the song ended and they went on throwing stones. It was really serious. You realize who you're dealing with here. These are kids.

References

Agamben, Giorgio. 2009. *"What Is an Apparatus?" and Other Essays.* Stanford, CA: Stanford University Press.

———. 2014. "What is a destituent power?" *Environment and Planning D: Society and Space* 32 (1): 65–74.

Amnesty International. 2014. *Trigger-Happy. Israel's Use of Excessive Force in the West Bank.* London: Amnesty International.

Ballas, Irit. 2012. "Regimes of impunity." In *On Torture*, edited by Amany Dayif, Katie Hesketh, and Jane Rice, 41–46. Adalah, The Legal Center for Arab Minority Rights in Israel.

Braun, Bruce. 2014. "A new urban dispositif? Governing life in an age of climate change." *Environment and Planning D: Society and Space* 32 (1): 49–64.

———. 2000. "Producing vertical territory: Geology and governmentality in late Victorian Canada." *Cultural Geographies* 7 (1): 7–46.

Braverman, Irus. 2011. "Civilized borders: A study of Israel's new crossing administration." *Antipode* 43 (2): 264–295.

Breaking the Silence. 2012. *Our Harsh Logic: Israeli Soldiers' Testimonies from the Occupied Territories, 2000–2010.* New York: Metropolitan Books.

———. 2011. *Children and Youth—Soldiers' Testimonies 2005–2011.* http://www.breakingthesilence.org.il/wp-content/uploads/2012/08/

Children_and_Youth_Soldiers_Testimonies_2005_2011_Eng.pdf. Last accessed August 19, 2015.

B'Tselem. 2013. *Abuse and Torture in Interrogations of Dozens of Palestinian Minors in the Israel Police Etzion Facility.* Jerusalem: B'Tselem—The Israeli Information Centre for Human Rights in the Occupied Territories.

———. "Press release: State Attorney's Office: Killing a wounded, fleeing boy by shooting him in the back merely a "reckless and negligent act." http://www.btselem.org/press_releases/20150414_state_attorney_decision_in_samir_awad_killing. Last modified April 14, 2015, accessed October 5, 2015.

Butler, Judith. 2009. *Frames of War: When Is Life Grievable?* London: Verso.

Delegation of British Lawyers (DBL). 2012. *Children in Military Custody.* DBL.

Defence for Children International, Palestine (DCIP). 2014a. *Growing Up between Israeli Settlements and Soldiers.* Jerusalem: DCIP.

———. 2014b. "How was 2014 for Palestinian children?" http://www.dci-palestine.org/how_was_2014_for_palestinian_children_1#MilitaryDetention. Last modified December 31, 2014, accessed August 5, 2015.

———. 2014c. *Solitary Confinement for Palestinian Children in Israeli Military Detention.* Jerusalem: DCIP.

———. 2009. *Palestinian Child Prisoners: A Systematic and Institutionalized Ill-Treatment and Torture of Palestinian Children by Israeli Authorities.* Jerusalem: DCIP.

———. 2012. *Bound, Blindfolded and Convicted: Children Held in Military Detention.* Jerusalem: DCIP.

———. 2013. *Palestinian Children Detained in the Israeli Military Court System: Reporting Period: 1 January 2012 to 31 December 2012.* Jerusalem: DCIP.

Elden, Stuart. 2007. "Governmentality, calculation, territory." *Environment and Planning D: Society and Space* 25 (3): 562–580.

Foucault, Michel. 2007. *Security, Territory, Population: Lectures at the College De France, 1977–1978.* Basingstoke: Palgrave Macmillan.

———. 2000. *Power: The Essential Works of Michel Foucault 1954–1984. Volume 3.* London: Penguin.

———. 1980. *Power/Knowledge: Selected Interviews and Other Writings, 1972–1977.* New York: Pantheon Books.

———. 1979. "Governmentality." *Ideology & Consciousness* 1979 (5): 5–21.

———. 1997. *Ethics: Subjectivity and Truth: The Essential Works of Michel Foucault 1954–1984. Volume 1.* London: Allen Lane, Penguin Press.

Ghanim, Honaida. 2008. "Thanatopolitics: The case of the colonial occupation in Palestine." In *Thinking Palestine,* edited by Ronit Lentin, 65–81. New York: Zed Books.

Habashi, Janette. 2013. "Children's religious agency: Conceptualizing Islamic idioms of resistance." *AREA* 45 (2): 155–161.

Hajjar, Lisa. 2013. *Lawfare and Armed Conclict: Comparing Israeli and US Targeted Killing Policies and Challeges against Them.* Beirut: Issam Fares Institute for Public Policy and International Affairs, American University of Beirut.

Häkli, Jouni, and Kirsi Pauliina Kallio. 2015. "Political geographies of childhood and youth. Virtual Special Issue. Editorial." *Political Geography*, http://www.journals.elsevier.com/political-geography/news/virtual-special-issue-on-political-geographies-of-childhood/

Hannah, Matthew. 2006. "Torture and the ticking bomb: The war on terrorism as a geographical imagination of power/knowledge." *Annals of the Association of American Geographers* 96 (3): 622–640.

Huxley, Margo. 2008. "Space and government: Governmentality and geography." *Geography Compass* 2 (5): 1635–1658.

Hyndman, Jennifer. 2010. "The question of 'the political' in critical geopolitics: Querying the 'child soldier' in the 'war on terror.'" *Political Geography* 29 (5): 247–255.

Israeli Military Order 1651 2009. Israeli Defence Forces.

Joronen, Mikko. 2015. "'Death Comes Knocking on the Roof': Thanatopolitics of Ethical Killing During Operation Protective Edge in Gaza." *Antipode* (forthcoming), doi:10.1111/anti.12178

———. 2013. "Conceptualising new modes of state governmentality: Power, violence and the ontological mono-politics of neoliberalism." *Geopolitics* 18 (2): 356–370.

———. 2011. "Dwelling in the sites of finitude: Resisting the violence of the metaphysical globe." *Antipode* 43 (4): 1127–1154.

Khoury, Jack. 2013. "IDF kills teenager in West Bank, fourth Palestinian death in a week." *Haaretz*, January 15, 2013.

Levy, Elior, and Yoav Zitun. 2013. "West Bank: Palestinian youth killed in clash with IDF." *Ynet*, January 1, 2013.

Marshall, David Jones. 2014. "Save (us from) the children: Trauma, Palestinian childhood, and the production of governable subjects." *Children's Geographies* 12 (3): 281–296.

———. 2013. "'All the beautiful things': Trauma, aesthetics and the politics of Palestinian childhood." *Space and Polity* 17 (1): 53–73.

Military Court Watch (MCW). 2015. *Children in Israeli Military Detention: Progress Report.* MCW.

———. 2013. *Two Boys, Two Laws: The Discriminatory Application of Law in the West Bank.* MCW.

———. 2014. *The UNICEF Report: Children in Israeli Military Detention.* MCW.

Millei, Zsuzsa, and Ken Cliff. 2014. "The preschool bathroom: Making 'problem bodies' and the limit of the disciplinary regime over children." *British Journal of Sociology of Education* 35 (2): 244–262.

Morrissey, John. 2011. "Liberal lawfare and biopolitics: US juridical warfare in the war on terror." *Geopolitics* 16 (2): 280–305.

Ndebele, Njabulo. 1995. "Recovering childhood: Children in South African national construction." In *Children and the Politics of Culture*, edited by Sharon Stephens, 321–334. Princeton, NJ: Princeton University Press.

No Legal Frontiers (NLF). 2011. *All Guilty! Observations in the Military Juvenile Court.* NLF.

Nolte, Amina, and Haim Yacobi. 2015. "Politics, infrastructure and representation: The case of Jerusalem's Light Rail." *Cities* 43: 28–36.

Office for the Coordination of Humanitarian Affairs (OCHA). 2015. *Fragmented Lives. Humanitarian Overview 2014.* East Jerusalem: United Nations OCHA occupied Palestinian territory.

Public Committee against Torture in Israel (PCATI). 2012. *Accountability Still Denied.* PCATI.

Rautio, Pauliina. 2013. "Children who carry stones in their pockets: On autotelic material practices in everyday life." *Children's Geographies* 11 (4): 394–408.

Scheper-Hughes, Nancy, and Carolyn Fishel Sargent. 1998. *Small Wars: The Cultural Politics of Childhood.* Berkeley and London: University of California Press.

Stephens, Sharon. 1995. *Children and the Politics of Culture.* Princeton Studies in Culture/Power/History. Princeton, NJ: Princeton University Press.

The Council for British-Arab Understanding (CAABU). 2012. *Palestinian Detainees: No Security in Injustice.* London.

United Nations Children's Fund (UNICEF). 2015. *Children in Israeli Military Detention: Observations and Recommendations, Bulletin no. 2: February 2015.* Jerusalem: UNICEF.

———. 2013. *Children in Israel Military Detention: Observations and Recommendations.* Jerusalem: UNICEF.

US Department of State. 2013. *Israel 2013: Human Rights Report.* Bureau of Democracy, Human Rights and Labor.

Wells, Karen. 2014a. "Children, youth, and subjectivity." *Children's Geographies* 12 (3): 263–267.

———. 2014b. "Marching to be somebody: A governmentality analysis of online cadet recruitment." *Children's Geographies* 12 (3): 339–353.

Yesh Din. 2014. *Data Sheet, September 2014. Law Enforcement upon IDF Soldiers in the Occupied Palestinian Territory.* Tel Aviv: Yesh Din.

———. 2013a. *Data Sheet, July 2013. MPCID Investigations into the Circumstances Surrounding the Death of Palestinians: Convictions and Penalties.* Tel Aviv: Yesh Din.

———. 2013b. "Significant drop in number of indictments—Out of 103 investigations opened in 2012, not a single indictment served to date." http://www.yesh-din.org/infoitem.asp?infocatid=249. Last modified February 3, 2013, accessed October 5, 2015.

PART II

Trans/National Subject Formation

CHAPTER 7

National Symbols and Practices in the Everyday of Irish Education

Marguerita Magennis

INTRODUCTION

This chapter considers issues on the often invisible symbols and practices of nationalism in education, and how it is received by nonnationals and Irish Travellers in Northern Ireland and the Republic of Ireland, with a particular focus on the potential to shape children's national identities. Through the theoretical lens offered by Michael Billig (1995) and further developed by Matthew Benwell and Klaus Dodds (2011), I explore constructions of national identity through symbols and practices within the education system and the everyday of schooling that influence children's formation of national identities and lead to inclusions and exclusions. During the analysis I raise questions about children's future identities and ask if national identities are in fact on the decline or whether these symbols heighten children's awareness of national belonging. This examination is particularly important in a context characterized by "hot nationalist passion" (Billig 1995, 44) continuously fuelling national unrest, as the case in Northern Ireland.

Moreover, national identity as it is shaped through education is examined here at the intersections of schooling with intercultural or, as others term it, multicultural education. Several models address ethnic, cultural, and religious diversity in education, with different consequences for children's experiences in schools. Greece and Ireland prefer to use the concept of intercultural education, whereas Britain, Canada, and Malaysia work with the concept of multiculturalism (Faas

2010). The existence of different conceptualizations of processes and practices to cater to different cultures and religious backgrounds in the latter three countries is similar to that in Northern Ireland where, since its formation in 1921, there have been two separate, religiously based educational systems with a focus on multicultural education for ethnic minority groups since the early 1990s,[1] which shaped children's national identities by intertwining religious and national values, ideals, and symbols in particular ways (Connolly 2001). Along with this two-armed system, there has also been an ongoing debate regarding the possibility and consequences of integrating these separate systems, with the main focus remaining that of religion (Hayes, McAllister, and Dowds 2007).

In this chapter I review existing literature that examines nationality and children's identifications with constructed notions and practices of the nation prevalent in schooling. By paying attention to how particular aspects of multicultural education is intended and received by nonnationals and Irish Travellers, I aim to highlight the problems with nationalism as it manifests in contemporary schooling, the possible inclusions and exclusions these approaches entail, and the shifting ways in which the nation and national belonging are understood by a young generation.

NATIONAL IDENTITY AND EDUCATION

Promoting a sense of national identity through reforms of practices, policies, and education is commonly accompanied with reservations that it may encourage xenophobia against nonnationals, leading to quarrels and social exclusion (Sindic 2008). A perspective offered by Billig (1995) highlights the everyday or banal ways in which children experience national identity. For Billig it is the less visible systems of national identity, the many little sociological processes through which national identities are continually sustained, that are intensely embedded in contemporary awareness, those affecting the psyche. Arguing that nationalism is universal even if it is, at times, understated, he shows how elapsed remedies function mindlessly in the subconscious, while we focus on the routine and familiar forms of nationhood and social life, such as thinking and using language and symbols (Billig 1995, 2006). Subsequently, rather than declining, Billig identifies national identity as very much alive, hovering just below the consciousness, encompassing the judgments, actions, and decisions one takes each day. Daily symbols of our national identity, such as flags, national language, social practices, sports, music, and dance, are often taken for granted and forgotten as a means of creating and preserving our national identity. For example, Paul Connolly (2002, 2008) showed how preschool children in Northern Ireland already categorized themselves based solely on symbols and flags. Joseph Moffatt (2011) offered some contradictions based on a study of older children from Dublin, where the children's categorizations of themselves and others included skin color, nationality, and language, with no focus on banal symbols.

Michael Skey (2009, 333) criticizes the concept of "banal nationalism" by arguing that while Billig claims national identity needs to be seen as a form of "life which is daily lived in"—and therefore becoming banal and unnoticed—there is a failure on Billig's part to engage with the impact of mass media and political speeches on different nationals and generations. A similar criticism is found in the work of Benwell and Dodds (2011) who studied everyday nationalism in Argentina and showed the different impact that the media had on people from different generations. The older generation held on to their claim that the Malvinas Islands were Argentinian and part of their heritage, while the younger generation saw them as British and showed no allegiance with them, despite symbols and representations that they encountered on a daily basis. Benwell et al. (2011) identify emotional investment, family history, geographic location, and generation as reasons for these differences within a sense of national belonging. Skey (2009) argued that the differences could be attributed to geographies, giving rise to what Billig (1995, 45) termed "hot nationalist passion" in relation to conflict over territory, as opposed to national identity performed on a daily basis or during a commemoration ceremony and sports events. This is similar to situations in Northern Ireland, where conflict and political discussion are continually high, as opposed to the Republic of Ireland where this conflict is rarely mentioned in everyday life. Accordingly Benwell et al. (2009) suggest the need to consider the everyday as not only being banal and secular, but also including a variety of hotter differences that affect people's lives on a regular basis. Thus highlighting the need to consider the different geographies, as is seen in Northern Ireland and the Republic, while supporting Skey in his suggestion, is that there is a need to consider nonnationals and the effects of globalization in everyday society.

If one examines the role of the school in promoting national identity according to Billig's theorization, then it is vital to consider how prevailing symbols and strategies are used, which lead to the inception and perpetuation of national identity, belonging, and exclusions.

To question where this feeling of belonging comes from and how it takes root become particularly pertinent for a nation that falls under two political and educational jurisdictions, but when considering the issues of nonnationals within the school system the issue becomes even more complex. Therefore, after introducing the context of study, I first examine what role school policy plays in the evolution of national identity and to what extent this role is shaped by politics.

CONSTRUCTING NORTHERN IRELAND IN A CHANGING WORLD

In recent years national identity has become a pertinent issue for educators to address due to the influx of nonnationals into an already unsettled society. In this chapter I understand identity as socially constructed. Consequently, national identity represents a highly volatile subject that, as Vamik Volkan (1988) expresses, reaches deeper into the human psyche than one is inclined to acknowledge. Billig (1995, 44) makes a differentiation between banal forms of nationalism and "hot nationality" that is actualized in conflicts or situations of resistance. Irish national identity became associated with the Catholic religion due to the British colonization (Muldoon 2010). Accordingly after colonization, Irish Catholics felt the need to reconstruct their identities, and in an attempt to do so, they saw the fusion of Catholic and nationalist identities as an opposition to the British attempts at imposing a single dominant religion (Moffatt 2011). The Irish efforts to attain liberation from Britain concluded with the Easter uprising in 1916, with Ireland being declared a republic in 1948. However, six counties in Northern Ireland remained under British rule, so the island became divided, as did national identity. The people in Northern Ireland, in particular, who have identified with the Catholic church for so long, clung to these religious practices, displaying "hot nationality" in an effort to resist the British rule. Ultimately Irish Catholicism emerged stronger and more connected to national identity than ever before, so much so that the education system in Ireland was predominantly overseen and controlled by the Catholic church, with some state-controlled schools in the north of Ireland mainly attended by protestant children (White 2010).

Anthony Smith (1991) suggests two models of national identity: a civic model and the ethnic genealogical model. Obviously, these are not mutually exclusive, and so looking for immutable categories is not a fruitful exercise. For example, evidence of the civic model can be found in Northern Ireland, where national identity is influenced by politics and a civic ideology, with Protestant members of the community retaining their British allegiances, while the majority of Catholics cling to their Irish roots (Smith 1991). In the Republic of Ireland, an ethnic genealogical view is dominant, emphasizing descent, ethnicity, and blood ties, with the ability to retain one's national identity outside of Ireland. An outsider thus will never become a full member of society despite gaining citizenship, as is evidenced throughout Ireland (Darmody, Byrne, and McGinnity 2012; Joyce, Stevenson, and Muldoon 2012). The term "blow-in" is often used to depict a person not born on Irish soil and thus never considered to be truly Irish. This complicates matters a great deal depending on the time frame for "ethnic" (Catholic) Irish born elsewhere, and "returning" to what would constitute Irish soil.

During the 1990s, as a result of what is termed as the "miracle of the Celtic Tiger," an oppressed nation suddenly became one of Europe's wealthiest countries, with unemployment levels falling, while incomes continuously increased (Smyth 2012). A further change was a fairly significant stream of immigration, opposite to what Ireland was familiar with, having been a net exporter of people since the famine in the mid-1800s. The more recent change left over 10 percent of residents in the Republic of Ireland as foreign born by 2007, leading to a multicultural society and schools (White 2010). Therefore along with the collapse of the Celtic Tiger in 2009, came instances of racism and prejudice with claims that nonnationals were taking the few jobs available. This situation has seen the beginnings of a form of "hot nationality" in the Republic of Ireland (Smyth 2012).

At the same time, the Catholic church came under scrutiny for corruption and exploitation. This left the once oppressed society struggling to reconstitute its national identity with questionable symbols, resulting in queries about whether the Catholic church should retain its influence on the education system in Ireland and subsequently on national identity, and encouraging a greater emphasis on multicultural education systems rather than religion.

INTERCULTURAL AND MULTICULTURAL EDUCATION

If one raises the question with Irish educators about what multicultural education is, and how they see their role in promoting the national identity of the children in their care, the answers would undoubtedly vary (Carr 2004). This is due to the many different interpretations of what is meant by multicultural education and the different requirements of the school curricula. Legislation requires that schools address issues of antidiscrimination practices by being inclusive and ensuring equality and diversity for all children (UNCRC 1989), with article 31 specifically addressing the need to encourage awareness of others' rights. The revised primary curriculum in Northern Ireland also highlighted these issues as the responsibility of the school system, while more recently in the Republic of Ireland the early year's frameworks, titled Aistear and Siolta, identified the need to encourage rights and awareness of identity of self and others (NCCA 2009). However, some of the strategies that are employed to do so are minimalistic and fail to take into account the psychological impact on the children of the everyday symbols within society and settings, those that Billig (1995) refer to as banal.

Some educators conceive the role of education to include multicultural materials and resources throughout the setting. The inclusion of multicultural dolls, or enhancing the home corner with multiple types of foods and utensils that represent different cultural experiences, does little to enhance the child's perception of cultural difference, if they have a preconceived idea about certain differences, including nationality (MacNaughton and Hughes 2007). Others offer posters and pictures depicting different ethnic groups as being successful, and incorporate initiatives such as international day into the curriculum. During these events children and parents share their home and cultural experiences, but without any consistency or critical discussion; thus these events often result in tokenistic efforts at multicultural education (MacNaughton and Hughes 2007; Devine 2011). Many studies highlight the importance of taking these tokens a step further, including the child's voice, encouraging exploration and investigation of the different experiences, and providing answers for the queries children raise instead of shying away for fear of causing conflict or confusion (Deegan, Devine, and Lodge 2004; Devine and Kelly 2006; Devine 2009, 2011). However, these attempts at highlighting the importance of children and the child's voice imply they can be passively socialized into one dominant national discourse (Scourfield 2005). Children are naturally curious, but they are also equally accepting of particular biases at this young age. Therefore it is important to encourage children to voice their concerns and queries, to ask questions, and open up debates around issues of difference and respect, thus ensuring schools are promoting critical inquiry, and allowing and facilitating the use of technology and interview techniques to support diversity within the classroom (Souto-Manning 2013).

One question identified by Connolly (2002) was whether educators could do anything to counteract the preconceived ideas that these children have about national identity. In a study of 3.5-year-olds in Northern Ireland, Connolly identified the color of flags, places. and religion as symbols with which children identified. Dympna Devine, Mairin Kenny, and Eileen Macneela (2008) showed similar findings in the Republic of Ireland. However, children from the Republic included skin color and language as contributing factors, which would suggest their ability to categorize themselves and identify with others who they perceived as different. Studies in Australia also report on very young children's awareness of skin color and how those contribute to the construction of national identity and particular exclusions and inclusions (MacNaughton, Cruz, and Hughes 2003; MacNaughton 2005, Srinivasan 2014, this book). Nevertheless, there are strong arguments to say that, for better or for worse, nationalism and national identities are here to stay; the question must then become, how can educators promote forms of nationality and at the same time elude the uninvited aftermath of racism and prejudice that is sometimes evident within the classroom (Sindic 2008)? It has also been suggested that national identity, rather than being on the decrease, is becoming an academic condition (Moffatt 2011), with educators throughout Ireland needing a raised awareness of not only cultural and banal symbols, but also taking account of the implications that "hot nationalism" will have on children from areas of conflict.

Nonnational children are often expected to fit into the school system, with little consideration given to their national identity (and more to their language issues; e.g., see Carr 2004; Department of Education and Skills 2010; Development and Intercultural Education 2014), with the main teacher education institutions in both Northern Ireland and the Republic of Ireland having no modular content relating to intercultural education or its importance. This often results in nonnational children being withdrawn for additional support (Devine 2008). The problem is that intercultural education is supposed to be an education for all children, not only those children from ethnic minority groups (Devine 2011), with schools being confronted and asked to deliberate on their structure and policies in relation to enrollment, class allocation, teaching materials, and relationships. An intercultural school is perceived to be fully inclusive with mutual recognition of everyone's values and ways of life and, in doing so, educators should aim to help all children maintain their individual national identity, while respecting and understanding those of others.

NATIONAL IDENTITY IN EVERYDAY SCHOOLING

National identity can be defined as the crucial principal of our being, forming a sense of belonging between people, underlining certain mutual aspects, while at the same time differentiating oneself from others (Weeks 1990). National identity is socially constructed and negotiated through multifaceted exchanges with others, rather than being forged in isolation. Accordingly a person's national identity is continually evolving throughout their life experiences (Carr 2004). By showing that children's identity varies depending on contexts, such as institution, teacher, school ethos, and peer group, and even the political state of the country, Daniel Faas (2010) suggests that the development of national identity has a proxy for fruitful integration into schools. John Carr (2004) agrees that national identity and identification are influenced by school and social circle and shows how Chinese children from Belfast, Northern Ireland, view themselves as "Northern Irish" in school, while still seeing their parents as Chinese. These children had experienced the Northern Irish Protestant education system, while retaining their Chinese national language and culture at home. This finding raises the importance of peer culture also, where children attempt to fit in with peers at school, which Dympna Devine (2008) highlights as being equally, if not more, important. Further comparisons can be found in studies by Sinead Meade and Michael O'Connell (2009) and Carmel Joyce, Clifford Stevenson, and Orla Muldoon (2012). They examine Irish Travellers' (Romani or Gypsy) national identification and show how they display "hot nationality" in an attempt to maintain their Irish national identity, while being rejected by other Irish children. Underpinning these findings Devine (2008) demonstrates that there is a greater acceptance of nonnational children than Irish-born Travellers in schools in the Republic of Ireland. Therefore attempting to define one's national identity and what influences it is often relative to how others see one, like the layers of an onion being peeled back throughout the child's life.

Irish children often associate their identity, like those from other nations, with the history and language of that nation (Scourfield, Dicks, Drakeford, and Davies 2006). Jonathan Scourfield and his colleagues' (2006) study outlines particular ways in which symbols and activities in schools, including traditional music and dance, language, sports, and religion, become channels of expression and formation of national identity. The Republic of Ireland has an added influence of Gaelscoils and Immersion schools, with similarities to

Welsh medium education (Scourfield 2005), with attempts to create a bilingual nation. If looked at through Billig's (1995) work, these symbols became "banal" to Irish children who see and experience them every day. However, it is important to consider how they affect nonnational children. Schools across Ireland, but particularly in the Republic, include such symbols of Irishness throughout the curriculum, with a particular emphasis placed on the Irish language and Irish sports and music. In doing so, these national displays not only influence nonnational children but also impact upon their "psyche" and identity formation and result in particular exclusions.

Irish Language

A common language plays an important part in developing a shared sense of identity, with Louis Balthazar (1993) highlighting language as a process of shaping some meaning of identity. Michael Peillon (1982) adds that the role of Irish language in Ireland is not only for nationals to celebrate Irish identity, but also a method of resisting the imminence of an EU nationality where language acts as a symbol of defense (Moffatt 2011). In Ireland the first experience of Irish language, for the majority of children, is in school. The Irish language is compulsory in the Republic of Ireland from junior infants (4 years of age) until the acquisition of leaving certificate at the age of 17 or 18 years. However, in Northern Ireland, Irish is rarely taught at the primary level, and is not a compulsory subject for final examination at the postprimary level. This promotion of the Irish language, although not the mother tongue of most nationals, would suggest that it is perceived as educationally formalized and attached to promoting a sense of Irishness throughout the school system.

Gaelscoils and Immersion schools are seen regularly throughout the Republic of Ireland, with an increased presence during the Celtic Tiger years and the availability of funding from the government to support their existence. The official support encourages the growth and continuity of the Irish language. In such schools the curriculum is delivered through the Irish medium, with preference given to children who come from Irish-speaking areas or homes. It has been suggested that these schools were an attempt at segregating the nonnationals, as these schools are usually situated in more affluent areas, with attendance from people from the middle and upper socioeconomic classes (McWilliam 2005; Carey 2008; Coolahan 2012). While the schools themselves present an ethos of being available to everyone, their carefully worded entry requirements sometimes suggest

otherwise, particularly in the case of Gaelscoils, where it is a require-
ment for a parent to be fluent in Irish. Similar situations can be found
in the more affluent national schools throughout Ireland, with nonnational children regularly being deprived entry. These schools are
considered to be "the better schools" and so nonnationals mainly
attend disadvantaged or oversubscribed schools where they receive
less of the necessary attention (Devine 2008). Therefore while the
ethos of the school and education system would portray inclusion and
equality for all, it would appear this is not always the case.

Immersion schools, however, encourage children from all nationalities and offer support to parents without Irish as a language, so
the children can have consistency at home. Once again this creates
its own difficulties, with children from nonnational families struggling to keep up with a new education system being delivered in a
foreign language. Nonnational children entering the education system are presented with two language hurdles: first, that of English
as a second language, and second, within the Republic of Ireland,
Irish as a third language. Children as young as three years often
encounter several languages around early childhood settings in an
attempt to provide and receive multicultural education. However, due
to attempts at maintaining the Irish national language, nonnational
children encounter extra difficulties, resulting in diminished educational attainment (Devine 2008; Faas 2013). This problem raises the
question: What have these children and families to gain from trying
to obtain an education through a different language, which some
would claim is dying? Further evidence suggests that nonnational
children who are encouraged to retain and taught through their
mother tongue have a more positive attitude to school and their own
culture (Carr 2004); some provision is made by such schools, in an
attempt to provide a link to their own national identity. However, this
is a rare experience and its feasibility with regard to funding needs to
be researched further.

Contesting the importance and value of the Irish language Moffatt's
(2011) study suggests that this emblematic sense of Irishness does
not necessarily support children's own understanding of Irishness.
Moffatt's (2011) study with children in an English-speaking school
in Dublin (Republic of Ireland) revealed that children did not associate the ability to speak Irish as a defining factor of their nationality.
With similarities to children of Northern Ireland who predominantly
do not speak or learn Irish, however, the majority still identify themselves as Irish, with religion and birthplace having a greater part to
play (Carr 2004).

Religion and the Catholic Church

In Ireland, Catholic education is currently at the forefront, with the educational arena becoming much more complex in recent years due to innumerable influences both directly and indirectly related to education. Ireland is no longer the hermetically watertight refuge it once was assumed to be (Kieran 2008; Coolahan 2012) and finds itself without the luxury of old certainties, with diversities becoming a facet of everyday life (Lynch and Baker 2005). Are the Irish Catholic schools up to the challenge? Could this multiculturalism provide a new opportunity for Catholic schools to renew and revitalize themselves, or will we see the demise of Catholic education as we know it in promoting Irish identities? Before looking into these issues it is necessary to consider the intimacy of the connection between culture and religion in Ireland that also helps to understand how schools respond to the need for multicultural education. David McWilliams (2005) provides a captivating insight into this aspect of Irish life in his book titled *Faith of the Nation*. He describes the ghostly rhythms of Irish identity and culture within a seamless presence of the sacred and secular. Some would claim that schools have become veritable slaves to the government regarding religion and multicultural education, and no responsibility is taken by either principals or government to ensure legislation is actually implemented, with teachers being left mostly to their own devices (Lynch and Baker 2005). However, according to Lynn Corcoran (2008) this defensiveness arises from a desire to protect something, but at times no one is sure exactly what, raising the question as to whether it is an attempt to hold onto a form of national identity. Writers and poets have succeeded in beautifully conjuring the interlacing of religion and culture, referring to the fact that influences of religion and words in childhood run at a very deep level in the human psyche, never really leaving the person (Corcoran 2008). This interlacing is seen, for example, in the reformulation of Catholic teaching into a confirmation of Christian values to appeal to the widest possible audience and remaining inoffensive to all (see, e.g., a portrayal of this by Lieven Boeve [2003] in an analysis of Catholic universities). This approach to Catholism and religion is evidenced in the north of Ireland where religious education is varied and includes the perspective of numerous identities and cultural beliefs in an attempt to accommodate both the national religions as well as those of the nonnationals.

Micheal Kilcrann (2003) attempted to identify the practical issues that we need to debate if we are to attempt to respond to the diversity in the Republic of Ireland primary education sector. Kilcrann (2003) developed these points through the evaluation of the Alive O program, the religious education program for Catholic schools in both jurisdictions, the Republic and Northern Ireland, but for different reasons. Alive O was designed to attempt to help children achieve a more valuable and active personal faith, providing links to the world around us with multicultural links to other religions and nations. Kilcrann's (2003) study concludes that primary education holds the key to developing an inclusive society, suggesting that educators have the key role. The problem is, how can one person (educator) cater for and share the experience of every child? How can children retain their home beliefs by being included in the religion of others?

The Northern Ireland curriculum is unique in its attempts to promote almost no influence of the Christian religion, similar to that of the United Kingdom (Moffatt 2011), emphasizing instead the need to consider different understandings of what it means to be a good citizen. We also find reference to the Christian character of religion in the Republic of Ireland: however, a strong Catholic ethos is evident in the Republic (Irwin 2010) as opposed to that in Northern Ireland. In Northern Ireland the curriculum centers on uplifting morals that are seen as an attempt to unite all communities despite sectarian divisions, by expressing principles such as interdependence. This delicate treatment of religion in Northern Ireland reflects historical tensions between Protestants and Catholics (O'Connor and Faas 2011), and often educators only tentatively broach the area of religion for fear of causing offense. Terms like "denomination" have Christian undercurrents (Faas 2011) and echo the nature and prevailing discourse in Ireland, while Christian overtones and prioritizing the Christian approach serve to potentially marginalize non-Christians and non-Catholic children. While most nonnational children will remain, some will be withdrawn from religious education at the request of their parents. Interestingly religion in Ireland, while still the focus of the curriculum and requiring examination at junior certificate, informs contemporary identity for children in a different way, with Moffatt (2011) showing how children in Dublin use religion to demonstrate how Irish identity is changing, seeing themselves as nonreligious in comparison to their parents. Though the degree of the secularization of Irish society may be argued, for these children a significant factor of secularism seems evident in their adoption of this voluntary stance toward religion. Having become prejudiced due to the forcing of religion upon the people of Ireland in both jurisdictions and the power that had been afforded to the Catholic church, these children clearly claim faith should be chosen, not imposed, and should remain at home, suggesting that Catholism, if not religion, is losing it clutches on the Irish national identity.

Irish History and Education

Bob Rowthorn and Naomi Wyne (1988) exhibit the power of schools in preserving a very specific commitment and disposition toward a nation, with their writing grounded in the argument that instruction in basic history and literacy is aimed at understanding the nation and one's national identity within it. They identify primary education as an almost hegemonic process through which literature was anchored in the British race at the expense of other identities. History is taught in a way that aims to nurture a bond with one's own country at the expense of other nations (Bourke cited in Koh 2010), with similarities found in the Republic of Ireland where history education strives to encourage a shared set of values and promote a national ethos. Roland Tormey (2006) suggests that while concepts of the nation may run throughout all subject areas in the curriculum, the teaching of history is an area that plays a key role in attempts to maintain the nation and sustain national identity. Accordingly Benedict Anderson (1991) claims that history is a memory creating a society or nation by bonding various people with the sharing of a past that none of them have experienced; therefore they are equal regardless of origin. This notion is validated further by emphasizing the lesson to be learnt as that of moral virtue, with reference to the troubles in Northern Ireland. The civics syllabus included patriotism in the form of singing, learning the national anthem, speaking Irish, and advice on purchasing only Irish goods (Tormey 2006). Consequently Ireland is defined through history as not being British, drawing on the sympathy of young children's minds and depicting their people as oppressed.

It is clear that history has some contemporary importance extending far beyond education, as research in education and social science has demonstrated (Tormey 2006). In Northern Ireland the significance of history is evidenced with both the cultural political organizations, Unionists and Nationalists,[2] having their own version of the past, each petitioning their historical narratives to justify contemporary attitudes (Walker 1996; McBride 1997; Conway 2007). Therefore history in the Northern education forms a fundamental part of promoting a sense of identity (Devine-Wright 2001), with symbols and representations of history being unavoidable features of life. For the nonnational children who look explicitly to school to provide them with an understanding of national history, this creates a somewhat biased interpretation. This confusion is clearly depicted in Kilcrann's (2003) thesis titled "Diary of a non-national child" and raise queries about why a nonnational needs to know about this new country, and this new language. Consequently, considering the value or importance Irish history holds for nonnationals, it becomes clear that history is an important part in attempts to reformulate their identities and to create alignments with their host nation (Carr 2004). This effect is in diametrical opposition to the philosophy of the Irish curriculum that aims to create a post-national identity with common values (Faas 2013). Avril Keating (2009) suggests that the curriculum portrays a European character particularly as part of efforts toward an intercultural approach. However, Faas (2013) questions whether this intercultural approach can improve and increase inclusion if it fails to form a national citizenship, raising further questions (e.g., see Koopman et al. 2005) as to the possibility of actually including multiple national identities simultaneously in the curriculum, which would appear to be what is happening in the everyday.

Gaelic Sport: Gaelic Athletic Association (GAA)

Further symbols and processes for national identity formation found in schools today, which are not always mentioned in the curricular guidance, are those of national sport, the GAA, traditional music, and dance. From an early age, children are encouraged to take up music or dance as part of their extracurricular activities and these usually involve learning Irish dancing and/or playing the accordion, wooden flute, or fiddle (violin). Most schools encourage the tin whistle as part of their music lessons and songs, and rhymes learned are Irish traditional. While these everyday cultural performances belong to forms of banal nationalism, these "traditional" performances of the nation still give little consideration to nonnational children, who are rarely given an opportunity to extend or trouble this experience, although they might be asked to demonstrate dance or music from their own culture. In fact, in some cases, the children may feel as though they are being made a spectacle of (Kilcrann 2003). Likewise with sport, from the start of the last century the GAA has had an influence on all forms of Irish culture specifically that of language; within the association itself, at meetings, in rules, and in many other ways, the Irish language is promoted and encouraged. In schools GAA sports are actively promoted during the physical education curriculum, with a particular emphasis on Hurling, Camogie, and Gaelic[3] in the Republic of Ireland, but mostly only the Catholic schools in Northern Ireland.

Sports influence identity (Scourfield et al. 2006) and there is no question that Gaelic sports both created and reinforced a distinctive sense of Irish Identity. Gaelic sports are judged to have promoted a particularized sense of Irishness steeped in history, which offers rejection of foreign nationals and embraces the Irish nation (Cronin 1999). Among the border schools in Northern Ireland, mostly among members of the minority Catholic community, the popular cultural pastime is sport, Gaelic football, hurling, and Camogie. These and other sports play a role in the construction of a unique identity for this section of Irish society. This is particularly evident in primary education where the majority of Catholic schools have a young Gaelic team or hurling team and are unlikely to participate in soccer, seen in Ireland but particularly in Northern Ireland as a British sport (Cronin 2001). Whereas Gaelic sports are seen to encourage the traditional manly attributes and fighting spirit needed to free Ireland (Cronin 2001) and save an oppressed nation, the Protestant schools favor soccer to promote and maintain their British identity; therefore, sport plays a significant factor in promoting a child's national identity. While schools participate in their respective sports, a small minority of integrated schools will either elect to have neither sport in the school, or attempt to have both, with specific rules about dress codes applying in these schools on nonuniform days, with no football jerseys being allowed to be worn for fear of causing conflict with a non-supporter, or nonnational (McGlynn 2003). In this way Gaelic sports are used to accentuate the continuity of Irish distinctiveness in the same way as language is promoted. Evidence of this influence is greater still in the Republic of Ireland where more emphasis is placed on hurling and Camogie as the national sport in most counties, with Gaelic football also evident as an indicator to Irish boys and girls that they are Gaels. Some view Gaelic sports as teaching resourcefulness, courage, and cooperation. Moffatt (2011) ascertains that the GAA have done more for Irish nationalism than any other organization.

For the nonnational child this might lead to several dilemmas with regard to national identity as Gaelic sports have no link to their home country. There is a further sense that for the majority of schools, there is no opportunity for nonnationals to play on the team, whether by personal choice or due to the staunch Irishness that emanates from within the GAA and the use of the Irish language during the activities. When school portrays this image of respected identity and inclusion through sports, nonnational children are either being forced to participate in activities that hold no meaning or value for them, or excluded and left to feel inadequate.

CONCLUSION

Undeniably contemporary Irish national identity has moved beyond the encompassing seamless garment that had been constructed, resembling rather a patchwork quilt of many colors and nationalities. While there is some recognition in contemporary Ireland of the complexity of national identities that cannot be narrowed to a universal form, which matches the ethnic genealogical model of Smith (1991), this remains a less-heard-of view. There is also an increased social acceptance that Irishness is not only Catholic or Gaelic and some consensus around the notion of what Irishness can mean in a multicultural society, which is, of course, not without problems and contestations. The analysis of literature that examined strategies and approaches to how nonnational children should be educated and included provided this chapter with a useful frame to examine the still strong biases associated with a constructed identity of Irishness that is prevalent in Irish education. Early multicultural education in Britain encouraged the concept of coexistence of cultures and nations, with everyone living side by side. However, based on the analysis in this chapter it is questionable whether this approach necessarily promotes positive national identities for all children including nationals. While I agree that teaching children about respecting another's color, ethnicity, and culture is useful, it is important to examine other realms of influence, such as those that stem from the home, school, media, and broader society, and it is important to remember the difference between multicultural education and inclusion as opposed to providing only an Irish perspective with regard to children's everyday. In Northern Ireland and the Republic of Ireland where a multitude of identities are being negotiated by educators in the multicultural settings, educational isolation and discursive exclusion through literacy, history, and the Irish language still cause frustration for nonnational children and their families, despite legislation to the contrary. Faas (2013) suggests the need for a more diverse system that will necessitate the inclusion of a plurality of national identities and provide a more flexible self-perception of nation-states, because he claims the identities of children in this century are not identical and perhaps ever more complex than before. Devine and colleagues (2008) draw attention to the fact that despite the best efforts of educators, prejudice and racism are not just aimed at nonnationals, but also at Irish Travellers.

These considerations suggest that power is part of the dynamics of inclusion and exclusion in the child's world and needs to be accounted for when challenging stereotypical or ethnic genealogical views regarding national identity. A focus on power then highlights the importance for educators to encourage and enable children to identify and explore their discriminatory behaviour, while considering its consequences for the minority group, with similarities to strategies employed in Mariana Souto-Manning's (2013) important work. It is also important to pay attention to and debunk how the ethnic genealogical model of Irishness is constructed and operates in the everyday as it attaches itself to a stereotypical kind of national identity.

The idea of promoting a sense of national identity through reforms of practices and education is frequently associated with fears that it may promote xenophobia against nonnationals, leading to quarrels and social exclusion. Nevertheless, it would appear that national identity is here to stay, with education making a contribution to the specific construction and meaning of being a national citizen and practices that uphold these differentiations. Therefore, there is a need to extend discussions with a greater input from the nonnational communities, so awareness could be raised to the specific symbols and practices that may seem banal to our children and their educators, yet have a major impact and meaning for those of another nation and their inclusion and exclusion from society as a whole (Sindic 2008).

ACKNOWLEDGMENTS

I would like to acknowledge Dr. Zsuzsa Millei and Dr. Robert Imre for their support and guidance as editors; your advice has been invaluable. I would also like to acknowledge my research assistant Michael Cooley, without whom my research would have taken much longer, my Boys for their proofreading, critique, and encouragement, and finally Professor Jim Deegan for those famous words: "Go for it!" It is their support that has encouraged me in an immeasurable way.

NOTES

1. In Northern Ireland it was 1989 before any legislation took account of multicultural education with a further emphasis being highlighted during the Good Friday Agreement in 1998. Until this time the main divide in the education system remained solely that of religion.

2. Unionists believe Northern Ireland should remain part of Britain with the Queen of England as their Sovereign, while Nationalists believe Northern Ireland should be reunited with the Republic of Ireland to reinstate the 32 counties (Timothy J. White, "The impact of British colonialism on Irish Catholicism and national identity: Repression, reemergence, and divergence," *Etudes Irlandaises* 35 (1) (2010): 21–37).

3. Hurling is a predominantly male GAA sport. Camogie is a predominantly female GAA sport. Gaelic is a GAA football game with male and female teams, although rarely played in mixed teams.

REFERENCES

Anderson, Benedict. 1991. *Imagined Communities*. London: Verso.

Balthazar, Louis. 1993. "The faces of Quebec nationalism." In *A Passion for Identity: An Introduction to Canadian Studies*, edited by Tara David, Rasporich Beverly,and Mandel Eli. Ontario: Nelson Canada.

Benwell, Matthew C., and Klaus Dodds. 2011. "Argentine territorial nationalism revisited: The Malvinas/Falklands dispute and geographies of everyday nationalism." *Political Geography* 30 (8): 441–449.

Billig, Michael. 2006. "A psychoanalytic discursive psychology: From consciousness to unconsciousness." *Discourse Studies* 8 (1): 17–24.

———. 1995. *Banal Nationalism*. London: Sage.

Boeve, Lieven. 2003. *Interrupting Tradition: An Essay on Christian Faith in a Postmodern Context*. Louvin, Belgium: Peeters Press.

Carey, Sarah. 2008. "Gaelscoil parents want to have their cake and eat it." *Irish Times* December 24. http://www.irishtimes.com/opinion/gaelscoil-parents-want-to-have-their-cake-and-eat-it-1.1275738

Carr, John. 2004. "Intercultural education in the primary school." *Proceedings of the Consultative Conference on Education*. Dublin, Ireland: INTO.

Connolly, Paul. 2008. *A Need to Belong: An Epidemiological Study of Black Minority Ethnic Children's Perceptions of Exclusion in the Southern Area of Northern Ireland*. Belfast: Centre for Effective Education, Queens University Belfast.

———. 2006. "It goes without saying (well, sometimes), racism, whiteness and identity in Northern Ireland." In *The New Countyside? Ethnicity, Nation and Exclusion in Contemporary Rural Britian*, edited by Jullian Agyeman and Sarah Neals. Bristol: Bristol Press.

———. 2001. "Qualitative methods in the study of children's racial attitudes and identities." *Infant and Child Development* 10 (4): 219–233.

Connolly, Paul, Alan Smith, and Berni Kelly. 2002. *Too Young to Notice? The Cultural and Political Awareness of 3–6 Year olds in Northern Ireland*. Belfast: Community Relations Council.

Conway, Brian. 2007. "Rethinking difficult pasts: Bloody Sunday (1972) as a case study." http://eprints.maynoothuniversity.ie/2874/1/BC_Rethinking.pdf

Coolahan, John. 2012. "The forum on patronage and pluralism in the primary sector." https://www.education.ie/en/Press-Events/Conferences/Patronage-and-Pluralism-in-the-Primary-Sector/The-Forum-on-Patronage-and-Pluralism-in-the-Primary-Sector-Report-of-the-Forums-Advisory-Group.pdf

Corcoran, Lynn. 2008. *Multiculturalism as a Phenomenon in Catholic Primary Schools*. www.mie.ie/getdoc/268e9249-a13f-493e-afb7.../Lynn-Corcoran.aspx

Cronin, Mike. 2001. *A History of Ireland*. Basingstoke: Palgrave.

———. 1999. *Sport and Nationalism in Ireland: Gaelic 1884*. Dublin, Ireland: Four Courts Press.

Darmody, Merike, Delma Byrne, and Frances McGinnity. 2012. "Cumulative disadvantage? Educational careers of migrant students in Irish secondary schools." *Race Ethnicity and Education* 17 (1): 129–151.

Deegan, Jim, Dympna Devine, and Anna Lodge. 2004. *Primary Voices: Equality, Diversity and Childhood in Irish Primary Schools*. Dublin, Ireland: Institute of Public Administration.

Department of Education and Skills (DES). 2010. "Intercultural education strategy: Executive summary 2010–2015." Dublin, Ireland: DES.

Development and Intercultural Education (DICE). 2014. "Within initial teacher education: DICE Project 2014–2016." St. Patrick's College, Dublin, Ireland: DICE.

Devine, Dympna. 2011. "Securing migrant children's educational well-being: Perspective of policy and practice in Irish schools." In *Changing Faces of Ireland, Exploring Lives of Immigrant and Ethnic and Minority Children*, edited by Merike Darmody, Naomi Tyrell, and Steve Song. Rotterdam: Sense.

———. 2009. "Mobilising capitals? Migrant children's negotiations of their everyday lives in school." *British Journal of Society Sociology of Education* 30 (5): 521–535.

Devine, Dympna, and Mary Kelly. 2006. "I just don't want to get picked on by everyone: Dynamics of inclusion and exclusion in a multi-ethnic Irish primary school." *Child and Society* 20 (2): 128–139.

Devine, Dympna, Mairin Kenny, and Eileen Macneela. 2008. "Naming the 'other': Children's construction and experience of racism in Irish primary schools." *Race Ethnicity and Education* 11 (4): 369–385.

Devine-Wright, Patrick. 2001. "History and identity in Northern Ireland: An exploratory investigation of the role of historical commemorations in context of intergroup conflict." *Peace and Conflict* 7 (4): 297–315.

Faas, Daniel. 2013. "Ethnic diversity and schooling in national education systems, issues of policy and identity." *Education Inquiry* 4 (1): 5–10.

———. 2010. *Negotiating Political Identities: Multi-Ethnic Schools and Youth in Europe*. Farnham: Ashgate.

Hayes, Bernadette C., Ian McAllister, and Lizanne Dowds. 2007. "Intergrated education, intergroup relations, and political identities in Northern Ireland." *Social Problems* 54 (4): 454–482.

Irwin, Jones. 2010. "Interculturalism ethos and ideology barriers to freedom and democracy in Irish primary education." *REA: A Journal of Religion, Education and the Arts* 6 (2).

Joyce, C., C. Stevenson, and O. Muldoon. 2012. "Claiming and displaying national identity: Irish Travellers' and students' strategic use of 'banal' and 'hot' national identity in talk." *British Journal of Social Psychology* 52 (3): 450–68.

Keating, Avril. 2009. "Nationalizing the post-national: Reframing European citizenship for the civics curriculum in Ireland." *Journal of Curriculum Studies* 41 (2): 159–178.

Kieran, Patricia. 2008. "Embracing change: The remodelling of Irish Catholic primary schools." 12: 4–1. dspace.mic.ul.ie/.../Kieran,%20P. (2008).%20'Embracing%20Change%3...

Kilcrann, Micheal F. 2003. "The challenge to primary religious education posed by a multicultural society." PhD thesis, St. Patricks College/Mater Dei Institute, Drumcondra, Dublin.

Koh, Serene S. 2010. "National identity and young children: A comparative study of 4th and 5th graders in Singapore and the United States." PhD thesis, University of Michigan.

Koopmans, Ruud, Ines Michalowsk, and Stine Waibel. 2012. "Citizenship rights for immigrants: National political processes and cross-national convergence in Western Europe 1980–2008." *American Journal of Sociology* 117 (4): 1202–1245.

Lynch, Kathleen, and John Baker. 2005. "Equality in education: An equality of condition perspective." *Theory and Research in Education* 3 (2): 131–164.

MacNaughton, Glenda. 2005. *Doing Foucault in Early Childhood Studies: Applying Poststructural Ideas*. London: Routledge.

MacNaughton, Glenda, and Patrick Hughes. 2007. "Teaching respect for cultural diversity in Australian early childhood programs: A challenge for professional learning." *Journal of Early Childhood Research* 5 (2): 189–206.

MacNaughton, Glenda, Merlyne Cruz, and Patrick Hughes. 2003. "Understanding and countering discrimination in early childhood." *Education for All* 2 (3): 1–5.

MaGlynn, Claire. 2003. "Integrated education in Northern Ireland in the context of critial multiculturalism." *Irish Education Studies* 22 (3): 11–27.

McBride, Ian. 1997. *The Siege of Derry in Ulster Protestant Mythology*. Dublin, Ireland: Four Courts Press.

McWilliams, David. 2005. *The Pope's Children: Ireland's New Elite*. Dublin, Ireland: Gill and Macmillan

Meade, Sinead, and Michael O'Connell. 2008. "Complex and contradictory accounts: The social representation of immigrants and ethnic minorities held by Irish teenagers." *Translocations: Migration and Social Change* 4 (1): 51–66.

Moffatt, Joseph. 2011. "Paradigms of Irishness for young people in Dublin." PhD thesis, National University of Ireland Maynooth, Ireland.

Muldoon, Orla, and Clifford Stevenson. 2010. "Socio-political context and accounts of national identity in adolescence." *British Journal of Social Psychology* 49 (3): 583–599.

National Council for Curriculum Assessment (NCCA). 2009. Aistear: The Early Childhood Curriculum Framework and Siolta, The National Quality Framework for Early Childhood Education. Dublin, Ireland: NCCA.

O'Connor, Laura, and Daniel Faas. 2012. "The impact of migration on national identity in a globalized world: A comparison of civic education curricula in England, France and Ireland." *Educational Studies* 31 (1): 51–66.

Peillon, Michael. 1982. *Contemporary Irish Society*. Dublin: Gill and Macmillan.

Rowthorn, Bob, and Naomi Wyne. 1988. *Northern Ireland: The Political Economy of Conflict*. London: Polity Press.

Scourfield, Jonathan. 2005. "Children's accounts of Wales as racialized and inclusive." *Ethnicities* 5 (1): 83–107.

Scourfield, Jonathan, Bella Dicks, Mark Drakeford, and Andrew Davies. 2006. *Children, Place and Identity: Nation and Locality in Middle School*. London and New York: Routledge.

Sindic, Denis. 2008. "National identities: Are they declining?" *Beyond Current Horizons: Technology Children, Schools and Families* December: 1–22.

Smith, Anthony D. 1991. *National Identity*. London: Penguin.

Smyth, Gerry. 2012. "Irish national identity after the Celtic Tiger." *Estudios Inlandeses* 7 (3): 132–137.

Souto-Manning, Mariana. 2013. *Multicultural Teaching in the Early Childhood Classroom: Approaches, Strategies, and Tools, Preschool–2nd Grade*. New York: Teachers College Press, and Washington, DC: ACEI.

Srinivasan, Prasanna. 2014. *Early Childhood in Postcolonial Australia, Children's Contested Identities*. New York: Palgrave Macmillan.

Skey, Michael. 2009. "The national in everyday life: A critical engagement with Michael Billig's thesis of banal nationalism." *The Sociological Review* 57 (2): 331–46.

Tormey, Roland. 2006. "The construction of national identity through primary school history: The Irish case." *British Journal of Sociology of Education* 27 (3): 311–324.

UN General Assembly. 1989. Convention on the Rights of the Child, United Nations. Treaty Series. http://www.refworld.org/docid/3ae6b38fO. html. Ratified in Ireland, September 1992, accessed March 15, 2015.

Volkan, Vamik D. 1988. *The Need to Have Enemies and Allies: From Clinical Practice to International Relations*. Northvale, NJ: Jason Aronson.

Walker, Brian M. 1996. *Dancing to History's Tune: History, Myth and Politics in Ireland, Belfast, Northern Ireland*. Belfast: Institute of Irish Studies, Queen's University of Belfast.

Weeks, Jeffrey. 1990. "The value of difference." In *Identity, Community, Cultural Difference*, edited by Jonathan Rutherford. London: Lawrence and Wishart.

White, Timothy J. 2010. "The impact of British colonialism on Irish Catholicism and national identity: Repression, reemergence, and divergence." *Etudes Irlandaises* 35 (1): 21–37.

CHAPTER 8

Palestinian Children Forging National Identity through the Social and Spatial Practices of Territoriality

Bree Akesson

INTRODUCTION

This chapter explores the development of national identity for Palestinian children and their families through the lens of territoriality. It suggests that the development of national identity is a process to which territoriality contributes in the forms of both social and spatial practices that delineate who is included and excluded in a particular space. It includes social practices as a collective experience passed down with the historical memory and present oppression of the occupation. Territoriality includes spatial practices, because it is reproduced and enacted through the construction and regulation of everyday spaces, creating regimes of inclusion and exclusion that become central to children's national identity construction. Ultimately, territoriality is a politically contested process that enacts particular geographies that are experienced and contested at multiple sites (Harker 2011).

In this chapter, after defining territoriality as related to place and Palestine, I outline the place-based methodology that I used to research Palestinian children and families living in the West Bank and East Jerusalem. I then explore how territoriality informs the formation of Palestinian national identity through intergenerational discourse and the everyday territory-bound politics of inclusion/exclusion. I also highlight the ways in which children and families challenge territoriality and therefore the dichotomy of inclusion/exclusion.

In exploring socio-spatial practices through the lens of territoriality, I unpack participants' connections to Palestine as a nation-state and argue that territoriality is a useful lens to view the development of individual and collective national identity.

UNPACKING TERRITORIALITY

Early scholarship on territoriality purports that it is a natural and instinctual behavior with evolutionary roots (Lorenz 1966; Ardrey 1967; Morris 1967; Hinde 1970). Subsequent scholars, such as Gerald Suttles (1972), Phil Cohen (1972), and Robert Sack (1983, 1986), challenged these claims by asserting that territoriality was not instinctual, but rather tied to people and place. Research since has noted that territoriality is a common human practice, exhibited in schools, organizations, neighborhoods, and nation-states (Brown, Lawrence, and Robinson 2005; Min and Lee 2006). Furthermore, Anssi Paasi (2000) concluded that territoriality is a conscious (rather than instinctual) act to specifically influence spatial behavior and exercise power over land and people. In addition, Sack (1983) noted: "To ignore territoriality or simply to assume it as part of the context is to leave unexamined many of the forces molding human spatial organization" (p. 55). In this way, I understand territoriality as a spatial process for claiming and controlling an identifiable geographical area, including its people and resources (Sack 1983, 1986), and "as a process of dividing, bounding and signifying space" (Kuusisto-Arponen 2003, 44). Sack (1986) continues that territoriality is

> an attempt to affect, influence, or control actions and interactions by asserting and attempting to enforce control over a geographic area. In everyday life territoriality is related to how people use land, how they organize themselves in space and how they give meanings to place. (2)

Within this definition, Sack emphasizes that territoriality is a spatial and human strategy. He continues by outlining three interrelated dimensions. First, territoriality must include the classification of a specific area. Second, territoriality involves communication, both verbal and nonverbal, that demarcates borders and boundaries. And third, territoriality must include an attempt of one group to exert control over access to the specific area, while affecting the interactions of others. In a contemporary application of territoriality to the context of violent conflict among young people, Jon Bannister,

Keith Kintrea, and Jonny Pickering (2013) insist that territoriality does not exist unless this third element is present. In other words, territoriality "is established through boundaries, rules, people, social processes, communication and places" (Kuusisto-Arponen 2003, 46).

Whereas Sack (1983, 1986) emphasizes the inner logic of territoriality as a strategy, Jouni Häkli's (1994) definition of territoriality includes its relationship with wider sociocultural developments, stressing its relationship to historical, administrative, and practical elements. For example, Paasi (2009, 213) emphasizes that the role of the state is not just as an organizer of space, but also as a "creator of meaning" in contemporary society. As Häkli (2008) suggests, the state has extraordinary power to propagate territorial arrangements. Likewise, Paasi (1996) notes: "Territorial units are historical products—not merely in their physical materiality but also in their sociocultural meanings" (3). Häkli's (1994, 2008) understanding makes territoriality a process, while Sack (1983, 1986) describes it as a strategy. In viewing territoriality as a socio-spatial process, Häkli's (1994, 2008) approach emphasizes the multiple relationships between people and place. Indeed, territoriality is always constructed in a specific social context, with its character depending on who has control over whom (Painter 1995).

Suttles (1972) argues that the group's defense of the place against others is a key feature of territoriality. This is supported by Leon Pastalan (as cited in Altman, 1970), who defines territoriality as

a delimited space that a person or a group uses and defends as an exclusive preserve. It involves psychological *identification* with a place, symbolized by attitudes of *possessiveness*. (4, emphasis added)

From this definition, the concept of territoriality includes both elements of identity and place attachment, with the emphasis on defense of place. Nevertheless, this form of defense can ultimately exacerbate a system of inclusion/exclusion.

A focus on territoriality emphasizes the importance of attachment to place in contributing to feelings of inclusion/exclusion related to identity. Setha Low (1992) describes place attachment as

a symbolic relationship formed by people giving culturally shared meanings to a particular space or piece of land that provides the basis for the individual's and group's understanding of and relationship to the environment. (165)

A significant scholarship is dedicated to the important influence of place attachment on addressing one's psychosocial needs (Altman and Low 1992), especially for children and youth developing individual and collective identities (Pretty, Chipuer, and Bramston 2003; Spencer 2005; Chow and Healey 2008). As a form of place attachment, territoriality has the potential to reinforce social networks and provide a sense of belonging and therefore identity for children and families.

Territoriality plays a critical role in the development of children's sense of security (Uzzell 1988). The process of territoriality can lead to a greater identification with home and the local community as a place of belonging, which results in feelings of greater sense of control over the environment. For example, Ade Kearns and Michael Parkinson (2001) defined the "home area" of a neighborhood community where the psychosocial benefits of belonging, identity, and community are based. Indeed, Jon Lang (1987) confirms that territories fulfill the basic human needs for security, identity, and stimulation, which are all vital for children's well-being and development. Several scholars have also underscored the importance of place to the development of "embedded identities" in children (McLaughlin 1993; Hall, Coffey, and Williamson 1999). More recent research has found that territoriality among youth is a source of social exclusion and conflict, which can be a root of gang behavior (Kintrea et al. 2008; Pickering, Kintrea, and Bannister 2012; Bannister, Kintrea, and Pickering 2013;). Furthermore, in their research on territoriality among 9–12-year-olds, Verkuyten, Sierksma, and Thijs (2015) explain that children develop a sense of psychological ownership of physical places that contributes to power struggles and conflict and shapes social relationships, thereby adding to the evidence that territoriality is a social and spatial practice.

Territoriality in Palestine

Scholarship on territoriality in Palestine has explained how the Israeli occupation has shaped Palestinian place and the role of the two main actors (i.e., Israeli and Palestinian) in crafting these places (Falah 1997; Newman 2001, 2006; Yiftachel 2002). Despite experiencing a multigenerational history of displacement, many Palestinians maintain a strong place attachment to their homes, villages, and communities. Rashid Khalidi (1997) explains that the lack of a formal, internationally recognized Palestinian state clearly has a great impact on the Palestinian sense of national identity.

Historically, territoriality and place attachment play out through Palestinians' loyalty to the place of Palestine, which has "served as the bedrock for an attachment to place, a love of country, and a local patriotism that were crucial elements in the construction of nation-state nationalism" (Khalidi 1992, 21). Yet, Suzanne Hammad (2011) notes, as the conflict progresses, Palestinians' sense of place is also in a constant state of flux, especially across different generations.

The concept of territoriality aptly addresses the complex mechanisms of belonging and exclusion that contribute to Palestinian national identity. In fact, the territorial dimension of the Israeli-Palestinian conflict is evident in the strong place-based identity of both groups. Furthermore, political geography emphasizes the politicization of spatial divisions when territorial control is invoked in the name of national security. For example, in the case of Israel and Palestine, the term "demographic threat" (Rouhana and Sultany 2003, 6) has been used in political circles to describe the minority Palestinian population increase that is perceived to be a threat to the majority Jewish Israeli population. Constructing this threat pressures Israeli policy-makers to create exclusionary and territorial policies that contribute to territorial conflict and antagonistic identities, while negatively affecting children and families. Anna-Kaisa Kuusisto-Arponen (2003) rightly notes that these sensitive sociocultural issues are absent from Sack's theorization of territoriality.

Nevertheless, Sack's (1986) dimensions of territoriality emphasize the importance of symbolic boundaries between groups and territories. In Palestine, territories are clearly named, defined, and marked in order to create a distinction between Palestinian and Israeli territories. Markers of territoriality include multiple bypass roads, some of which are designated for use only by Israeli settlers (Halper 2000; Falah 2003; B'Tselem 2004; UNOCHA 2007; Ma'an Development Center 2008), as well as the selection of place-names, which have become a powerful tool for reinforcing competing territorial ideologies (Cohen and Kliot 1992). The 709-km wall represents an extreme exercise in territoriality, slicing deep into the Palestinian territories (Halper 2000; Falah 2003; Parsons and Salter 2008; Fields 2010;). Furthermore, the whole West Bank has been territorially segmented with certain areas designated for either Palestinian or Israeli access (Newman 1996; Falah 2003; Hanafi 2009). Symbols of belonging and exclusion mark the people and permeate the places of Palestine and Israel. For example, license plates indicate whether the car is from Israel or Palestine; the Jewish *kippah* (cloth head cover) and the Palestinian checkered *kuffiya* (headscarves) serve as symbols of the resistance movement and the ultimate symbol of nationalism. Palestinian and Israeli flags dot the landscape and symbolize which piece of land belongs to whom. Graffiti also marks territory, indicating spaces that are for one group or another. These ubiquitous symbols are everyday reminders of the ongoing territorial conflict and the potential for physical violence, who belongs to one side and who belongs to another. The many facets of place reflect and signify social divisions and inequality resulting from variations in influence and power over the course of history. In this way, territory frames social meanings and opportunities for multiple generations of Palestinians.

By delineating groups and one's inclusion and exclusion to these groups, territoriality represents a process of Othering (Paasi 1996). Othering is the practice of an individual (or group) comparing oneself (or itself) to others while at the same time distancing oneself from these same others (Bauman 1991). The Other is depicted as being somehow different. The distance helps to solidify one's own identity as the norm. One could say that by concentrating on the difference between oneself and the Other, identity is created. Othering is a way groups form and gain cohesion, including notions of being different from others, from those who do not belong to our own group. Heidrun Friese (2001, 67) explains that Othering "create[s] boundaries between conceptions of us and them." It helps form imagined groups and more importantly separates one group from another, a manifestation of territoriality.

It is imperative to note that the emergence of Palestinian identity was not the sole result of the birth of the Israeli state and the Israeli Other. Important as the creation of the state of Israel in 1948 was to the formation of Palestinian national identity, further factors were also at play, namely, a broad process among Middle Eastern countries, which involved identification with new states created by post-World War I partitions (e.g., Egypt, Lebanon, and Jordan). Indeed, individual and collective obstacles and traumas related to Israel have played a role in shaping Palestinian identity (Khalidi 1997). However, although the events between Israel and Palestine have certainly shaped Palestinian national identity over the past century, Israel is not the sole defining characteristic. Identity is steeped in the rich historical elements of Palestinian identity such as culture, tradition, and language. As Khalidi (1997) explains, if this core sense of national identity was not already in place, the catastrophic events of the occupation might have shattered the Palestinians as a people so that they were scattered to neighboring Arabic countries. Instead of shattering their national identity, these events "reinforced preexisting elements of identity, sustaining and strengthening a Palestinian self-definition that was already present" (Khalidi 1997, 22). Rather than Israel being *the* Other, these historical events highlighted Israel as *an* Other (Kelman 1999).

Territoriality and Children's Identity

Previous research has examined the complexity of war-affected children's identity in contexts such as Cyprus (Leonard 2012), Sudan (Bixler 2005), northern Uganda (Cheney 2005), and Palestine (Mahjoub et al. 1989; Habashi 2008; Netland 2013). Most relevant to this chapter is the research of Habashi (2008). Emphasizing Gearoid Ó Tuathail's (1996) concern for geopolitical discourse and "the power struggle between different societies over the right to speak sovereignly about geography, space and territory" (11), Janette Habashi (2008) identifies multiple dimensions of Palestinian children's national identity, which she describes as a continuous emerging process that is fragmented in nature. Habashi (2008) categorizes Palestinian national identity by dimensions of *self*—historical self, ennobled self, traitor self, religious self, resistance self, and geographic self—and *Other*—oppressor Other, scattered Other, allying Other, and religious Other. In light of Habashi's (2008) important contribution, this chapter conceptualizes territoriality as a complex socio-spatial process with many dimensions that can be used to explore the construction of Palestinian children's national identity development. The task remains to probe the socio-spatial facets of identity in the face of contemporary politics and shifting geopolitical realities (Ó Tuathail 1996; Harker 2011) and unpack territoriality's role in how children forge their identities.

While emphasizing the importance of collective understandings of national identity, the chapter also reinforces the recent trend in children's geographies emphasizing that children are active agents in their own lives and therefore contribute to the crafting of their own individual identities. They react to, engage with, and challenge the social structures imposed upon them by the occupation and its institutions, as well as the historical weight of previous generations' manifestations of Palestinian national identity. As Jonny Pickering,

Keith Kintrea, and Jon Bannister (2012) note, territoriality can therefore also be a learned process "with an intergenerational adherence to historical boundaries and rules of engagement" (951).

METHODOLOGY

This chapter represents a part of a larger qualitative research project exploring the concept and meaning of place—specifically the place of home, school, neighborhood community, and nation-state—for children and families living in Palestine (see Akesson 2014 for a detailed description of the larger research study). In 2010, pilot interviews were conducted with Palestinian children, families, and organizations. Research continued in 2012, with a sampling of three families from each administrative region of the occupied West Bank and annexed East Jerusalem. Altogether, 18 families agreed to participate in the study, with a total of 149 individual family members (48 percent male and 52 percent female)—50 adults and 99 children.

A minimum of three family members (parent, older child [aged 9–18], and younger child [8 and under]) from the *'a'ila* (or primary family system of father, mother, and children) were invited to take part in a collaborative interview focusing on their experiences with place. Collaborative family interviews often included members of the larger extended family, or *hamula* (including aunts, uncles, cousins, and so on), with some interviews including up to 12 family members. There were 103 family members who were from the primary index family (*a'ila*) and 46 family members who were part of the extended family (*hamula*). Ten key informants—chosen for their knowledge of the context—were also interviewed for the study.

Dedoose—a web-based platform for qualitative data analysis—was used to facilitate coding and analysis. Using a grounded theory approach (Charmaz 2006), analysis of the data involved careful reading and annotation of the collated information so as to ascertain the meaning and significance that participants attributed to their experiences. A comprehensive list of tentative units of meaning was created, and using the constant comparative method (Glaser and Strauss 1967; Maykut and Morehouse 1994), these lists were further combined and categorized by merging any overlapping ideas. Themes were grouped around places that children and families interacted with: home, school, neighborhood community, and nation-state. This chapter addresses the fourth theme, nation-state, exploring the relationship between territoriality and the development of national identity of Palestinian children and families.

The Social and Spatial Practices of Territoriality and the Development of Palestinian National Identity

As discussed above, from a territorial perspective, the development of Palestinian identity linked to the nation-state is a process comprised of both social and spatial practices. It includes social practices through lines of action related to national identity that are transmitted from generation to generation and thereby collectively constructed anew. It also includes spatial practices, because national identity is very much tied to place through concepts, such as place attachment and Othering. In this section, the data is viewed through the lens of territoriality. The first section explores how territoriality informs Palestinian national identity through generational understandings and how it manifests when children actively engage in geopolitical discourses that play out in Palestinian homes, schools, and communities. The second section addresses inclusion/exclusion as a significant component of territoriality. The third and final section provides examples of the ways in which participants challenge territoriality and the dichotomy of inclusion/exclusion inherent in territoriality.

"Speaking Politics": Territoriality through the Generations

Territorial identification with the nation-state of Palestine was very much related to participants' collective memory and current experience of living under Israeli occupation. Families described the harsh conditions of the occupation including restricted movement due to checkpoints and the separation barrier, home searches and demolitions, confrontations with Israeli soldiers and settlers, and high unemployment and poverty related to a crippled economy. All these spatial strategies enacted by the Israeli government are aligned with Sack's (1986) third element of territoriality incorporating an attempt to exert control over an area and the actions of the Other. This aspect of territoriality became a part of the everyday local Palestinian discourse related to identity.

The complexity of national identity is illustrated in the following story from Samira,[1] a mother of three young boys, who laughed when describing her nine-year-old son's school lesson titled "Palestinian Society Development":

> And they put in it—oh, it is so funny!—"1917, we have British occupation. 1948 we handed it to Israeli occupation. 1948 we have *al-Nakba.*

1967 we have *al-Naqsa*. And then we have 1998 the first *intifada*. 2000 we have the second *intifada*." And the title of the lesson was "Palestinian Social Development". So that makes me laugh.

Samira found humor in the local Palestinian discourse equating these historical events with the development of Palestinian collective identity. The description of the development of Palestinian identity with these critical historical memories also helps construct what Habashi (2008, 15–18) has identified as "the oppressor Other". Indeed, historical memories play a key role in the formation of national identity (Anderson 1983). But as Habashi (2008) points out, memories are conditional upon the geopolitical discourse that plays out in Palestinian homes, schools, and communities. Samira continued to explain how her son had a difficult time remembering the dates, because he did not understand what these events—*al-Nakba*, *al-Naksa*, *intifada*—meant:

> So, I make it like a drama, [and] I said, we were like a village people sitting in very nice land with our neighbors. We have tents. We are happy working in the lands. Then, some people came and said, "This is not your [land]. This is British land, right?" . . . I give that sad story [to my son], but [I make it] very positive. And my older boy [was listening, and] he said, "Mom, can't I change the title?" I said, "Like what?" He wanted to rename it the biggest (shyly demonstrating an offensive gesture indicating strong defiance and contempt).

By acknowledging and at the same time reshaping historical events, Samira is contributing to her sons' complex understanding of their national identity. She calls upon a geopolitical identity, defined by Gearóid Ó Tuathail and Simon Dalby (1998), that focuses on the intersection of global discourse and local identity. As Samira's older son also demonstrated, Palestinian children are not just repeating the previous generations' understandings of national identity. Rather, the construction of Palestinian identity is a cross-generational discourse (Habashi 2008). Even though the cultural inheritance of identities are passed down and serve to frame the development of identity, they are also constructed anew in each generation (Clarke et al. 1976). In other words, children are reconstructing their sense of identity, both in light of the generational commitment to territoriality and according to their own sense of self.

The ubiquitous oppression under occupation and resulting territoriality contributed to the politicization of children through their participation in narratives passed down from generation to generation.

In this way, territoriality can also be understood as a learned process, with the current generation reenacting the geopolitical activities of previous generations of their older siblings, parents, and grandparents. Many participants noted that Palestinian children "speak politics" at a very young age. Phrases such as "Palestinians have politics born in their blood," "politics is life," and "you breathe politics" were common expressions from both children and adult participants. Families noted children's understanding of and involvement in politics as being related to the global discourse, and therefore contributing to national identity. For example, young political activist Sanaa explained how politics affects her everyday life: "I go to the checkpoint, [I] speak politics. I am seeing the police, [I] speak politics. I speak politics normally. You are not thinking about it." Sanaa speaks to how individual, social, and spatial practices can become intertwined and complicated by geopolitics. And, as she explains in the following quote, these intertwined practices contribute to her Palestinian national identity:

> Here when you go and speak to children two-years-old, you find them speaking politics, speaking about settlers, speaking about police, speaking about Israelis. Outside [Palestine], the kids are speaking about games, about having fun. Our kids [in Palestine] are speaking about politics.

Sanaa and her family described how they were recently forcibly displaced from their home in East Jerusalem and how younger Palestinian children, such as her ten-year-old brother Mourad, reacted to the incident:

> You know what they are thinking about? When we come to speak with our kids, we say, "OK, what do you think for tomorrow?" [My brother responds,] "I am not thinking for tomorrow. I want to be a man, to fight, and to have my house back. I want to say about what is happening in the evacuation, how the police are throwing us, how the police beat my dad and my mom." They are not thinking about [being children].

Mourad's desire to defend against the loss of his home—reflecting Suttles's (1972) key element of territoriality—is framed by a strong attachment to place. Mourad also reproduced his older sister's geopolitical awareness of and activism against the occupation. Sanaa continued: "Like when you ask our kids what you want to do in the future, [they say,] I want to bring Palestine back. It is the only thing we are thinking about, to save our country." As Sanaa implied, Palestinian children define themselves as highly politicized, actively struggling against the occupation and its effects. Their perceptions of the political situation contribute to their depictions of national identity and make them active agents in the geopolitical discourse.

Territoriality Framed by Inclusion/Exclusion of the Other

The exclusion of Palestinians from areas where their families once lived heightens the importance of the place of Palestine and the development of collective national identity. Who belongs and who does not belong is a significant element of territoriality. When discussing the place of Palestine—specifically their past and present homes and neighborhood communities—participants noted an acute perception of boundaries—the separation wall, the Green Line, the checkpoints—aligned with Sack's (1986) delineation of territoriality as involving demarcations of borders and boundaries. While these borders and boundaries of inclusion/exclusion have been inherited through history from previous generations, like understandings of Palestinian national identity, the meanings behind the borders and boundaries have been renegotiated and reinvented anew through the local and geopolitical discourse, which oftentimes further propagated the inclusion/exclusion that characterizes territoriality. For example, Mufid described his fear, anger, and frustration when he witnessed the Israeli incursion into his home community during the second *intifada*. When I asked how he dealt with those complex feelings, he explained:

> My mom...would tell me, "Don't worry. They are weak. They are scared of us. With their tanks and their [guns], they can't walk in the streets, because we will do something to them."...And, yeah, I remember a song from when I was young. It says: "They come knocking on our doors, just like beggars. And we tell them to go."...So there's this picture in my mind—and this is like a true fact actually—that they are weak in their mind, you could say, and just scared people. So that actually boosts me. I am like, OK, I am not going to be scared of someone who is already scared of me. And I am just a little child. So that has actually boosted me up.

In another example, Abu-Ahmed asked his ten-year-old daughter, Farida: "Are you afraid from them [the Israeli soldiers and settlers]?" To this she replied: "No, because they are not stronger than us." These examples emphasize separation, difference, and exclusion. They also resonate with Habashi's (2008, 67) description of "the oppressor Other," which contributes a piece to the complicated Palestinian

PALESTINIAN CHILDREN ❖ 153

national identity. By depicting Israelis—the Other—in this way, the participants contextualized the complexities of war, which contributed to an understanding of Palestinian identity as being in opposition to Israel. But a reliance on only this interpretation may eclipse the nuances that comprise and complicate individual and collective Palestinian national identities.

Families gave multiple examples of how they resist the occupation through engaging in activities that reinforce territoriality through processes of inclusion/exclusion. In Hebron, Umm-Yacoub described how she and her family engage in protests against the occupation:

> When we are holding the stones and we are just sitting, repeating and saying, "Free Palestine!" Also, by singing national songs for Palestine, that will bother them a lot. [One time] our children were singing a national song. Then they [soldiers] said to them, "Lower your voice." They don't want to hear those songs.

Umm-Yacoub's example shows how territoriality's verbal and nonverbal communication to further demarcate borders and boundaries can also produce nationalism. Activities of resistance such as these also represented the ways that Palestinian families constantly yearned for an independent national state and their community's ongoing efforts on behalf of this ideal. While deeply tied to the political movement for an independent state of Palestine, the experiences of these Palestinian families illustrate the complexity of negotiating national identity in light of complicated geopolitical discourse.

Participant narratives illustrated that Othering is a bidirectional process, with language reinforcing the territorial process of inclusion/exclusion. For example, Riad, a community-based volunteer for Palestinian children in East Jerusalem, told the following story:

> Once I was a taxi driver. Once four young teenagers, they ride with me in the taxi, and they told me, "We speak Arabic," and they were proud that they speak Arabic. "Oh good, what [do] you know in Arabic?" He said, "OK, *Wakif willa batokh*" [meaning "Stop, or I will shoot you!"] I asked him, "Is that what they taught you?" Yeah, it's like all that they know at 16 or 17-years. And they said, "I am speaking Arabic. I am speaking Arabic." I said, "What do you know in Arabic? *Wakif*? You know, to stop or I will shoot you?" They grow their children up just like to hate the Arabs.

There were numerous examples like this that work to create exclusionary and symbolic boundaries between Israelis and Palestinians.

If identity is constructed through direct reference to and interaction with the Other, these repeated experiences are implicated in both the fracturing and solidifying of contemporary Palestinian identity. Palestinian children and families therefore see themselves as both victims and victors, oppressed and resisters, included and excluded, dueling notions contributing to complex notions of individual and collective national identity. These competing positions—informed by the geopolitical discourses (Ó Tuathail and Dalby 1998) that play out in Palestinian homes, schools, and communities—are instilled in Palestinian national identity. As awareness of them increases, "the meaning of territorial space becomes more uncertain" (Habashi 2008, 18).

Challenging Territoriality: Beyond Inclusion/Exclusion

Constructing two opposing sides affords significant value to an individual or group by establishing a sense of belonging and reducing uncertainty. Yet, reliance on inclusion/exclusion to explain Palestinian national identity is overly simplistic as it negates any exceptions that may be inherent in or challenge national identity. As much as participants gave examples that illustrated the divisive nature of territoriality, they gave an equal number of examples of how they also troubled this rift. Several participants told stories of their interactions with Israelis, often soldiers, speaking to Palestinians' efforts to move beyond simple territorial dichotomies. For example, Samira, a mother of three working for a local nongovernmental organization (NGO), told a story from the second *intifada*. Samira was driving a car with her mother-in-law, three-year-old son, and nine-month-old infant as passengers. She was so scared to be near the Israeli checkpoint that she got into an accident near a checkpoint manned by Israeli soldiers. She quickly tried to get her mother-in-law and young children extracted from the vehicle. When the Israeli soldiers approached, she heard her three-year-old son address one of the soldiers: "Uncle! Uncle! I did not do anything wrong! I did not throw stones. I am a good boy." Samira said: "I started crying. Look how he viewed them! [My son] is calling [the soldier] uncle, even with his gun." Samira continued:

> I know the soldiers are also human being. And I know that they are doing bad things, but on the other side, they are human beings. There is a moment when they realize that what they are doing is wrong, you know? So I can't generalize that *you* are bad. You know, I can't. I am not teaching my kids this. I teach them like about being peaceful,

accept others, and you know resist the occupation and humiliation for sure.

Samira's claim about Israelis being human also reflects Habashi's (2008, 19–20) categorization of Palestinian identity as "the allying Other," which is "characterized by conditions in which the *other* is not alienated from the *self* but rather is affirmed and integrated as a positive dimension" (emphasis in original). Similarly, NGO worker Adam explained how not all interactions between Israelis and Palestinians are negative, speaking to the diversity among individuals, rather than stereotyping and excluding members of a particular group:

It's very much up to the soldier how they are. It seems that, like most things they do actually, it's individual. So there are soldiers who are nicer than others. There are soldiers with an Arabic background, or speak the language, like the Druze also. It doesn't necessarily make them much nicer. But, yeah, there are individuals who seem to get along better with Palestinians, they have a little bit of a chat on the street, and things like that.

Metaphorically stripping soldiers of their uniform and associated behavior and positioning them as everyday people troubles the strict dichotomy of us-versus-them and the inclusions/exclusions they create. Hence, examples such as these serve to challenge the inclusion/ exclusion of territoriality.

Participants' descriptions of individual and collective freedom engendered a powerful and profound Palestinian national consciousness. The longing for freedom is underscored by generations of Palestinians living under territorial restrictions imposed by the Israeli Others and involving many socio-spatial practices deeply embedded into everyday Palestinian life (e.g., checkpoints, the separation barrier, and the permit system). For example, Sanaa explained:

The only thing we are thinking about is to have the freedom, and our kids want to walk in the same way we walk. They want to have freedom in the future...they say, "I don't have the freedom for me. I want the freedom for my kids." Because of that, always we have this hope. I will...someday Palestine will have the freedom. When we have the freedom, maybe we will think normally, like all the people. But the only thing, the best thing is to just think about the freedom.

Sanaa spoke in terms of her connection to the Palestinian collective, including not just the Palestinians in her home community of East

Jerusalem, but also those in the "imagined community" (Anderson 1983) spread over the territorially separated places of Palestine:

> Always, I am feeling [that] many people [should] have a freedom, not just [my neighborhood]. Like for me, I say I want freedom for [my neighborhood], but also, I want this thing for my Palestinian people...if I came back to my house, I will not feel good, because I will think about my brothers and sisters, the Palestinian people...[on] the TV, I see Gaza, I see the West Bank. And always, I am thinking about them. When I am looking at them, I am feeling they are my family. I want all the Palestinian people to have [a] normal life.

Sanaa articulated the importance of freedom not only for herself, but also for Palestinians as a people, thereby indicating that the collective struggle for freedom is also an element of modern Palestinian identity. Sanaa's experience indicates that geopolitical discourses and engagement revolving around the Palestinian struggle for freedom and justice—rather than territorial acts that contribute to Othering—can serve as a strong base for developing a sense of identity.

CONCLUSION

In my analysis, I showed how the social and spatial practices of territoriality classify areas of inclusion/exclusion, demarcate borders and boundaries through verbal and nonverbal communication, and illustrate the attempt of one group to exert control over another through interactions and the defense of place. The participant voices indicate that Palestinian national identity is more complex than Sack's (1986) delineation, not just because of the history of the Palestinian people, but also because of contemporary geopolitics that influence territoriality and thereby influence individual and collective national identity. Territoriality's contribution to the geopolitical discourse inherent in the development of individual and collective national identity is clearly a process that includes social and spatial practices.

Paasi (2009, 226) calls for more attention to be paid to spatial socialization, "the specific processes by which peoples and groups come to be socialized as members of specific territorially bounded spatial entities." My analysis answers Paasi's call by illustrating that territoriality is comprised of social practices with elements of identity forged through interactions: collective understandings of historical events, generational influences, and exchanges with the Other. Individual identity is constructed in concert with the larger Palestinian community, but also through interactions with those who do not belong to the broader Palestinian imagined community. That the development of Palestinian identity is related to collective understandings of past historical events and the current geopolitical discourse provokes a reflection of the dynamic relationship between the collective and the development of identity. Spatial identity for the participants was therefore both historically embedded and fluid (McDowell 1999; Robinson 2000). Furthermore, I showed through the analysis how social and spatial practices are intertwined. Territoriality involves spatial practices, because of its connection to participants' attachment to both present and past places. Place attachment offered a sense of belonging to the Palestinian nation-state for the participants in this study. Place attachment was intensified by a long history of territoriality and the present geopolitical discourses. Therefore, territoriality is a way to express control over a place, especially when a group has little control over the access and use of space, as is the case for the participants in this study.

Territoriality implies fixed images and homogeneity of those on one "side" or another. Indeed, the role of the nation-state as the primary global organizing agent has been referred to as the "territorial trap" (Agnew 1994; Agnew and Corbridge 1995; Paasi 1999), stressing fixed images of nation-states and their related identities (Kuusisto-Arponen 2003). Yet, this research suggests that the Palestinian participants in this study are attempting to challenge those fixed images and their related identities at different levels (individual and collective) and through a variety of social and spatial practices. In this way, Palestinians are not homogeneous in their identification with the nation-state (and, by extension, a collective Palestinian national identity), oftentimes resisting the inclusion/exclusion dichotomy. If, as Paasi (2000) and other contemporary geographers assert, territoriality is a conscious act (rather than an instinctive response) to influence spatial behavior and exercise power over land and people, then it can be consciously challenged. Such is the case for the participants in this study, who each expressed diverse facets of an individual and collective Palestinian national identity by challenging the dichotomy of inclusion/exclusion.

Palestinian national identity continues to shift and change under the impact of a cascade of startling events and powerful historical forces that are broadly changing the Middle East almost beyond recognition. In these contemporary events, the public discourses and socio-spatial practices that reinforce territoriality have continued to reflect a deep-seated distrust, anger, and demonization of the Other and continue to affect the relationship between Palestinians and

Israelis. Nevertheless, it is promising to acknowledge the above examples that elucidate Palestinians' engagement with the geopolitical discourse through activism, reconceptualizing the Other, and challenging notions of inclusion/exclusion. Focusing on everyday social and spatial territorial practices thereby offers valuable insight into the potential challenges and opportunities for ameliorating the negative effects of conflict for children and families.

NOTE

1. All names and identifying details about the participants have been changed to ensure anonymity.

REFERENCES

Agnew, J. 1994. "Territorial trap: The geographical assumptions of international relations theory." *Review of International Political Economy* 1: 53–80.

Agnew, J., and S. Corbridge. 1995. *Mastering Space: Hegemony, Territory and International Political Economy*. London: Routledge.

Akesson, B. 2014. "Contradictions in place: Everyday geographies of Palestinian children and families living under occupation." PhD diss., McGill University, Montréal, QC.

Altman, I. 1970. "Territorial behavior in humans: An analysis of the concept." In *Spatial Behavior of Older People*, edited by L. A. Pastalan and D. H. Carson, 1–24. Ann Arbor: University of Michigan—Wayne State University, Institute of Gerontology.

Altman, I., and S. M. Low. 1992. *Place Attachment*. New York: Plenum Press.

Anderson, B. 1983. *Imagined Communities: Reflections on the Origin and Spread of Nationalism*. London and New York: Verso.

Ardrey, R. 1967. *The Territorial Imperative: A Persoanl Inquiry into the Origins of Property and Nations*. Glasgow: Fontana.

Bannister, J., K. Kintrea, and J. Pickering. 2013. "Young people and violent territorial conflict: Exclusion, culture and the search for identity." *Journal of Youth Studies* 16 (4): 474–490.

Bauman, Z. 1991. *Modernity and ambivalence*. Ithaca: Cornell University Press.

Bixler, M. 2005. *The Lost Boys of Sudan: An American Story of the Refugee Experience*. London: University of Georgia Press.

Brown, G., T. B. Lawrence, and S. L. Robinson. 2005. "Territoriality in organizations." *Academy of Management Review* 30: 577–594.

B'Tselem. 2004. *Forbidden Roads: Israel's Discriminatory Road Regime in the West Bank*. Information Sheet. Jerusalem: B'Tselem.

Charmaz, K. 2006. *Constructing Grounded Theory: A Practical Guide through Qualitative Analysis.* London and Thousand Oaks, CA: Sage.

Cheney, K. 2005. "'Our children have only known war': Children's experiences and the uses of childhood in northern Uganda." *Children's Geographies* 3 (1): 23–45.

Chow, K., and M. Healey. 2008. "Place attachment and place identity: First-year undergraduates making the transition from home to university." *Journal of Environmental Psychology* 28 (4): 362–372. doi:10.1016/j.jenvp.2008.02.011.

Clarke, J., S. Hall, T. Jefferson, and B. Roberts. 1976. "Subcultures, cultures and class." In *Resistance through Rituals*, edited by S. Hall and T. Jefferson, 3–59. London: Hutchison.

Cohen, P. 1972. *Subcultural Conflict and Working-Class Community.* Working Paper No. 2. Centre for Contemporary Cultural Studies, University of Birmingham.

Cohen, S. B., and N. Kliot. 1992. "Place-names in Israel's ideological struggle over the administered territories." *Annals of the Association of American Geographers* 82 (4): 653–680.

Falah, G-W. 2003. "Dynamics and patterns of the shrinking of Arab lands in Palestine." *Political Geography* 22 (2): 179–209. doi:10.1016/S0962-6298(02)00088-4.

———. 1997. "Re-envisioning current discourse: Alternative territorial configurations of Palestinian statehood." *The Canadian Geographer/Le Géographe Canadien* 41 (3): 307–330. doi:10.1111/j.1541-0064.1997.tb01316.x.

Fields, Gary. 2010. "Landscaping Palestine: Reflections of enclosure in a historical mirror." *International Journal of Middle East Studies* 42 (1): 82a. doi:10.1017/S0020743809990821.

Friese, H. 2001. "Pre-judice and identity." *Patterns of Prejudice* 35 (2): 63–79.

Glaser, B. G., and A. L. Strauss. 1967. *The Discovery of Grounded Theory: Strategies for Qualitative Research.* Chicago, IL: Aldine.

Habashi, J. 2008. "Palestinian children crafting national identity." *Childhood* 15 (1): 12–29.

Häkli, J. 2008. "Regions, networks and fluidity in the Finnish nation-state." *National Identities* 10 (1): 5–22.

———. 1994. "Territoriality and the rise of the modern state." *Fennia* 172 (1): 1–82.

Hall, T., A. Coffey, and H. Williamson. 1999. "Self, space and place: Youth identities and citizenship." *British Journal of Sociology of Education* 20 (4): 501–513. doi:10.1080/01425699995236.

Halper, J. 2000. "The 94 percent solution: A matrix of control." *Middle East Report* 216: 14–19.

Hammad, S. H. 2011. "Senses of place in flux: A generational approach." *International Journal of Sociology and Social Policy* 31 (9–10): 555–568.

160 ✢ BREE AKESSON

Hanafi, Sari. 2009. "Spacio-cide: Colonial politics, invisibility and rezoning in Palestinian territory." *Contemporary Arab Affairs* 2 (1): 106. doi:10.1080/17550910802622645.

Harker, C. 2011. "Geopolitics and family in Palestine." *Geoforum* 42 (3): 306–315. doi:10.1016/j.geoforum.2010.06.007.

Hinde, R. A. 1970. *Animal Behavior.* New York: McGraw-Hill.

Kearns, A., and M. Parkinson. 2001. "The significance of neighborhood." *Urban Studies* 38 (12): 2103–2110.

Kelman, H. 1999. "The interdependence of Israeli and Palestinian national identities: The role of the other in existential conflicts." *Journal of Social Issues* 55: 581–600.

Khalidi, R. 1997. *Palestinian Identity: The Construction of Modern National Consciousness.* New York: Columbia University Press.

Khalidi, W. 1992. *All That Remains: The Palestinian Villages Occupied and Depopulated by Israel in 1948.* Washington, DC: Institute for Palestine Studies.

Kintrea, K., J. Bannister, J. Pickering, M. Reid, and N. Suzuki. 2008. *Young People and Territoriality in British Cities.* York, UK: Joseph Rowntree Foundation.

Kuusisto-Arponen, A.-K. 2003. *Our Places—Their Spaces: Urban Territoriality in the Northern Irish Conflict.* Tampere, Finland: University of Tampere.

Lang, J. 1987. *Creating Architectural Theory: The Role of the Behavioral Sciences in Environmental Design.* New York: Van Nostrand Reinhold.

Leonard, M. 2012. "Us and them: Young people's constructions of national identity in Cyprus." *Childhood* 19 (4): 467–480. doi:10.1177/0907568211429209.

Lorenz, K. 1966. *On Aggression.* New York: Harcourt, Brace & World.

Low, S. M. 1992. "Symbolic ties that bind." In *Place Attachment*, edited by I. Altman and S. M. Low, 165–185. New York: Plenum Press.

Ma'an Development Center. 2008. *Apartheid Roads: Promoting Settlements, Punishing Palestinians.* Ramallah: Ma'an Development Center.

Mahjoub, A. W., J.-P. Leyens, V. Yzerbyt, and J.-P. Di Giacomo. 1989. "War stress and coping modes: Representations of self-identity and time perspective among Palestinian children." *International Journal of Mental Health* 18 (2): 44–62.

Maykut, P., and R. Morehouse. 1994. "Qualitative data analysis: Using the constant comparative method." In *Beginning Qualitative Research: A Philosophic and Practical Guide*, edited by P. Maykut and R. Morehouse, 126–149. New York: Falmer Press.

McDowell, L. 1999. *Gender, Identity, and Place.* Minneapolis: University of Minnesota Press.

McLaughlin, M. W. 1993. "Embedded identities: Enabling balance in urban contexts." In *Indentity and Inner-City Youth: Beyond Ethnicity and Gender*, edited by S. B. Heath and M. W. McLaughlin, 36–68. New York: Teachers College Press.

Min, B., and J. Lee. 2006. "Children's neighborhood place as a psychological and behavioural domain." *Journal of Environmental Psychology* 26: 51–71.

Morris, D. 1967. *The Naked Ape.* New York: McGraw-Hill.

Netland, M. 2013. "Exploring 'lost childhood': A study of the narratives of Palestinians who grew up during the first intifada." *Childhood* 20 (1): 82–97. doi:10.1177/0907568212461329.

Newman, D. 2006. "The resilience of territorial conflict in an era of globalization." In *Territoriality and Conflict in an Era of Globalization,* 85–110. Cambridge, UK, and New York: Cambridge University Press.

———. 2001. "From national to post-national territorial identities in Israel-Palestine." *GeoJournal* 53 (3): 235–246.

———. 1996. "Shared spaces—separate spaces: The Israel-Palestine peace process." *GeoJournal* 39 (4): 363–375. doi:10.1007/BF02428499.

Ó Tuathail, G. 1996. *Critical Geopolitics: The Politics of Writing Global Space.* Minneapolis: University of Minnesota Press.

Ó Tuathail, G., and S. Dalby. 1998. "Introduction: Rethinking geopolitics." In *Rethinking Geopolitics,* edited by G. Ó Tuathail and S. Dalby, 1–15. New York: Routledge.

Paasi, A. 2009. "Bounded spaces in a 'borderless world': Border studies, power and the anatomy of territory." *Journal of Power* 2 (2): 213–234.

———. 2000. "Classics in human geography revisited: Commentary 2." *Progress in Human Geography* 24 (1): 91–99.

———. 1999. "Boundaries as social processes: Territoriality and the world of flows." In *Boundaries, Territory and Postmodernity,* edited by D. Newman, 69–88. London: Frank Cass.

———. 1996. *Territories, Boundaries and Consciousness: The Changing Geographies of the Finnish-Russian Border.* Chichester, UK: John Wiley.

Painter, J. 1995. *Politics, Geography & "Political Geography."* London: Arnold.

Parsons, N., and M. B. Salter. 2008. "Israeli biopolitics: Closure, territorialisation and governmentality in the occupied Palestinian territories." *Geopolitics* 13 (4): 701. doi:10.1080/14650040802275511.

Pickering, J., K. Kintrea, and J. Bannister. 2012. "Invisible walls and visible youth: Territoriality among young people in British cities." *Urban Studies* 49 (5): 945–960.

Pretty, G. H., H. M. Chipuer, and P. Bramston. 2003. "Sense of place amongst adolescents and adults in two rural Australian towns: The discriminating features of place attachment, sense of community and place dependence in relation to place identity." *Journal of Environmental Psychology* 23 (3): 273–287. doi:10.1016/S0272-4944(02)00079-8.

Robinson, C. 2000. "Creating space, creating self: Street-frequenting youth in the city and suburbs." *Journal of Youth Studies* 3 (4): 429–443.

Rouhana, N. N., and Sultany, N. 2003. "Redrawing the boundaries of citizenship: Israel's new hegemony." *Journal of Palestine Studies* 33 (1): 5–22. doi:10.1525/jps.2003.33.1.5.

Sack, R. D. 1986. *Human Territoriality, Its Theory and History.* Cambridge, UK: Cambridge University Press.

———. 1983. "Human territoriality: A theory." *Annals of the Association of American Geographers* 73 (1): 55–74. doi:10.1111/j.1467-8306.1983. tb01396.x.

Spencer, C. 2005. "Place attachment, place identity and the development of the child's self-identity: Searching the literature to develop a hypothesis." *International Research in Geographical and Environmental Education* 14 (4): 305–309.

Suttles, G. 1972. *The Social Construction of Communities.* Chicago, IL: University of Chicago Press.

United Nations Office for the Coordination of Humanitarian Affairs (UNOCHA). 2007. *The Humanitarian Impact on Palestinians of Israeli Settlements and Other Infrastructure in the West Bank.* East Jerusalem: UNOCHA.

Uzzell, D. L. 1988. "An environmental psychological perspective on learning through landscapes," Appendix 5. In *Learning through Landscapes: A Report on the Use, Design, Management and Development of School Grounds,* edited by E. Adams. Winchester, UK: Learning through Landscapes Trust.

Verkuyten, M., J. Sierksma, and J. Thijs. 2015. "First arrival and owning the land: How children reason about ownership of territory." *Journal of Environmental Psychology* 41: 58–64.

Yiftachel, O. 2002. "Territory as the kernel of the nation: Space, time and nationalism in Israel/Palestine." *Geopolitics* 7 (2): 215. doi:10.1080/714000930.

CHAPTER 9

Constructing Narratives of Political Identities: Young People in the "New" European States

Alistair Ross

INTRODUCTION

This chapter analyzes how some young people in postcommunist Europe construct narratives of identity with their country, their sense of agency, and their constructions of themselves as generationally different from their parents and grandparents. Based on data from focus groups with young people between 12 and 19 years from 12 countries that joined the European Union in 2004–2013, I argue that many of these young people demonstrate a sophisticated ability to construct a range of narratives with their country and with the European Union that show a complex and contingent pattern of identities. They talk about politics, their political self and agency, and of belonging to various geopolitical entities such as the nation/country and the European Union.

These 12 countries have both elements in common and some significant differences in their political histories. Some of them were new, or newly independent, following the breakup of the Soviet Union (Estonia, Latvia, and Lithuania), or of Yugoslavia (Slovenia, Croatia, and Macedonia [in the process of joining the European Union]), or of Czechoslovakia (the Czech Republic and Slovakia); others had been countries under Soviet hegemony (Poland, Hungary, Romania, Bulgaria, and Czechoslovakia itself). None of these states existed in their present boundaries in 1914, all had been devastated by the 1939–1945 war, and all had experienced various forms of authoritarian repression between 1945 and 1989.

The teenagers whose constructions are analyzed in this study were all, therefore, members of the first generation born after the fall of the Berlin Wall and the dissolution of the Warsaw Pact. This is not to homogenize the histories of all these countries, each had its own particular trajectory, but in each the construction of a political narrative of the state in which these young people live is being carried out under very different circumstances to those of their parents or grandparents when they were young. These young people have no direct experiences of the regimes, wars, uprisings, and assertions of independence with which many of their parents and grandparents were involved.

Carmen Leccardi and Carles Feixa (2012) have suggested that young people in Eastern Europe are more tied to the memories of the family than young people in Western Europe. They argue that their prolonged and necessary cohabitation with their parents means that they continue to be brought up within the remnants of the post-communist context of their family life, they "have to come to grips on a daily basis with the legacy of the former Soviet-style socialism" (Leccardi and Feixa 2012, 5). Such a hypothesis is not borne out by the evidence of the young people in this study (see also Macek et al. 1998; Dimitrova-Grajzl and Simon 2010). More compelling is the argument put forward by Mary Fulbrook (2011), whose study of German identities in the twentieth century suggests that not only are there significant differences in the ways that identities are constructed between generations, but also these are the consequence of political fractures and dissonance in national society. Fulbrook (2011) argues that the age at which people experience key historical moments, such as the transitions within German society in 1933, 1945, and 1989, can be a critical explanatory factor behind an individual or group's "availability for mobilization" for political expression. This "construction of a collective identity on the basis of generationally defined common experiences" (Fulbrook 2011, 11) is used to explain the rise of National Socialism and the postwar politics of the Germanys. Age, she suggests, is "crucial at times of transition, with respect to the ways in which people can become involved in new regimes and societies" (Fulbrook 2011, 488).

Identification with a geopolitical institution—such as a state or the European Union—is multidimensional. Michael Bruter (2005, 12) suggests two major components of identity with a political community:

A *cultural* perspective would analyze political identities as the sense of belonging an individual citizen feels towards a particular political group. This group can be perceived by him [sic] to be defined by a certain culture, social similarities, values, religion, ethics or even ethnicity. A *civic* perspective would see...the identification of citizens with a civic structure, such as the State, which can be defined as the set of institutions, rights, and rules that preside over the political life of the community.

Bruter was writing specifically with reference to the development of a "European identity," but his model also holds with respect to the construction of state or national identities. He contends that these two components exist in parallel in citizens' minds, and need to be differentiated when possible. For example, individuals may have stronger civic or cultural elements to their (European) identity, with differences between individuals, countries, and over periods of time. Using a questionnaire with UK, French, and Netherlands respondents ($n = 212$) Bruter (2005) offers evidence of "a civic component...[that] makes people identify with the European Union as significant 'super-state' identity, and...a cultural component that makes people identify with Europe in general as an area of shared civilization and heritage" (114). He speculates that a common European heritage might be too much of abstraction, and supports this with focus group data from the same three countries: "Civic unity is a major determinant of the level of European identity of citizens" (2005, 162).

This differentiation of cultural and civic references is core to the analysis of young people that follows, in how they identify with both Europe and their country. Their identification with each of these employs aspects of these two components in varying degrees, depending on the particular moment and the particular focus of discussion. What political discourses do they utilize in constructing their identities as members of a country that is so different to the nation of their parents' youth? How do they respond to these constructions—do they feel empowered to actively engage in social and political affairs, or do they feel that they lack agency and alienated from the political? Do they construct themselves politically as different: has there been a generational shift?

YOUNG PEOPLE'S POLITICAL DISCOURSE

Political discourse is sometimes presumed to be solely the domain of the politician, but Teun van Dijk (1997) argues we "should also include the various *recipients* in political communicative events...once we locate politics and its discourses in the public sphere, many more participants in political communication appear on the stage" (13). Deliberation, decision, and action are defining political activities, and politics is about discourse in the context of disagreement, conflicts, and inequalities in power (Fairclough and Fairclough 2012). In this chapter I argue that young people are not simply recipients of political communications, but actively debate and internalize such discourse, and use it to contribute to the construction of their own political and social identities.

Many studies of political socialization have cast young people as passive recipients of political messages from the social environment (e.g., Hahn 1998). The attitudes of teachers and education policy-makers toward dealing with political and social controversies in school may be critical: teacher and institutional resistance to the controversial may be part of a denial that young people can understand or have an interest in the political (Maitles 1997). Qualitative studies that seek out political understanding suggest that there is more taking place. As Coles (1968), a psychiatrist reviewing his transcripts of 25 years, explains:

> We have found ourselves surprised by our chronic inability even to recognize the political implications of what we were hearing from children...We have tried to understand why it took us so long...to regard our data...as a sort of running political commentary by boys and girls who were...involved in dramatic moments in history. (8–9)

Adrian Furnham and Barrie Stacey (1991) point out that most research on political socialization regards young people as "passive interpreters of the political information that they receive" (33). However, they also point out that young people seek political information, and sometimes reject it, selecting and changing it to fit their own interpretive framework. Nigel Thomas's (2009) study of children and young people's political participation argues that many studies over the past two decades have focused on adult-led activities, in which children's spaces and autonomy have been restricted. What is needed, he claims, are studies of children as political actors and of the micropolitics of children's interactions with each other and with adults. But Priscilla Alderson (2010) has pointed to Thomas's (and others) tendency to focus on small empirical personal micro-communication studies that exclude and disadvantage children making only fairly brief references to political context, and consequently politics remains a "crucially neglected topic in childhood studies" (429).

In the field of political geography, Christopher Philo and Fiona Smith (2003) suggest that there is a common disregard for young people's conceptions of geopolitical spaces (such as countries), and that this is a consequence of young people's limited availability to directly influence the more obvious "political" phenomenon and structures that are to do with nation and states. Tracey Skelton (2008, 26) attempts to addresses this omission in her conceptualization of young people as "agentic in making their own socio-spatial worlds" (26). She argues that because they are part of our social structures, we "need to capture their commentaries on the social world around them" (2008, 26). She elsewhere develops this argument: the very fact that their position is "liminal...within political-legal structures and institutional practices...makes them extremely interesting political subjects" (Skelton 2010, 146). This chapter provides some examples of young people offering critical commentaries on their relevant political practices and structures, as they construct their identities within various available geopolitical spaces.

Marc Jans (2004) observes that young people are "strikingly sensitive about global social themes like the environment and peace." Again, this chapter offers a range of empirical evidence in support. But Jans also notes that society mainly plays upon this sensitivity and these observations in a limited educative manner. This sensibility of children is mainly considered as a "solid base for future citizenship and only rarely as a base for actual citizenship" (2004, 31). In the present study, it was notable how often young people said that they would not, or could not, talk about these issues in an educational setting.

Kirsi Pauliina Kallio, analyzing largely data from children younger than those considered in this chapter, offers a definition of children's politics as "intentional social activity which has particular meaning to its performer" (2009, 8). She argues that children's empowerment and agency is situational, a tactical use of opportunities to "momentarily...politicize an issue important to them" (Kallio 2008, 12). Katz argues that such agency needs to be more widely recognized: "Children are not just repositories of adults' desires and fantasies, but also subjects and social actors in their own rights" (Katz 2008, 9; also Habashi 2009). The data analyzed in this study evidences the active engagement of many young people with social and political ideas, and their recognition that they have decisions to make and options to choose that are not simply personal choices, but ones that influence and interact with their societies. They have agency, and they are very aware of this. Kirsi Pauliina Kallio and Jouni Häkli (2011) have identified and criticized what they see as the two major current research streams. First, those that focus on children's agency and role in local and national policy (such as Thomas 2009 and Skelton 2008,

2010)—but although these seek to empower children's voices in the public agenda, they also determine and constrain this agenda and thus exclude some young people by requiring specific forms of political action (Kallio and Häkli 2011, 22–23). Second, there is a research stream that addresses children's everyday lives in relation to political issues relevant to particular young people, which may be, for example, economy or war (such as Katz 2008 and Habashi 2009)—but such a research agenda excludes the voices of those who are not activists or involved in conflicts (23).

What I attempt in this analysis is to offer these particular young people—most of whom are not activists, or involved in conflicts as their parents may have been—an opportunity "to be taken seriously, to engage in dialogue with adults and each other, and to have an appropriate degree of autonomy" (Thomas 2010, 188) and to use the outcome to allow them to create their own agenda for constructing their relationships to their countries or larger geopolitical regions

This Study

The chapter is based on a one-person study I made, with the assistance and support of a great many people in these countries and the United Kingdom, for which I am grateful.[1] I worked with young people between 11 and 19 years old, in 15 different countries in Europe (the whole study also included countries that are candidates for joining the European Union—Turkey, Iceland and Macedonia, and Cyprus) (Ross 2015). I carried out focus groups in several locations in each country between January 2010 and October 2012, visiting cities and towns in which I had colleagues willing to assist me. In each location in each country I usually visited two schools, trying to select those with different socioeconomic intakes: this was the most efficient way to access groups of approximately the same age. In each school there were two groups of approximately six students. My aim was to include young *residents* of each country, not necessarily citizens, and I tried to include some young people from significant minority groups. Table 9.1 shows the numbers of locations, schools, focus groups, and students in the study.

This was not a representative sample of young people, but a convenience sample of the range of potential views across each country: from different regions within the country, different social backgrounds, and different cultural groups. Consent was obtained from the schools, parents, and the young people themselves, and all data has been made anonymous. Most interviews were in English: where the young people

Table 9.1 Number and location of informants in focus groups

Country	Locations (towns and cities)	n schools	n focus groups	n young people
Bulgaria	Blagoevgrad, Sofia, Veliko Tarnovo	6	11	72
Croatia	Rijeka, Zadar, Zagreb	6	11	68
Czech Republic	Hradec Králové, Ostrava	4	8	47
Estonia	Tallinn, Tartu, Luunja, Püünsi	4	8	44
Hungary	Budapest, Pécs, Szeged	6	10	64
Latvia	Jūrmala, Rēzekne, Riga	4	8	50
Lithuania	Elektrėnai, Kaunas, Vilnius	4	6	40
Macedonia	Prilep, Skopje, Tetovo	6	11	72
Poland	Białystok, Kraków, Olsztyn, Warszawa	9	16	96
Romania	Bucureşti, Iaşi, Oradea, Timişoara	10	16	105
Slovakia	Banská Bystrica, Prešov	3	7	42
Slovenia	Koper, Ljubljana, Novo Mesto, Prade	7	13	76
Total in this analysis		*69*	*125*	*776*
Other countries in study not included in this analysis				
Cyprus	Lapta, Larnaca, Lefkoşa, Nicosia	4	8	55
Iceland	Akureyri Reykjavík Selfoss	8	10	58
Turkey	Çanakkale Eskişehir İstanbul Tokat	15	16	85
		27	*34*	*198*

were not able to do this, a native-speaking colleague translated (an academic acquainted with issues of citizenship and identity who was not known to the young people). In the English-language interviews this colleague supported the young people when needed. Discussions were transcribed and examined and systematically analyzed against a country-specific index of themes built partly on the Bruter and Fulbrook studies (above), partly on country-specific literature, and partly on the groups' specific narratives. These country analyses were then combined into a meta-analysis (Rabiee 2004, 657).

Identities are open to change, because their origin lies in communal exchanges. They are constantly reconstituted through shared understandings and discursive explorations with others (Shotter and Gergen 1989; Burr 1995). This chapter explores some of the discursive practices employed in young people's talk about identity. Vivien Burr observes that "our ways of understanding the world come not from objective reality but from people, both past and present" (1996,

7). The young people in these groups negotiate meanings between themselves using their previous social experiences, each other's observation, and my questions and probing.

I used focus group discussions to allow participants to collaboratively construct their views and position themselves in discourses, and as my principal data source (Krueger and Casey 2009). These were not a series of semi-structured interviews, but discussions between members into which I introduced issues to focus on (Hess 2009). I phrased to indicate that I did not know what the answer might be. I acted as a naïve foreigner asking for explanations of the self-evident. My participation kept conversations flowing with requests for clarification and occasionally drawing out apparent contradictions or changes in a participant's position. I did not intend to challenge points of views, but rather aimed to elicit more conversations.

My opening questions were designed to put everyone at ease: I accepted all responses as valid, welcome, and useful, and ensured that everyone spoke. I then focused on aspects of location: were they all from the same country? Those from other countries were asked how they felt about their country of origin and their country of residence. I spoke of "the country," not of the state or the nation. I sometimes contrasted answers from different people to prompt debate. Asking how the young people thought their parents and grandparents thought about these issues allowed the opportunity to compare themselves with earlier generations. Some responded literally about their own families, others talked more generally about older people. I invited comments on social and regional differences, and possible minorities.

The contexts of these discussions inevitably affected their nature and content. Each focus group was heterogeneous and served as an audience for itself and for a stranger, enacting a specific and unique set of identities through the discourses invoked. The data generated in this project is the consequence of particularities that are partially a reaction to the insertion of my identity(ies) (or what the group members constructed as my identities) into the group. It is their retort both to that act and to the expressed identities of the other group members. By working with several groups (within schools, locations, and countries) I have attempted to crystallize my data through multiple reflections or iterations, but I, as the interlocutor in each situation, remained the same (but not necessarily constant) participant. Examining the social construction of identities can only be attempted in a social context, and social contexts cannot be reproduced (Shotter 1990). The counterpoint to this is that it now becomes my subjectivities that seek to interpret the "meaning" of their discourses. Having taken up a particular position as my own, I inevitably see the world from the vantage point of that particular position, in terms of the particular images and metaphors relevant within particular discursive practices (Davies and Harré 1990).

As mentioned earlier, the discourses were systematically analyzed against a country-specific index of themes built partly on the Bruter and Fulbrook studies (above), on examples of expressions of feelings of agency, or lack of this (Katz 2008), and partly on country-specific literature.

CONSTRUCTIONS OF THE NATION

One very common expression of national identity was reference to pride in the history and cultural practices that were thought to be unique to the country. Several young people referred to how they had become aware of having a particular culture. A Czech young woman, Milenka (14) described making a study visit to Denmark: "It was the moment when I discovered what it was to be Czech... only then did I realize what it meant to me, to be Czech, to have traditions." Cultural specifics were often seen as the significant differentiators between European countries: Olesia from Kraków (♀12) said: "We are not different when you think about rights, but we are different if you think about culture. We have different music, different songs... [our] own language." Rostek (16♂) in Warszawa linked Polish culture to the motto *Bóg, Honor, Ojczyzna* [God, honor and fatherland]: "Many people identify themselves with these values," going on to argue that while the current liberalization in Poland seemed to diminish Poland's historical experience, "we should find a center between these two different visions." In Presov (Slovakia) a group of 12-year-olds competed to list attributes: "dances," "handcrafts," "cooking—national dishes and food," and "language—all Slovaks have language in common."

Others cited national literature and music, writers and composers as evidence of their culture, and spoke in detail and verve about their distinctive contributions, often linking this to the development of nineteenth-century romantic nationalism. These positive cultural markers were strongly foregrounded in most of the discourses about why they identified with the country, and there were, in the conversations about the country per se, very few references to civic institutions such as parliament, presidents, or flags.

There were a significant number of expressions of internationalism, of a desire to make national differences as little as possible. In Poland, Patrycja (♀18) argued: "Now for young people [it] isn't so important that we are Polish—we'd rather say that we are western European Union." Tomasz (♂17) described himself as "a citizen of the world, not just of Europe, but of the world." But some saw these changes as a threat, globalization potentially attacking the country's distinctive values. In Białystok, Ida (♀18) reflected: "We have a great culture, and we are proud of it—but nowadays...we maybe don't have much difference between many countries."

References to the country's politicians were nearly always negative. In the Baltic states they were seen as argumentative and not competent: Hillar (♂16) said "they fight each other. They don't agree on important decisions—they are like children [laughter]. Always fighting...Estonian politicians seem to be a bit stupid." A common theme in many countries was that politicians were self-seeking and sought to personally benefit from office. This was seen as endemic in Slovakia by Bohuslav (♂14) as he argued: "If you go to other countries everything is clean, and [here] the politicians grab everything...we have nothing, everything is corrupt." Such a perception was found in many countries—their own national politicians were thought to be more venal than those of other countries. In Bulgaria, Todor (14♂) claimed politicians "lie to people [to get elected]...they care only for themselves when they get power."

Many young people were critical of their compatriots, particularly about the way that they engaged in civic activities. For example, Małgorzata (♀ 16) pointed out that though many Poles disliked the government, "they don't bother to go to the elections to do anything about it. Poles are passive about politicians' activities." There were similar charges of electoral apathy in Bulgaria. In a heated discussion, Nikola (♂16) said: "In some countries when the Government makes a change which is not liked by the people—they stand up and protest about that change...but whatever our government changes, we just say 'OK'...'Oh, it doesn't matter'. I think we should stand up and fight for our rights."

In the former Yugoslav states, and Bulgaria in particular, some young people tended to describe their position as liminal on the threshold of Europe, but not within it. This was sometimes expressed in spatial terms referring to Europe as situated to the northwest and the Balkans to the southeast, themselves on the border. At other times liminality was related to temporality, for example, the phrase "not yet European" was used quite often—it was a condition yet to be achieved.

This negative portrayal of civic leaders of the country in relation to politicians, and to the political behavior of some citizens was strikingly different from the stress on cultural affiliations that were so prominent in the great majority of the focus groups. Michael Bruter's (2005) civic-cultural perspectives seem to be an appropriate analytic framework to characterize constructions of identification with the country (the "nation" being rarely referred to). There was a strong and positive stress on culture, history, language, and traditions as features of their affiliation with the country, and a much more negative portrayal of the country's civic institutions, a striking reversal of the way in which Bruter described European identities.

However, when the focus group moved on to discuss the potential for also having a European identity, Bruter's analysis was confirmed. A European Union identity was strongly linked to its institutions and civic practices (mobility, schemes for study opportunities, economic support through trade and regional support, and the promotion of human rights), and the possibilities of a cultural identity across Europe were generally dismissed (see Ross 2015 for a more extensive analysis of this). But when the focus groups moved on to discuss the hypothetical enlargement of the European Union to include countries, such as Belarus or Russia, then many young people objected strongly on the grounds of what they perceived as a lack of democracy and respect for human rights in those states—and, at this point, contrasting them with the civic *virtues* of their own countries. To give some brief examples of this: in Estonia, Imre (♂15) referred to Russia as "not a very democratic country...[here we] make sure that human rights are protected," and in Poland Onufrius (♂15) said Russia was "deep in communist times—they have fewer rights and freedoms than in Europe." In southeast Europe attitudes to Russian membership varied. Bulgaria and Serbia historically had strong positive connections with Russia, and the view that Russia was a champion or protector of the Serbs colored the views of the Slovenians and Croatians against Russians. In Romania, Cristian (♂16), having denounced his country's political institution as corrupt, then contrasted it with Russia, stating: "We try to be sort of politically correct here, and they don't really—they have...a history, a habit, of exploiting underdeveloped countries."

Viewing the possibility of other states as potential partners threw up different orientations of their own country. Othering states with a different political order, with different civic cultures and values, led them to see their own countries in a somewhat different light. When asked to consider their own country in isolation, it was constructed in cultural terms, and the country's political institutions were downplayed—sometimes with savage criticism. When filtered through the lens of potential partnership with some other states, their own country became constructed as political, and civic virtues were paraded to demonstrate difference. Both of Bruter's (2005) perspectives, the civic and the cultural, are used contingently as the conversations move between the use of different lenses.

CONSTRUCTING A GENERATIONAL NARRATIVE

As discussions progressed from initial protestations of familial affection and continuity, a sense emerged that participants' identities were different from those of their parents and grandparents. Most young people described parental views as rooted in past history, which helped explain their parents' identities and preoccupations but were not considered as very relevant to their own identities, their present, or their futures. The discussion by a group in Warszawa (Warsaw) that follows illustrates this.

In April 2010 Russia invited a delegation of Polish politicians and military leaders to a memorial for the Katyn massacre of 1940. The airplane taking the Polish president and others crashed as it landed, and all 96 on board died. Polish society was devastated, and a memorial cross was erected outside the presidential palace in Warszawa. When the president asked for this to be moved to emphasize the separation of state and church, there were protests from the "defenders of the cross." There were clashes with the police and then with the young supporters of a countermovement who argued that Poland was secular (BBC 2010; Leszczynski 2011).

In November 2010, I spoke with a group of 15- and 16-year-olds in a central Warszawa *Gimnazjum* (high school) a couple of kilometers from the presidential palace:

> *Lech* I think that there's false patriotism in Poland, a false concern with politics—however, if a nation unites during catastrophes, like the Smolensk catastrophe, when one could sense an explosion of Polishness, and for a moment the nation unites, and the arguments don't matter for a moment, for a while—show-off patriotism. I have never met a real patriot...The majority of my friends and people I know aren't, because we don't have major national problems, national issues. My friends are not concerned with national identity...The older generation from the times of communism, when Poland was not wholly independent—back then this was necessary to free Poland—now, we don't have this problem.
>
> *Sergiusz* There's a huge difference between the older and the younger generations. The patriotism of older people has developed into

egoism. This is changing, but we can still see this in small towns—and the patriotism of older people isn't a good patriotism. We can say that older people feel like Poles, but younger people feel less citizens of Poland and more citizens of Europe. They are more like Europeans, they are more open to other people from different countries.

Kinga The younger generation doesn't care if it's Polish or something else—it doesn't feel a bond with the nation. The older people who fought for our independence feel more strongly the statement "I am a Pole"...When they put the cross before the presidential palace, the older generation was very pro putting a monument there, to commemorate the deaths, and they wanted the accident to be remembered, and the younger generation just stood there for fun, just to watch the whole cross affair, and to see these people.

Lech begins by talking of "false patriotism," and then concedes there could be moments of national catastrophe, such as the Smolensk crash, that created feelings of national unity. But the younger generation was not patriotic, he argued, and did not need to be. Echoing Fulbrook (2011), he argued that "the older generation from the time of communism" justifiably needed to be patriots "to save Poland," and that "they" thought it should not be forgotten. He articulated an opposing discourse with "friends and people that I know" that disagreed with the views of his parents. Sergiusz also picked up intergenerational differences. Older people were egotistical, conservative, and did not show "good" patriotism. Younger people were less Polish and more European. Kinga supports this with her analysis of how the different generations behaved in the affair of the cross.

Many young people saw their parents and grandparents as locked into a view of the country that was conditioned by histories of struggle and resistance that were no longer so relevant. Parents and grandparents were described, fairly consistently, as being more patriotic and as having a greater attachment to the country than their own generation. These young people were not generally disrespectful of their parents' position, but argued that conditions now were different for themselves and for their futures. Given the lens of generational change, their constructions of their country seemed to shift. They defined the differences between their views and their parents' views of the country less in terms of cultural identification, and more in terms of historical perceptions of the changes in the nation and national identity.

In the various narratives I collected, the construction of difference from the older generations was striking, sometimes almost with a sense of loss: "Now we don't feel the necessity of solidarity so much," explained Jolánka (♀15) in Hungary. Gosia's (♀17) account is full of references to grandparents and parents positioning them in a binary of "they" and her own generation as "we":

> Maybe not our parents, but our grandparents feel the most Polish, because they or their parents were fighting for Poland in the wars... my grandma and my grandfather... tell me about the wars and how they lived—how it was hard, and how Russians came to my grandfather's house and stole everything. I think because of these moments in history they feel the most Polish... We've got an easier life—we can't really understand how hard it was for these people.

The notion of a cohort—meaning those born within a particular period of time, rather than a particular year—is a useful analytic tool with which to examine the different experiences and societal constructs of different age groups. The concept of generation was used by Fulbrook (2011) to characterize "the differential impact of the times people live through and the significance of the 'social age' at [the] time of particular historical contexts and developments" (2011, 9). Many of the young people in this study stress that they saw themselves as *politically* a different generation, and attributed this difference to the changed "social age" and political context. Many of them said that they were thinking of how they might act to safeguard their futures, some by participating in sociopolitical processes, which will be considered in the following section, and others by taking the opportunity to migrate, permanently or temporarily. They were, as Katz observed, "subjects and social actors in their own right" (2008, 9).

Power and Agency

Running through many of these discussions about the faults of national society were discourses of power and powerlessness. Some of these young people felt dispossessed, lacking any sense of agency or ability to influence the system. For example, in Latvia, although Klinta (♀15) was able to say: "I feel satisfied with my country," she went on: "We cannot change what is happening. We cannot change the future of Latvia." In Romania, there was sometimes debate about whether political activity was possible, as in this exchange in Bucureşti:

> *Olga* (♀16) We don't have the power to change. We've tried to change the President and our parents to vote for someone else—but it's still the same—men want power, and when they have it, they make use of it.

Mihai (♂15) I'm sorry, but we are the people—we have the power—we are democratic, so the power should be with the people.

Most young people were broadly optimistic, professing faith in the future development of their country, sentiments sometimes tinged with expressions of powerlessness but mostly affirmative. Many were like Ivana (♀17) in Bulgaria, who suggests that emigration is a selfish solution: "If you go abroad, you will not change anything." Migration was a contested issue in almost every country, and offered yet another lens through which to define identity connected to one's country. Borislav (♂16) argued that there were two types of people: "People who want to leave, who don't want to live here and think that if they go abroad they will have a better life, and people who are proud of being Bulgarian, who love the country and want to stay." The thought of leaving a country produced in some an urge to talk about their attachment to the country.

This focus on the cultural rather than the civic, coupled with the respective positive and negative attitudes toward each, created a quandary for those who felt that they possessed agency or at least that they could contribute to the control of civic structures and political processes (Ross 2014). Could they—or should they—attempt to achieve the necessary solidarity to challenge systems that they felt to be inefficient or even corrupt when their allegiance to the country was primarily to its cultural practices, rather than its civic institutions? A recent study has suggested that college students may be particularly sensitive to perceived violations of agency, such as political corruption (Metcalfe, Eicha, and Castel 2010, 281). An exchange between a group of 16-year-olds at a school in northeastern Poland illustrates this:

Maria (♀) You all say that this...should be changed so we'll be better, but are you able to say that in two years' time, when you're 18, you'll go to vote? Because many young people usually don't.
Dominik (♂) Yes, of course. [does not sound very convinced]
Małgorzata (♀) I can't tell, because now I could say yes I will, but then it could turn out that I won't.
Olgierd (♂) The election itself is not the solution—what really counts is the willingness to change. Will you [Maria] stay here in Poland and try to change and make better what can be made better around us? Most young people will not—they'll choose an easier way and emigrate to the West. It takes real effort to try to change something knowing that you're alone...the willingness to change must really

be ours and not of the one who's going to represent us. It's us who
should want to change something in our country.

Maria and Olgierd appear to construct themselves as potentially
agentic. She argues that at least they should participate in elections
(she thinks most young people will not), while he says that real agency
lies in staying in Poland and participating in change. Dominik's hesi-
tancy, and Małgorzata's franker acknowledgment suggest that they, at
least, feel less powerful. Emigration was, for many, a very real option
made possible by their country's accession to the European Union
in the few years before these discussions. The prospect of leaving,
whether for the short or the long term, was vigorously discussed
in many groups. Talking about these options required these young
people, particularly those in their later teens, to concentrate on their
relationship to the country in a more focused way with a greater sense
of realism, than might otherwise have been the case.

There was a counter-narrative of individual self-interest, exempli-
fied by Monta (♀15) in Latvia, who said (after a long discussion on
this issue): "Well, I think more about myself, not about the country.
If we speak honestly, I think more about what *I* am going to do,
what *I* need, and what *I* want—not about what the country needs,
what will happen to our country." To some, this was unproblematic.
In Lithuania Aušra (♀15) argued: "I am not only a Lithuanian, but I
am also a European. It's great! It's easier to go abroad. I'm not planning to stay in Lithuania—the economic situation is not very good."
This was a different sense of empowerment that reflects an individual,
self-interested sense of being able to decide on one's future—in a way
that had not been possible for their parents and grandparents at the
same stage of their lives. Katheryne Mitchell (2006) has noted that
the expansion of the European Union in 2004 could be construed as a
shift from a former policy of "upward harmonisation" to a "discipline
of neo-liberalism" (395) that encouraged the development of flexible
and mobile workers, and the constructions put forward by Monta
and Aušra appear to underline the extent to which some young people have strategically used the possibility of movement to construct a
sense of individual agency.

Conclusions

Participating young people discussed political issues in an articulate
manner and with a high degree of cogency. Their comments were
critical and relevant to their personal context, but were informed with

knowledge about the history and politics of their countries and the European Union. Participants' views were different within each country and between countries. More significantly, participants asserted their identities in different ways depending whether they looked through the lens of their country or Europe.

Bruter's (2005) civic-cultural perspectives were evidenced in most accounts of participants' identification with their country. Positive cultural empathy contrasted with a range of dissatisfactions with civic structures. The strengths of their countries' political values became more evident (to some of them) when they considered some neighboring states. The lens of the European Union also sometimes led to similar nuances. It was sometimes said that the country's civic structures had been positively supported by membership, though economic support, some said, offered opportunities for political corruption. This critique underpins the argument that youth in this study were informed about politics and political values and skillfully leveled their evaluations on these grounds. Skelton's (2008, 2010) observations on the way that young people are able to construct commentaries on the social world about them are evident in the critical and informed remarks that they made, often focusing (as Jans 2004 noted) on global social themes.

Generational differences offered another lens through which to construct one's country. The events described by parents and grandparents—of the Second World War, of the communist period, or of the times of national independence were known of, but seen as part of a parental discourse that was necessary to the young people only to provide another form of political engagement from which they can distance themselves. There was sympathy and understanding of parents and grandparents' patriotism, but also an expression of being part of a modern cohort or generation that no longer needs loyalty to one's country in the same form. Generally, their patriotism is constructed in terms of affection and gentle affinities, rather than of struggle and resistance. This appears to reflect Fulbrook's (2011) concept of generational dissonance following key political transitions, and contrasts with the hypothesis advanced by Leccardi and Feixa (2012) that young people in Eastern Europe construct their identities largely within the collective family memories of the communist period. These young people's perception of the older generations of their family appears to be that parents and grandparents are locked into a reaction to their experiences of those times, and that the new generation that these young people belong to are able to dissociate themselves from these reactions.

Accession to the European Union created a very real dilemma for many young people. They were now able to migrate, temporarily or permanently, to other European countries with relatively little restriction. They argued that doing so would perhaps leave their country in a liminal, non-European status, but bring them personally social and economic advantages. Staying in their country, they reckoned, to which many expressed strong cultural ties, might possibly advantage the country as a whole. Despite the often expressed frustrations with local politics, a number of participants felt they should stay. The neoliberal labor flexibility within the enlarged European Union (Mitchell 2006) gave these young people a very real sense of agency and an ability—even a need—to make decisions about the directions their lives could take (Skelton 2010).

This interviewed cohort of young people positioned themselves as politically very different to earlier generations. They are engaged with politics, sometimes through criticisms of local political practices, and at other times striving for political agency. They have, in a very real sense, a set of choices to make about their political identities. Moreover, not only are they aware that such choices exist but they are also approaching the age when they will be able to make decisions.

NOTE

1. I had been awarded a Jean Monnet Chair, which helped fund this study: I am grateful to the European Commission for this. I also relied on many colleagues and friends across Europe, the majority of whom I had previously collaborated with in the European Commission's CiCe Academic Network (Children's Identity and Citizenship in Europe).

REFERENCES

Alderson, Priscilla. 2010. "Review of children, politics and communication: Participation at the margins." *Children and Society* 4 (5): 428–430.
BBC News. 2010. "Poland clash over memorial cross for Lech Kaczynski." August 3. http://www.bbc.co.uk/news/world-europe-10853307.
Bruter, Michael. 2005. *Citizens of Europe? The Emergence of a Mass European Identity*. London: Palgrave Macmillan.
Burr, Vivien. 1995. *An Introduction to Social Constructivism*. London: Routledge.
Coles, Robert. 1986. *The Political Life of Children*. Boston, MA: Houghton Mifflin.
Davies, Bronwyn, and Rom Harré. 1990 "Positioning: Conversation and the production of selves." *Journal for the Theory of Social Behavior* 11 (3): 341–361.

Dimitrova-Grajzl, Valentina, and Eszter Simon. 2010. "Political trust and historical legacy: The effect of varieties of socialism." *East European Politics & Societies* 24 (2): 206–228.

Fairclough, Isabela, and Norman Fairclough. 2012. *Political Discourse Analysis*. London: Routledge.

Fulbrook, Mary. 2011. *Dissonant Voices: Generations and Violence through the German Dictatorships*. Oxford: Oxford University Press.

Furnham, Adrian, and Barrie Stacey. 1991. *Young People's Understanding of Society*. London: Routledge.

Habashi, Janette. 2009. "Child geopolitical agency: A mixed methods case study." *Journal of Mixed Methods Research* 3 (1): 42–64.

Hahn, Carole. 1998. *Becoming Political: Comparative Perspectives on Citizenship Education*. New York: State University of New York Press.

Hess, Diana. 2009. *Controversy in the Classroom: The Democratic Power of Discussion*. London: Routledge.

Jans, Marc. 2004. "Children as citizens: Towards a contemporary notion of child participation." *Childhood* 11 (1): 27–44.

Kallio, Kirsi Pauliina. 2009. "Between social and political: Children as political selves." *Childhoods Today* 3 (2): 1–22.

———. 2008. "The body as battlefield: Approaching children's politics." *Geografiiska Annaler: Series B* 90 (3): 285–297.

Kallio, Kirsi, and Jouni Häkli. 2011. "Are there politics in childhood?" *Space and Polity* 15 (1): 21–34.

Katz, Cindi. 2008. "Childhood as spectacle: Relays of anxiety and the reconfiguration of the child." *Cultural Geographies* 15 (1): 5–17.

Krueger, Richard, and Mary Casey. 2009. *Focus Groups: A Practical Guide for Applied Research*, 4th ed. Thousand Oaks, CA: Sage.

Leccardi, Carmen, and Carles Feixa. 2012 "Introduction: Youth in transition(s)." In *1989—Young People and Social Change after the Fall of the Berlin Wall*, edited by Carmen Leccaerdi, Carles Feixa, Siyka Kovacheva, Herwig Reiter, and Tatjana Sekulić. Strasbourg: Council of Europe.

Leszczynski, Adam. 2011. "A very Polish protest party." *The Guardian*, April 6.

Macek, Petr, Constance Flanagan, Leslie Gallay, Lubomir Kostron, Luba Botcheva, and Beno Csapo. 1998. "Postcommunist societies in times of transition: Perceptions of change among adolescents in central and eastern Europe." *Journal of Social Issues* 54 (3): 547–561.

Maitles, Henry. 1997. "Teaching political literacy." Paper presented at the Scottish Educational Research Association Annual Conference, University of Dundee. http://www.leeds.ac.uk/educol/documents/000000417.htm

Mannheim, Karl. 1964. "Das Problem der Generationen." In *Wissensoziologie: Auswahl aus dem Werk*, edited by Kurt Wolff. Berlin: Luchterhand.

Metcalfe, Janet, Teal Eicha, and Alan Castel. 2010. "Metacognition of agency across the lifespan." *Cognition* 116 (2): 267–282.

Mitchell, Katheryne. 2006. "Neoliberal governmentality in the European Union: Education, training and technologies of citizenship." *Environment and Planning D: Society and Space* 24: 389–407.

Philo, Christopher, and Fiona Smith. 2003. "Guest editorial: Political geographies of children and young people." *Space and Polity* 7 (2): 99–115.

Rabiee, Fatemeh. 2004. "Focus-group interview and data analysis." *Proceedings of the Nutrition Society* 63 (4): 655–660.

Ross, Alistair. 2015. *Understanding the Constructions of Identities by Young New Europeans: Kaleidoscopic Selves*. London: Routledge.

———. 2014. "Intersecting identities: Young people's constructions of identity in south-east Europe." In *Educational Inequalities in Schools and Higher Education*, edited by Kalwent Bhopal and Uvanney Maylor. London: Routledge.

Shotter, John. 1990. "Social individuality versus possessive individualism: The sounds of silence." In *Deconstructing Social Psychology*, edited by Ian Parker and John Shotter. London: Routledge.

Shotter, John, and Kenneth Gergen (eds.). 1989. *Texts of Identity: Inquiries in Social Construction*. Thousand Oaks, CA: Sage.

Skelton, Tracey. 2010. "Taking young people as political actors seriously: Opening the borders of political geography." *Area* 42 (2): 145–151.

———. 2008. "Research with children and young people: Exploring the tensions between ethics competence and participation." *Children's Geographies* 6 (1): 21–36.

Thomas, Nigel. 2009. *Children, Politics and Communication: Participation at the Margins*. Bristol: Polity.

van Dijk, Teun. 1997. "What is political discourse analysis?" In *Political Linguistics*, edited by Jan Blommaert and Chris Bulcaen. Amsterdam: Benjamins.

CHAPTER 10

"Let's Move, Let's Not Remain Stagnant": Nationalism, Masculinism, and School-Based Education in Mozambique

Esther Miedema

INTRODUCTION

In this chapter, I examine the role of public schools in shaping young people's gendered understanding of citizenship and their "sense of place" in Mozambique. I seek to illuminate two interrelated features of processes of civil enculturation, which is defined as education for and about citizenship (Baumann 2004). First, I discuss the centrality of public education to nation-building efforts in Mozambique, examining the approach taken by the country's ruling party Frelimo to creating and consolidating the Mozambican nation during postindependence days and at the time of data collection. I analyze how current school-based education shapes young Mozambicans' geographical and cultural imagination, that is, how it seeks to provide them particular ways of imagining and making sense of their place in the world and their nation. In doing so, and drawing on feminist scholars such as Iris Marion Young (1990), Joane Nagel (1998), Cynthia Enloe (2000), Isabel Casimiro (2004), and Signe Arnfred (2010), I investigate the masculinist underpinnings of Frelimo's nation-building project and the core goals of secondary education as reflected in policy and curricular documents, political speeches, and participant accounts.

Second, I argue that investigating perspectives on, and processes of, civil enculturation and nation-building through formal education requires examining underpinning understandings of childhood and youth. Drawing on the work of scholars who have sought to describe and deconstruct "other" non-Western childhoods (e.g., McIlwaine and Datta 2004; Kesby et al. 2006), I engage with the ways in which secondary school-based education in Mozambique is grounded in a particular construction of desirable young Mozambican women and men. In the process, I highlight the ways in which the aims of school-based education build on local articulations of globally circulating discourses (Peters 2001; Robertson 2005) of, for example, "active citizenship" and "entrepreneurship." To conduct this analysis, I examine the sociohistorical underpinnings of postindependence and more current thinking about the role of education in Mozambique through an examination of key policy and curricular documents of the Ministry of Education and Culture (MoEC), political speeches, and policy-makers and educators' narratives.

Points of Departure: Gender and the Role of Education in the Construction of Space, Place, and Culture

Within the social sciences, including the field of education, there is a growing recognition that notions of space and place are crucial to the analysis of social life, practices, and relationships (Massey 1994; Holloway et al. 2010). Similarly, there has been a growing awareness of the spatial nature of the production, performance, and contestation of (cultural) identities and citizenships, including through school-based education (Paechter 2004; Allen 2013). Within dominant discourse, "space" and "place" are often conceptualized in scalar and territorial terms, whereby space is conceived of as the abstract and global "out-there," and place as the bounded, local, and intimate "in-here" (Amin 2002, 388). Building on scholars such as Doreen Massey (1994) and Ash Amin (2002), this chapter is premised on a relational interpretation of space and place, that is, one where space and place are understood as co-constitutive and "folded together," which makes it impossible to ontologically separate proximate from distal happenings (Amin 2002; see also Miedema and Millei 2015).

Another central premise underpinning this chapter is that spaces, places, and cultures are made meaningful through embodied practices that are mediated by power, rather than preexisting, coherent entities (Gupta and Ferguson 1997). Furthermore, as feminist scholars have argued, notions of space and place are given meaning in gendered ways, and space and gender relations need to be understood as mutually constitutive (Martin 1982; Massey 1994). Understanding how spaces are created through, for instance, school-based education, and who has the power to do so (e.g., policy-makers and educators) thus requires critical examination. Similar to space and place, associations of places, citizens, and cultures are understood as sociopolitical and historical constructions that are shaped by the past, present, and future and, furthermore, are open to (re)negotiation and resistance (Bryant and Livholts 2007). Therefore, rather than treating associations between places and cultures as pre-given points of departure, they, too, should be understood as objects of research and examination (Gupta and Ferguson 1997).

Given the chapter's focus on processes of civil enculturation, that is, the ways in which the state seeks to educate young people for and about citizenship, *and* given Mozambique is a multiparty democracy that has effectively been governed by one party (Frelimo) since independence, I am particularly concerned with the relationship between the state and the citizen. The work of Luke Desforges, Rhys Jones, and Mike Woods (2005) is helpful in this regard. As the authors observe, states serve a central role in the configuration of the *scales* at which citizenship is determined and expected to be performed (see also Dickinson et al. 2008). While the citizen has long been associated with the nation-state, Desforges and colleagues (2005) argue that recent changes in modes of government have (re)forged the relationship between citizen and place, with the citizen defined by, and in relation to, her/his (active) role in subnational communities. In the context of Mozambique, within both policy and curricular documents, and participant narratives, the Mozambican citizen is construed at various levels or scales, with a particular emphasis on her/his place and role at the local level and her/his sense of national identity.

Feminist scholars have not only problematized the gendered nature of the category of citizenship, but also highlighted the masculinist underpinnings of national politics and nation-building processes (see, e.g., Young 1990; Enloe 2000; Casimiro 2004; Lister 2007; Casimiro, Andrade, and Jacobson 2009). Feminist theorists have done much to problematize and redress the pervasiveness of masculine exclusiveness of political and scholarly thinking. According to Nagel (1998), however, feminist scholarship has failed to address one central issue: that the masculinist exclusiveness of sociologists and political scientists may need to be understood as reflective of the masculinist nature of the enterprise of nation-building *in and of itself.* While women do play a role in the "making and unmaking of states," Nagel points out that "the scripts in which these roles are embedded are written primarily by men, for men, and about men" (1998, 243; see also Lyons 2004). Women need to be understood as "supporting actors" in these masculinist endeavors, their functions reflecting masculinist conceptions of the feminine and "women's proper 'place'" (Lyons 2004, 243).

I concur with Nagel that restricting the study of gender in politics to women may miss the main way in which gender structures politics, that is, "through men and their interests, [and] their notions of manliness" (Nagel 1998, 243). For this reason, this chapter seeks not so much to examine the absence of women in educational discourse on citizenship and the nation in Mozambique, but instead to make explicit the predominance of men, notions of manhood, and (what are deemed to be) men's interests. In particular, I seek to highlight how, in important ways, nation-building in the context of Mozambique needs to be understood as grounded in what Enloe (2000) has referred to as "masculinized memory, masculinized humiliation and masculinized hope" (44).

Methodology

The data discussed in this chapter were gathered in the framework of a qualitative study that was conducted over a period of seven months (2010–2011). In this chapter, I focus on selected MoEC policy and curricular documents. This analysis is complemented by an examination of speeches delivered by leading political figures, and transcripts of semi-structured interviews with MoEC policy-makers and secondary school staff.

Publications were purposively selected using a snowballing technique that generated a range of relevant policy documents, curricular guidelines, secondary school textbooks, and speeches. The documents presented in this chapter constitute key ministerial texts that, in principle, inform all other MoEC policies, strategies, and curricular and programmatic documents. The selected political speeches were those that were held by the former president, prime minister, and minister of education to mark important national and international days and events, such as World AIDS Day, the publication of the State of the Nation Report, and the opening of the academic year. All documents discussed here were developed shortly after former president Armando Guebuza first took office in 2005, and the Ministries of Education and Culture were merged to form the MoEC.

Semi-structured interviews were held with a gender-balanced sample of policy-makers, and school principals and teachers working in three different public secondary schools. It is important to note that public schools in Mozambique are often regarded to provide low-quality education and those who can afford to do so, namely, the political and business elite, send their children to private schools (Müller 2014). Educators (n = 9) were recruited on the basis of their involvement in the delivery of HIV- and AIDS-related education to grade nine learners. The sampling of policy-makers (n = 8) was geared toward a recruitment of senior officials who were responsible for ensuring HIV- and AIDS-related issues were addressed within the strategies and work plans of their particular directorate/institution.

All interviews lasted between one and two hours and were conducted by the author in Portuguese, the official language of Mozambique. Following consent, interviews were audio-recorded and transcribed ad verbatim, and cross-checked with participants for accuracy. Translation of documents and interview transcripts was primarily done by the author. In the discussion of the data derived from interviews, the date of the interview is stated, and the title "Sr." (Mr.) or "Sra." (Mrs.) is used in combination with a pseudonym to refer to participants. When citing policy-makers, the acronym "MoEC" is stated, and when quoting an educator, a fictive name is used to refer to the school in question. To ensure confidentiality, no reference is made to the department or directorate to which a policy-maker was connected.

The analysis concentrated on identifying statements in documents and participant narratives with regard to (a) the aims of education, (b) the expected qualities of secondary school graduates, and (c) the role of education in the context of Mozambique. The analysis followed a systematic and iterative process, clustering statements according to thematic focus. On the basis of this analysis, a number of key themes were identified relating to the three broad areas stated above.

Nation-Building in Postcolonial Mozambique: Examining Masculinized Humiliation, Memory, and Hope

Struggles to liberate the nation from the colonizer, Akhil Gupta (1997) observes, could only take place and were deemed politically legitimate where the nation was, however fragile, already discursively recognized as a potential geographically bounded entity. Decolonization thus departed from, and reaffirmed, the modernist ideological creation of the nation-state. In addition, Gupta (1997) argues, decolonization involved a process of mapping a national past, present, and future vision on to a territorial entity that was often only consolidated during or directly after colonial rule (see also Anderson 2006). Nationalism and construction of national identities have been the subject of much postcolonial scholarship and critique (e.g., Said 1979; Chatterjee 1986; Spivak 1988; Bhabha 1990; Dirlik 2002; Lazarus 2002; Loomba 2005; Ndlovu-Gatsheni 2009). Preeminent postcolonial scholars, such as Edward Said and Partha Chatterjee, have convincingly demonstrated the *structural* homology between, and elitist and coercive underpinnings of, anticolonial nationalist and Orientalist (read: Western) discourses (see also Spivak 1988; Bhabha 1990). Meyda Yeğenoğlu's (1998) analysis of the sexualized nature of nationalism in Algeria and Turkey is particularly illuminative in this regard. The author elucidates the ways in which anticolonial discourse in Turkey and Algeria builds on the distinction between East and West, and, crucially, reproduce the epistemological structure of Orientalist male hegemony. Building on scholars such as Chatterjee and Yeğenoğlu, I contend that nationalist movements in the Global South can neither be reduced to reactive phenomena that are characterized only by their resistance to colonialism nor be interpreted as mere duplication of colonial epistemologies. Instead, nationalist movements need to be understood as being *selective* about what they have adopted and rejected from the West.

In the case of Mozambique, its territorial boundaries had been agreed upon by Portugal and other colonial powers in neighboring regions, "uniting" as well as dividing a widely diverse range of ethnic and linguistic groups, most of which transcended the country's borders (Shelley 2013). After more than ten years of armed struggle, independence from Portugal was gained in 1975, and the one-party state of the People's Republic of Mozambique was proclaimed. Samora Machel, the political leader of the former guerrilla movement *Frente de Libertação de Moçambique* (Liberation Front of Mozambique, Frelimo) became the country's first president. Frelimo, which declared itself a Marxist-Leninist party in 1977, set out a program of social reform to construct a modern nation and mentality (Sumich and Honwana 2007; Cabaço 2010).

The process of mapping of meaning onto the territory of the new Mozambican nation consisted of creating a shared identity based on a collective memory of external and internal oppression (Meneses 2012; Miedema and Millei 2015). The former was partly defined in relation to colonial institutions, which Frelimo set about dismantling following independence. Fundamental to Frelimo's approach to end the *internal* oppression of people resided in combating a range of issues, including humiliation suffered at the hands of the colonizers, illiteracy, and traditional practices such as *lobolo* ("bride wealth"), polygamy and traditional healing, which were deemed "irrational" (Cabaço 2010; Arnfred 2011). Traditional beliefs and practices were to be replaced by "modern" norms and values, including the ideal of the nuclear family, monogamy, scientific knowledge, and rationality (Cabaço 2010; Arnfred 2011).

The notion of a unified—"tribe-less"—people was central to Frelimo's vision for the nation's present and future. Frelimo perceived the ethnolinguistic and cultural diversity of the country as a potential threat and a barrier to progress (Macagno 2009). One of Frelimo's central aims, therefore, was to instill a national vision of Mozambique as "one people, one nation, one culture…from Rovuma to Maputo" (Machel 1977, cited in Macagno 2009, 22). The expression "from Rovuma (the river on the far northern border of Mozambique) to Maputo (located in the very south of the country)" refers to Samora Machel's epic journey just before independence to demarcate the totality of the new state (Stroud 1999). The expression is regularly used in official speeches (see, e.g., Guebuza 2009, 2010, 2014) and is part of the national anthem, which young school-going people jointly sing at the start of their school day. Arguably, the metaphorical reiteration of the territorial boundaries of the country may be understood as indicative of an effort to link Mozambicans to Mozambique and promote the national "geographic imagination" (Malkki 1995; Gupta and Ferguson 1997).

Equally crucial to Frelimo's postindependence vision was that of the *homem novo*: the new—generic—man. The new man, who was modeled on the guerrilla nationalist of the recent past, and defined as a person liberated from the external and internal forms of oppression and exploitation described above, became "the icon of the truly Mozambican citizen" (Cabaço 2010; Meneses 2012, 129). Crucially, the *homem novo* was a man freed of the past. The following interview excerpt highlights the external, colonial shackles that Mozambicans needed to shed after gaining independence. According to school director Sr. Mateo, the new man was one "who ha[d] liberated himself from that colonial conception of the Black man," for

the colonisers, the Portuguese used to teach us to despise ourselves, right? We felt "inferiorised" (*inferiorizados*), incapable…They said we had to become civilised, [saying] the Mozambican man was not civilised and had to learn to *live like a man*, right? A civilised man, a primitive man who emerged from a primitive culture [and turned] into a civilised or modern man. (Gandhi school, November 19, 2010, emphasis added).

The excerpt is illustrative of an imperial masculinity whereby Mozambicans were cast as the racial Other: primitive, childlike, and not fully human, but partially redeemable when tamed by "real," middle-class, European men (see also Meneses 2012; Spronk 2014). Furthermore, as the following quote from a 1977 speech delivered by one of Frelimo's founding members Sergio Vieira suggests, the sense of inferiority and humiliation Sr. Mateo alludes to above needs to be understood in spatiotemporal terms. According to Sergio Vieira, the "colonised man . . . is a person unable to locate himself historically [and] in space [for] he was taught to despise his own personality" (cited in Barnes 1982, 409).

Thus, the masculinized humiliation and memory that Enloe (2000) speaks of need to be understood in relation to two intersecting processes of colonialization: that of Othering, and silencing and forgetting (Spronk 2014). By imposing its own Portuguese memory on Mozambicans, Maria Paula Meneses (2012) asserts: "The Eurocentric memory became the beginning of history for all the colonized—a process that mean[t] the loss of their own history" (123). As Meneses observes, the erasure of memories, combined with the removal of land and power, entailed an obliteration "of the base from which [Mozambicans] could launch themselves into the world" (2012, 123). To an important degree, therefore, the (memory of the) humiliation of, and suffered under, colonial rule needs to be understood in relation to the historical and cultural *dis*location of native Mozambicans.

Education was critical to what might be understood as the relocation of the formerly colonized man. Samora Machel, for example, defined the school as a "combat center," declaring it to be necessary to "win the war, create the new society and develop the homeland" (1978/1981, cited in Macagno 2009, 21, 25). The combination of efforts made to (forcibly) reorganize rural space (e.g., by dis- and relocating smallholders into communal villages) and to remove those considered incompatible with the ideal of the "new man" to remotely located reeducation camps (party dissidents, "unproductive" urbanites, such as alcoholics and sex workers, and "collaborators" of the colonial regime) is indicative of the geographic, exclusionary, and often violent nature of the strategies deployed by Frelimo in the construction of the new nation (Stroud 1999; Lyons 2004; Hamann 2006).

Frelimo's postindependence approach to women is similarly indicative of the exclusionary character of its nation-building program. Peasant women were actively involved in the fight for independence, including as guerilla fighters, and Frelimo is said to have actively supported women who challenged patriarchal hierarchies and sought to enact new female identities (Arnfred 2010). However, the gains made in the creation of more equitable gender relations rapidly dissipated following the end of the war, women reporting a sense of abandonment by the party in the struggle for emancipation (Arnfred 2010; Casimiro 2004). The process of constructing postindependence Mozambique and the "new man" was characterized by new forms of silencing and forgetting, from which—the mostly illiterate, non-Portuguese speaking—female guerilla fighters were largely excluded. Following independence, women's "emancipation" was defined in modernist terms, and would result from the integration of women in processes of (large-scale) industrial or agricultural production on equal footing with men. "Traditional" society was portrayed in terms of women's subjugation, the possibility of emancipation located in the future socialist state (Arnfred 2010; Casimiro 2004; Casimiro et al. 2009).

With regard to the new man and the idea of tradition, it is important to note that while Frelimo was vehemently opposed to manifestations of "the traditional," this notion was mainly defined in terms of practices and structures such as initiation rites. Furthermore, while the party did pay explicit attention to women's emancipation and this did lead to a degree of female participation in national politics, Frelimo's reform program was not geared to a critical analysis of women's place in the socio-spatial hierarchy (Casimiro 2004; Casimiro et al. 2009). Frelimo's postindependence nation-building project negated the ways in which women in "traditional" society had maintained (and expanded) "spheres of autonomy" (Arnfred 2010, 12), and attempts to defend aspects of the past were deemed "reactionary" and barriers to progress (Arnfred 2010, 12).

As Arnfred (2004) notes, the model of the "socialist family" promoted by the party, for example, was indistinguishable from a puritan Protestant ideal of the family. As noted elsewhere (Miedema and Millei 2015), the family was both women's primary domain and constituted "the first cell of the party" (Machel 1973, as cited in Newitt 1995, 548). Additionally, while Frelimo was against traditional marriage ceremonies and the practice of *lobolo* (bridewealth), young people who sought to marry without their parents' consent or ceremony were severely condemned (Arnfred 2004). Referring to these kinds of errant young people, Machel reputedly stated that "they behave like animals, and they [think] that this is Independence" (Machel 1982, cited in Arnfred 2004, 118). Thus, while traditional marriage was considered an "outdated" practice, not marrying was worse, and in these cases Frelimo sided with (the typically more traditional) caregivers. This ambivalence in Frelimo thought led the party to draw a distinction between "positive and negative aspects of tradition" (Arnfred 2004, 118).

A final illustration of Frelimo's vision for the future of the country may be found in an early party statement on education, which was described as a prerequisite for the creation "of a prosperous and advanced economy" (Frelimo Education and Culture Department 1970, cited in Mabunda 2005, 66). A fairly extensive excerpt is offered not only to illustrate the pervasive use of militaristic terminology, but also to draw attention to the underpinning ideals of an economically productive society and the spatial terms in which the party's vision was presented. According to Frelimo, education was necessary to

> create, develop and consolidate a new society,...a unitary Mozambique, internationalist, self-sufficient economically, politically and militarily;...to contribute to the destruction of the old mentality...; to form a new man...aware of the power of his intelligence and the power of his work to transform society and nature; to create the Mozambican persona who, without any subservience...should know, in contact with the exterior world, to assimilate critically the ideas and experiences of other peoples, transmitting to them also the fruits of our reflection and practice; to create a conscience of responsibility and collective solidarity;...of participating in the production,...freeing the capacity [to take] initiative; and to create and develop a scientific attitude, open, free of all superstitious influences [and] dogmatic traditions. (Frelimo Education and Culture Department 1970, cited in Mabunda 2005, 65)

The excerpt sums up a range of important themes introduced in this section, namely, those of a unified Mozambique and the new Mozambican mentality that Frelimo set out to create and the critical importance (re)education was seen to have in this regard. References to "production" and "a scientific attitude" allude to Frelimo's modernist ambitions to create a society based on scientific insights rather than traditional beliefs and a technologically advanced economy (see also Mabunda 2005). However, as numerous authors have shown, processes of modernization favor male power and masculine interests (e.g., Jayawardena 1986; Escobar 1995; Nagel 1998; Casimiro et al. 2009; Arnfred 2010; Meneses 2012). Thus, while in theory the "new man" designates a person of unspecified gender, the analysis shows that the notion needs to be understood as inherently masculinist, excluding women and others considered not conforming to the underpinning revolutionary ideals (see also Meneses, 2012).

The mention of the various forms of national self-sufficiency and the Mozambican "persona" who can interact with the world outside "without any subservience," points to a view of the modern state as a distinct and bounded territory that mapped directly onto a discrete cultural identity, that is, a "people" (see also Gupta and Ferguson 1997). These statements suggest, furthermore, that a sense of cultural rootedness and self-confidence was deemed a prerequisite for the ability to establish equitable relationships with the outside world (see also Meneses 2012).

The attempt to erase all traces of the former colonizer's presence as well as the remnants of "the traditional" suggests, furthermore, that the mapping of the past, and present and future vision, involved the *destruction* of the old man, which involved an "organized forgetting" and "Othering" of that which was considered undesirable (Pitcher 2006, 88). Frelimo's postindependence nation-building efforts, on the other hand, can be understood as driven by what are typically considered to be a masculinist definition of the desirable Mozambican man: as one who had destroyed the oppressive and downgrading vestiges of colonialism and "traditions," and internalized Frelimo's modern production-oriented mentality. Frelimo's *homem novo* may be understood as the embodiment of the "masculinized hope" of postindependence Mozambique.

In conclusion, the process of construing postindependence Mozambique involved imagining a national past, present, and future vision (Gupta 1997; Pitcher 2006). As the analysis shows, "locating" the new Mozambican, furthermore, entailed an emphasis on unity, and processes of forgetting, silencing, and "Othering." Finally, the discussion revealed that despite the centrality of the "new," from a gender and generational perspective, Frelimo's nation-building efforts need to be understood as geared to a masculinist interpretation of "emancipation" as involvement in industrialized production, and a "re-traditionalization" of society, understood in the patriarchal sense of entrenching women and children's place under the guardianship of a male elder (Nagel 1998; Kesby et al. 2006; Miedema and Millei 2015).

"Consolidating Mozambicanness": School-Based Education, Capable Citizens, and Nation-Building

This section engages with education policy and curricular documents developed in, and pertaining to, the period between 2006 and 2011, and speeches delivered by key political figures in the same period. The analysis highlights how schools continue to serve as a critical site for the construction of the political, cultural, and geographical imagination in the minds of Mozambique's young citizens. The intention to shape the contours of young people's imagination of the nation-state and their sense of "Mozambicanness" is apparent in, for instance, the Ministry of Education's 2006–2010 strategy (MoEC 2006), which is titled *Turning the school into a centre of development, consolidating Mozambicanness*. The title captures two essential and interlinked goals of the strategy: to provide education that contributes to "development" and to enhancing young people's sense of cultural identity. These two issues will be examined in turn, beginning with the latter.

As discussed, Frelimo promoted the idea of "consolidating Mozambicanness" during the period leading up to, and directly after, independence. The importance attached to achieving this goal is apparent throughout recent MoEC publications and additional government statements. Illustrative of the role accorded to education in furthering young people's sense of Mozambicanness, for example, is the following excerpt from the section "Strengthening Mozambicanness: [creating] unity in diversity" in the MoEC strategy (MoEC 2006):

> The construction, consolidation [and development] of the Mozambican Nation..., requires [its] citizens [are instilled] with proper personalities and identities, [who are] committed to the nation...Mozambique is a diversified Nation in all its dimensions and from its beginnings [and the] challenges of [achieving] economic and social development of the Mozambican Nation require, above all, a national consciousness that supersedes the differences between the persons and groups it is composed of. [While] culture makes differences [between ethnic and linguistic groups] apparent, it equally [contributes to enhancing] cohesion. In this regard,...cultural values are crucial to the development of solidarity between members of a group. (131)

Noteworthy in the passage above is the use of terms such as "construction" and "consolidation," and Mozambique being a diversified nation "from its beginnings." The latter notion in particular suggests a conception of Mozambique as having "come into being," or, to paraphrase Gupta (1997), as discursively recognized as a geographically bounded entity from a certain point in time onward. Whether these discursive beginnings are conceived of in relation to Mozambique as a Portuguese colony or as an independent nation-state is not clarified, but the excerpt implies an acknowledgment that Mozambique as a nation, and—by extension—Mozambican culture was *made* meaningful, and, furthermore, is open to resistance and negotiation (Bryant and Livholt 2007). The recent upsurge in violent conflict between the ruling party Frelimo and Renamo (Frelimo's main contender since independence), which emanated from unresolved and new geopolitical disputes, and the solution to which has been construed in terms of a redrawing of the boundaries of the country, arguably further highlights the "negotiability" of the territorial boundaries of the country. The development of the nation is understood as requiring transcendence of difference and the consolidation of a sense of "national consciousness" as a means to overcome resistance to Mozambique *as an entity.*

While the MoEC strategy refers to the importance of recognizing and "valuing" diversity, and "local communities, identities and cultural norms" (MoEC 2006, 114), equally strong emphasis is placed on the need to strengthen young people's "identif[ication] with national values [and] culture" (MoEC 2006, 132), and that this is "fundamental to the success and sustainability of all development programmes" in the country (MoEC 2006, 114). The document acknowledges, in other words, the Mozambican citizen as emplaced within a specific sociolinguistic group at a local level, but that socioeconomic success of the nation "in the global economy" (MoEC 2006, 9) depends on an overarching *national* identity (see also MoEC 2007b). The positioning of Mozambican citizens at these different scales, that is, local, national, and (ultimately) global, resonates with the observation of Desforges et al. (2005) that states serve a crucial role in the configuration of the scales at which citizenship are determined and expected to be enacted.

Although the MoEC strategy does not explicitly indicate what the national culture or value system consists of, the following statement provides further clarity: education, the document states (MoEC 2006, 14), should "inculcate in its citizens…good behaviour,…a civilized mentality, order, cleanliness and hygiene, modesty, love of self, respect for one's next and society, [and in doing so] contribute to [Mozambicans] sense of pride in being Mozambican." Furthermore, the document clarifies that "education should be grounded in family values, respect for [Mozambican and] African [culture and] traditions [as well as] "universally recognized values of modernity" (MoEC 2006).

With regard to "the family," it is important to note that the MoEC strategy indicates that it is especially important to invest in the education of women, "given [their] role as mother educator of new generations" (MoEC 2006, 13). The conception of women as "mother educator" was echoed in participants' accounts, Sra. Adelaide (Gandhi school, October 26, 10) indicating, for instance, that in Mozambique we have an expression: to educate a girl is to educate the nation. In other words, girls have a responsibility to educate themselves to ensure the progress of the nation.

Participants, furthermore, stressed the importance of the family and community in educating or raising the young. The following quote illustrates the value attached to education in the sense of upbringing and the responsibility placed on women to ensure future generations were, to paraphrase Sr. Simião (MoEC, January 4, 2011), "well-oriented":

Education "of the cradle" [upbringing], from the first moment one enters the world, is critical. Because if...you did not have this cradle [base], basic things, orientation for life, going to school or not going to school is like water on top of a duck—it would make no difference, [it] would fall. (Sra. Vania, MoEC, December 3, 2010)

Speaking of the role of elders, Sr. Carlos explained, furthermore:

[Elders] are people with...a lot of experience [in terms of] social and cultural life and above all who have been able to stabilize their emotions, right?...[Whilst] a young person...likes this and likes that...he doesn't have a solidified personality. (MoEC, December 2, 2010)

The quotes indicate that, similar to postindependence days, young people were expected to listen to and heed their (more traditional) elders, and that without this form of education or "orientation," young people would not become "rooted" (Sra. Vânia, MoEC, December 3, 10). The excerpts above illustrate a number of additional issues. To begin with, while reference is made to Mozambican and African culture and the "values of modernity" (MoEC 2006, 14), the list of values provided echo those expounded by Machel in a 1982 speech in which he explicitly acknowledged the similarities between Frelimo and Protestant Christian morals (Arnfred 2004). In his speech, Machel is said to have stressed the importance of "individual and collective hygiene and cleanliness, of clean nails and well-combed hair, and of the dignity of the family" (Arnfred 2004, 117). The values the MoEC seek to instill in the young Mozambican citizen an equally conservative set of standards, rather than an articulation of "authentic" Mozambican, African, or "modern" values. Civil enculturation taking place in schools, therefore, continues to be geared to the "re-traditionalization" that Nagel (1998) refers to, and nation-building efforts directed at maintaining and (further) entrenching patriarchal values.

The second core theme referred to in the title of MoEC strategy was that of the school as a "center of development." According to the MoEC strategy, "accelerated economic growth and poverty reduction" constitute "explicit," national priorities for Mozambique (MoEC 2006, 5; see also MoEC 2007a). Moving from the local to a national scale, the document goes on to clarify that education should be designed to ensure that "all citizens have the opportunity to acquire basic knowledge and necessary capacities to improve their lives, that of [their] communities and the country" (MoEC 2006, 6). The use of international development terminology of "sustainable economic growth" and "human capital" (see, e.g., MoEC 2006, 10, 18) suggests an important discursive shift has been made from the postindependence rhetoric of the school as a "combat center" (Machel 1981, cited in Macagno 2009, 25). The emphasis on the role of education in relation to socioeconomic development in the MoEC documents is, furthermore, in line with the Mozambican government's most important financial donors, such as the World Bank and United Kingdom's Department for International Development (see, e.g., Fox et al. 2012).

The curricular outline for secondary education (MoEC 2007a) provides insight into the kind of citizen deemed necessary to achieve sustainable economic growth. According to this outline, the curriculum reflects the "aspirations of Mozambican society in [that it seeks to develop] responsible, active . . . and entrepreneurial citizens" (MoEC 2007a, 1). The guidelines clarify, furthermore, that the curriculum aims to develop citizens who can "contribut[e] to the political, economic and social victories (*conquistas*) [already] attained and to poverty reduction within the family, community and the country" (MoEC 2007a). The notion of the "good" citizen is further clarified in the MoEC curricular guidelines for crosscutting issues (MoEC 2007b), which indicate that schools need to tackle the "degradation of patriotic, moral, ethical and civic values, especially among young [Mozambican] people [such as personal and collective responsibility] in order to [be able to bring about] the change in attitude [and] skills needed to . . . solve very complex problems," such as HIV and AIDS (8).

The responsible citizen invoked in the two sets of curricular guidelines, that is, as an active entrepreneurial and morally responsible contributor to the developmental process of the country resonated with the views expressed by research participants. School director Sr. Mateo (Gandhi school, November 9, 2010), for instance, spoke of education as enabling young people "to walk on their own [two] feet

[and] help Mozambique to get out of the situation in which it [finds] itself," while according to Sr. Reís:

> Our education is not about creating intellectuals but...to enable people to live in harmony in the locality they find themselves, to help the people to help themselves to live better: produce better, communicate better, carry out work, create [better] conditions in the community. This is the basic purpose of education. Not neglecting the fact that some may reach higher levels but our education is primarily formative, [so that] people have abilities to live in their locality. (MoEC October 9, 2010)

The importance of young Mozambicans learning to "stand on their own feet" and, crucially, "to help themselves" and "take initiative" was clarified against the backdrop of Mozambique's change from a "socialist system...[to] a market economy" (Sra. Matilda, December 7, 2010) in which, as Sra. Alinda (Maxaquene school, December 4, 2010) clarified, young people could no longer expect the state to provide jobs, they should learn "not simply to wait, [but that] they can also create [their own employment opportunities]." Poignant in this regard were the words of policy-maker Sra. Matilda (MoEC, December 7, 2010), who, during the interview stated, laughingly: "The whole world [has] this thing of the entrepreneur, which I think really stems from an American ideology, don't you think? That a man takes care of himself. So, let's move, let's not remain stagnant."

A final theme worth addressing here relates to the strong focus in MoEC texts and participants on the role of (secondary) education in providing learners with technical and vocational skills. The need for these skills was conceptualized in two different ways: on one hand, references to the need to prepare young people for a "rapidly changing" global market and an increasingly knowledge-based economy (MoEC 2006, 8) suggest a view that education needs to prepare young people for a world of work that is complex and in a constant state of flux. A closer inspection of the curricular outlines reveals an emphasis on (small-scale) farming skills, suggesting that, to an important extent, learners are prepared for traditional and local markets. Sr. Reís's earlier statements underscore this view.

Similar to the MoEC documents, therefore, the excerpts from participant interviews resonate with the kind of scaling downward and upward of the definition and (expected) performance of the "active citizen" to the local and national levels that Desforges et al. (2005) speak of. The quotes conjure a very particular image of the "good" secondary school graduate, namely, a person who will be able to live in harmony with, and have a skill set that is directly applicable in, and relevant to, her/his *direct* surroundings. A simultaneous scaling upward of the notion of citizenship is evident in the references to the well-educated citizen contributing to the "development of the country." Finally, the mention of the "American ideology" and frequent references to the notion of entrepreneurship and "the knowledge economy" in both the MoEC texts and participant narratives indicate a vision of education that was grounded in global discourse on education contributing to young people's entrepreneurial skills and ability to partake in the "knowledge economy" (see, e.g., Peters 2001; Robertson 2005), but that the activity of the Mozambican entrepreneur was primarily envisaged to take place at the local level.

In important ways, participant narratives and MoEC policy documents stress inculcating in learners "a sense of pride in being Mozambican" (MoEC 2006, 14) and "patriotic, moral, ethical and civic values" (MoEC 2007b, 8), emphasizing the importance of doing so in view of the need to ensure a coherent Mozambican identity was maintained in the "global village" that Mozambique is a part of and the perceived "degradation" of values among young Mozambican women and men. The frequent mention of notions such as "taking initiative," "not remaining stagnant," and the centrality of entrepreneurship in the secondary curriculum suggest that the "desirable" young Mozambique man and woman was defined in two central interlinked ways: (a) his/her patriotism and (b) the ability to "take care of him/herself."

The data suggests that, for women, "patriotism" largely entailed that they took on their "proper" role as "mothers of the nation" (Sra. Adelaide, Gandhi school, October 26, 2010). Therefore, the combination of the emphasis on the notion of entrepreneurship and women's perceived role as educators of the young suggests that education was geared to further entrenching women's double workload located in the economic and domestic domain (on this point see also Çagatay 2003; Robinson 2006; Miedema and Millei 2015). In addition, from a gender perspective, while the emphasis on entrepreneurship in the secondary school curriculum may be interpreted as encouraging in that young women were stimulated to enter domains that traditionally were seen to be the preserve of men, the "emancipatory" potential of the notion is undermined by the considerable gender-based discrimination female entrepreneurs are faced with in practice. As the International Labour Organization (2011) reports, for example, women face important constraints in accessing necessary capital to start or expand their business, in part due to lower levels of education and (concomitant) lack of understanding of the financial language and related laws required to access formal finance mechanisms. In practice, therefore, female entrepreneurship is smaller in scale and mainly takes place in informal local markets (Manuel 2015).

CONCLUSIONS

As Mohamed Hamoud Kassim Al-Mahfedi (2011) observes, state-maintained schools present young citizens with the official version of a national geography through an understanding of, for instance, national borders. In addition, formal education shapes the sociopolitical imagination of young people, by providing the contours of what is deemed to constitute the "good" national citizen. Emplacing young women and men within a bounded territory, and instilling a "geographic common sense of belonging" (8) thus need to be understood as an integral part of the nationalistic process of constructing and "consolidating" the nation.

The analysis presented in this chapter has highlighted a number of key aspects of the process of inculcating this "geographic common sense" in young Mozambicans. To begin with, the chapter has elucidated the different scales at which citizenship in Mozambique is construed and expected to be practiced: rooted in the citizen's locality, while committed to the nation and its people in their entirety (Desforges et al. 2005). The chapter has, furthermore, highlighted that across the years, creating and maintaining young Mozambicans' geographical and sociopolitical imagination and, crucially, their sense of cultural pride, have been perceived to be critical to the country's ability to progress socioeconomically.

As discussed, during the period leading up to, and directly after, independence, "Mozambicanness" was defined in relation to the notion of the new socialist person and his/her contribution to "production," while during the more recent period between 2006 and 2011, the patriotic, "good" Mozambican citizen was defined in terms of the neoliberal entrepreneur, the person capable of taking care of her/himself. Despite this important political and economic transition, the analysis highlighted that, in various ways, the national imagination across these two broad periods has remained strikingly constant (see also Miedema and Millei 2015). First, across these periods, these imaginations drew on, and further entrenched, a fairly consistent presentation of a shared national past, and vision of the present and future, and that in important ways these "maps" were grounded in a sense of humiliation, memory, and hope (Enloe 2000). Second, during both periods, emphasis was placed on "the Mozambican people," defined as those residing in the territory between the river Rovuma in the very north of the country and Maputo in the very south.

Third, Mozambicans were construed as united in their diversity: the Mozambican *citizen* was defined as "tribe-less," determined in the first place by her/his belonging to the nation-state rather than to a particular ethnic or linguistic group or locality (Macagno 2009). Indeed, the focus on cultural pride, patriotism, and the importance of a collective solidarity to increase production during the postindependence period and during the more recent period to tackle "concrete social problems" (MoEC 2007b, 8), such as HIV and AIDS, highlight the emphasis placed on, and perceived value of, Mozambique as a discrete, place-based culture. Furthermore, while the more recent MoEC texts are predicated on modernist ideals of nation-state and the liberal autonomous man who is capable of "taking care of himself" without much state intervention, the purpose of education was conceived of in terms of delimiting the individual to the "traditional" setting of the community. The analysis thus elucidates that the good Mozambican citizen was largely construed in place-based terms.

The analysis also revealed the gendered nature of nation-building politics in Mozambique in the sense that these are largely defined by men, men's interests, and conceptions of what counts as masculine and feminine (Nagel 1998). While, like in many other settings, women in Mozambique were central to the struggle for independence, they were quickly sidelined in postcolonial Mozambique (Casimiro et al. 2009; Arnfred 2010). Similarly, while Frelimo is said to have provided a degree of support to women who sought to forge new gender roles and identities within the home during the fight for independence, thereafter, women's emancipation was located in the public realm of economic production. As noted by Isabel Casimiro, Ximena Andrade, and Ruth Jacobson (2009), a critique of power relations within the *domestic* sphere and discussion of sexual relations was deemed reactionary, an example of "undesirable, western-derived feminism" (110; see also Arnfred 2010). Frelimo's conception of feminism—in the sense of providing a critique of gender and sexual relations and broader agitation for equal rights—as a Western phenomenon resonates with perceptions of feminism in both the Global South *and* North, noted by Jayawardena (1986). Furthermore, Frelimo's interpretation of women's emancipation in largely economic terms needs to be understood as illustrative of Chatterjee's (1986) argument that anticolonial nationalist movements were grounded in the very colonial structures and hierarchies they strove to discard (see also Yeğenoğlu 1998; Spronk 2014).

From a gender perspective, a crucial commonality across both the postindependence and the more recent periods relates to the masculinist conception of the value of education for women. While education was expected to create the modern Mozambican man and woman across both periods, women were expected to retain what Yeğenoğlu refers to as their "essential feminine virtues" (1998, 134), or, as Sra. Adelaide put it, to continue to fulfil their role as "mothers of the nation." As authors such as Chatterjee have argued, women were deemed responsible for striking an "appropriate" balance between modernization and "authenticity": they were to become educated and modern while keeping the "original" Mozambican culture intact.

Frelimo's approach with regard to women and their role in Mozambican society is reflective of Yeğenoğlu's (1998) argument as to women serving as "the discursive instrument" (136) in the drawing of borders between newly independent countries and their former colonizers, and the process of creating new nation-states and identities (see also Chatterjee 1986). The policing of women's bodies and subjectivities in Mozambique thus needs to be understood as central to establishing and maintaining both the symbolic and territorial boundaries of what was construed as the authentic (precolonial) Mozambican culture and people (Chatterjee 1986).

In important ways and irrespective of gender, school-based education in Mozambique appears to be geared to shaping young people who will heed what are construed as "positive" authentic *Mozambican* traditions, such as respect for elders and traditional marriage ceremonies (Arnfred 2004). Additionally, as the analysis revealed, young people were only deemed full members of the community once they had been educated into the existing socio-spatial hierarchy. Sr. Reís's statement that public education in Mozambique was not about "creating intellectuals" but enabling young people to live in harmony in their locality is particularly salient in this regard. Given virtually all but the children of the political and business elite attend state-maintained schools, his remark arguably suggests a conception of education as geared to a "containment" of young lower-class Mozambican women and men, that they were educated, in other words, to stay put.

REFERENCES

Allen, Louisa. 2013. "Behind the bike sheds: Sexual geographies of schooling." *British Journal of Sociology of Education* 34 (1): 56–75.

Al-Mahfedi, Mohamed Hamoud Kassim. 2011. "Edward Said's "imaginative geography" and geopolitical mapping: Knowledge/power constellation and landscaping Palestine." *The Criterion: An International Journal in English* 2 (3): 1–26.

Amin, Ash. 2002. "Spatialities of globalisation." *Environment and Planning* 34, 385–399.

Anderson, Benedict. 2006. *Imagined Communities: Reflections on the Origin and Spread of Nationalism. Revised edition.* London and New York: Verso.

Arnfred, Signe. 2011. *Sexuality & Gender Politics in Mozambique: Rethinking Gender in Africa.* New York: Boydell & Brewer.

———. 2010. "Women in Mozambique: Gender struggles and gender politics." In *African Women: A Political Economy,* edited by Meredeth Turshen. New York: Palgrave Macmillan.

———. 2004. "Conceptions of gender in colonial and post-colonial discourses: The case of Mozambique." *Gender Activism and Studies in Africa.* Codesria Gender Series, Vol. 3. Dakar: CODESRIA, 108–128.

Barnes, Barbara. 1982. "Education for socialism in Mozambique." *Comparative Education Review* 26 (3): 406–419.

Baumann, Gerd. 2004. "Nation-state, schools and civil enculturation." In *Civil Enculturation: Nation-State, Schools and Ethnic Difference in Four European Countries,* edited by Werner Schiffauer, Gerd Baumann, Riva Kastoryano, and Steven Vertovec. New York and Oxford: Berghahn Books.

Bhabha, Homi (ed.). 1990. *Nation and Narration.* London: Routledge.

Bryant, Lia, and Mona Livholts. 2007. "Exploring the gendering of space by using memory work as a reflexive research method." *International Journal of Qualitative Methods* 6 (3): 29–44.

Cabaço, José Luís. 2010. *Moçambique, Identitdades, Colonialismo e Libertação.* Maputo: Marimbique.

Çagatay, Nilüfer. 2003. "Gender budgets and beyond: Feminist fiscal policy in the context of globalisation." *Gender and Development* 11 (1): 15–24.

Casimiro, Isabel. 2004. *Paz na terra, guerra em casa: Feminismo e organizações de mulheres em Moçambique.* Maputo: Promédia.

Casimiro, Isabel, Ximena Andrade, and Ruth Jacobson. 2009. "Mozambique: War, peace and women's movements." In *Independent Women: The Story of Women's Activism in East Timor,* edited by Irina Cristalis and Catherine Scott. London: CIIR.

Chatterjee, Partha. 1986. *Nationalist Thought and the Colonial World: A Derivative Discourse.* London: Zed Books.

Desforges, Luke, Rhys Jones, and Mike Woods. 2005. "New geographies of Citizenship." *Citizenship Studies* 9 (5): 439–451, doi: 10.1080/13621020500301213.

Dickinson, Jen, Max Andrucki, Emma Rawlins, Daniel Hale, and Victoria Cook. 2008. "Introduction: Geographies of everyday citizenship." *ACME: An International E-Journal for Critical Geographies* 7 (2): 100–112.

Dirlik, Arif. 2002. "Rethinking colonialism: Globalization, postcolonialism, and the nation." *Interventions* 4 (3): 428–448.

Enloe, Cynthia. 2000. *Bananas, Beaches and Babes: Making Feminist Sense of International Politics*. Berkeley: University of California Press.

Escobar, Arturo. 1995. *Encountering Development: The Making and Unmaking of the Third World*. Princeton, NJ: Princeton University Press.

Fox, Louise, Lucrecia Santibañez, Vy Nguyen, and Pierre André. 2012. *Education Reform in Mozambique: Lessons and Challenges*. Washington, DC: World Bank.

Guebuza, Armando Emílio. 2014. *Discurso do Presidente Armando Guebuza na abertura da IV Conferência Nacional Sobre Mulher e Género*. https://www.facebook.com/notes/govdigitalmz/discurso-do-presidente-armando-guebuza-na-abertura-da-iv-confer%C3%AAncia-nacional-so/239982386202544, retrieved on January 5, 2015.

———. 2010. *Discurso de Investidura de Armando Emilio Guebuza— 14/01/2010*. http://armandoguebuza.blogspot.nl/2010/01/discurso-de-investidura-de-armando.html, retrieved on January 5, 2015.

———. 2009. *O Combate Contra A Pobreza: Concentrando as Nossas Acções no Distrito. Comunicação de Sua Excelência Armando Emílio Guebuza, Presidente da República de Moçambique, sobre o Estado Geral da Nação*. Maputo: GoM.

———. 2004. "Podemos, merecemos e somos capazes de ser ricos." *Domingo*, November 28, 2004.

Gupta, Akhil. 1997. "The song of the nonaligned world: Transnational identities and raw reinscription of space in late capitalism." In *Culture, Power, Place. Explorations in Critical Anthropology*, edited by Akhil Gupta and James Ferguson. Durham, NC: Duke University Press.

Gupta, Akhil, and James Ferguson (eds.). 1997. *Culture, Power, Place: Explorations in Critical Anthropology*. Durham, NC: Duke University Press.

Hamann, Hilton. 2006. *Days of the Generals: The Untold Story of South Africa's Apartheid Era Military Generals*. Cape Town: Zebra.

Holloway, Sarah, Phil Hubbard, Heike Jöns, and Helena Pimlott-Wilson. 2010. "Geographies of education and the significance of children, youth and families." *Progress in Human Geography* 34 (5): 583–600.

International Labour Organisation (ILO). 2011. *The Enabling Environment for Women in Growth Enterprises in Mozambique: Assessment Report ILO-WEDGE-Southern Africa*. http://www.ilo.org/wcmsp5/groups/public/---ed_emp/---emp_ent/---ifp_seed/documents/publication/wcms_184769.pdf, retrieved on February 18, 2015.

Jayawardena, Kumari. 1986. *Feminism and Nationalism in the Third World*. London: Zed Books.

Kesby, Mike, Fungisai Gwanzura-Ottemoller, and Monica Chizororo. 2006. "Theorising other, 'other childhoods': Issues emerging from work on HIV in urban and rural Zimbabwe." *Children's Geographies* 4 (2): 185–202.

Lister, Ruth. 2007. "Why citizenship? Where, when and how children?" *Theoretical Inquiries in Law* 8 (2): 693–718.

Lazarus, Neil. 2002. "The politics of postcolonial modernism." *The European Legacy: Toward New Paradigms* 7 (6): 771–782.

———. 1993. "Disavowing decolonization: Fanon, nationalism, and the problematic of representation in current theories of colonial discourse." *Research in African Literatures* 24 (4): 69–98.

Loomba, Ania. 2005. *Colonialism/Postcolonialism.* London and New York: Routledge.

Lyons, Tania. 2004. *Guns and Guerilla Girls: Women in the Zimbabwean Liberation Struggle.* Trenton and Asmara: Africa World Press.

Mabunda, Moisés. 2005. "Nation building in Mozambique: An assessment of the secondary school teacher's placement scheme 975—1985." Master's thesis, University of Pretoria, Pretoria.

Macagno, Lorenzo. 2009. "Fragmentos de uma imaginação nacional" (Fragments of a national imagination). *Revista brasileira Ciencas Sociais* 24 (70): 17–35.

Malkki, Liisa. 1995. "Refugees and exile: From "refugee studies" to the national order of things." *Annual Review of Anthropology* 24: 495–523.

Manuel, Sandra. 2015. In discussion with the author, February 2015.

Martin, Jane. 1982. "Excluding women from the educational realm." *Harvard Educational Review* 52 (2): 133–148.

Massey, Doreen. 1994. *Space, Place and Gender.* Cambridge: Polity Press.

McIlwaine, Cathy, and Kavita Datta. 2004. "Endangered youth? Youth, gender and sexualities in urban Botswana." *Gender, Place & Culture: A Journal of Feminist Geography* 11 (4): 483–512.

Meneses, Maria Paula. 2012. "Images outside the mirror? Mozambique and Portugal in world history." *Human Architecture: Journal of the Sociology of Self-Knowledge* 10 (1): 121–136.

Miedema, Esther, and Zsuzsa Millei. 2015. "'We reaffirm our Mozambican identity in the fight against HIV & AIDS'; examining educational perspectives on women's 'proper' place in the nation of Mozambique." *Global Studies of Childhood: The Cultural Politics of 'Childhood' and 'Nation': Space, Mobility and a Global World* 5 (1): 7–18.

Ministry of Education and Culture (MoEC). 2006. *Fazer da escola um polo de desenvolvimento consolidando a Moc ambicanidade: Plano Estratégico de Educação e Cultura 2006—2010/11.* Maputo: MoEC.

MoEC. 2007a. *Plano Curricular do Ensino Secundário Geral (PCESG); Documento Orientador: Objectivos, Política, Estrutura, Plano de Estudos e Estratégias de Implementação.* Maputo: MoEC/INDE.

MoEC. 2007b. *Temas Transversais: Texto de apoio para os professores do ESG.* Maputo: MoEC/INDE.

Müller, Tanya. 2014. *Legacies of Socialist Solidarity: East Germany in Mozambique.* London: Lexington Books.

Nagel, Joane. 1998. "Masculinity and nationalism: Gender and sexuality in the making of nations." *Ethnic and Racial Studies* 21 (2): 242–269.

Ndlovu-Gatsheni, Sabelo. 2009. *Do "Zimbabweans" Exist? Trajectories of Nationalism, National Identity Formation and Crisis in a Postcolonial State.* New York: Peter Lang.

Nelson, Lise. 1999. "Bodies (and spaces) do matter: The limits of performativity." *Gender, Place & Culture* 6 (4): 331–353.

Newitt, Malyn. 1995. *A History of Mozambique.* London: Hurst.

Paechter, Carrie. 2004. "Space, identity and education." *Pedagogy, Culture and Society* 2 (3): 307–308.

Peters, Michael. 2001. "National education policy constructions of the 'knowledge economy': Towards a critique." *Journal of Educational Enquiry* 2 (1): 1–22.

Pitcher, Anne. 2006. "Forgetting from above and memory from below: Strategies of legitimation and struggle in postsocialist Mozambique." *Africa* 76 (1): 88–112.

Robertson, Susan. 2005. "Re-imagining and rescripting the future of education: Global knowledge economy discourses and the challenge to education systems." *Comparative Education* 41 (2): 151–170.

Robinson, Fiona. 2006. "Care, gender and global social justice: Rethinking 'ethical globalization.'" *Journal of Global Ethics* 2 (1): 5–25.

Said, Edward. 1979. *Orientalism.* New York: Random House.

Shelley, Fred. 2013. *Nation Shapes: The Story Behind the World's Borders.* Santa Barbara, CA: ABC-CLIO.

Spivak, Gayatri Chakravorty. 1988. "Can the subaltern speak?" In *Marxism and the Interpretation of Culture*, edited by Cary Nelson and Lawrence Grossberg. Basingstoke: Macmillan, 271–313.

Spronk, Rachel. 2014. "The idea of African men: Dealing with the cultural contradictions of sex in academia and in Kenya." *Culture, Health & Sexuality: An International Journal for Research, Intervention and Care* 6 (5): 504–517. doi: 10.1080/13691058.2014.889755.

Stroud, Christopher. 1999. "Portuguese as ideology and politics in Mozambique: Semiotic (re)constructions of a postcolony." In *Language: Ideological Debates*, edited by Jan Blommaert. Berlin: Walter de Gruyter, 343–381.

Sumich, Jason, and João Honwana. 2007. *Strong Party, Weak State? FRELIMO and State Survival through the Mozambican Civil War: An Analytical Narrative on State-Making.* Crisis States Working Papers Series No. 2. London: LSE.

UNAIDS. 2013. *Global Report. UNAIDS Report on the Global AIDS Epidemic 2013.* Geneva: UNAIDS.

Yeğenoğlu, Meyda. 1998. *Colonial Fantasies: Towards a Feminist Reading of Orientalism.* Cambridge: Cambridge University Press.

Young, Iris Marion. 1990. *Justice and the Politics of Difference.* Princeton, NJ: Princeton University Press.

CHAPTER 11

Polish Children in Norway: Between National Discourses of Belonging and Everyday Experiences of Life Abroad

Paula Pustulka, Magdalena Ślusarczyk, and Stella Strzemecka

INTRODUCTION

I would like to live in a place that is a blend of Norway and Poland. It seems so strange to go for summer holidays to your own country, your home country. It somehow doesn't sound right. (Adrian, ten years old)

This chapter revolves around the issue of "blending" or hybridizing, as well as seeking to unpack the "why" in Adrian and other children's accounts of feeling peculiar or strange as youths with migratory backgrounds. To start with some illustrations, seven-year-old Marek, who arrived in Oslo three years ago, begins his meeting with the researcher by underscoring that he is not Norwegian; Norway-born Jan, also aged seven, keeps switching between talking about life and events in Poland and Norway—indicating that his life is happening "here and there." Finally, Sylwia, 12, browsing international fashion stores and websites on her iPad throughout the interview, states that English is her language of choice, thus demonstrating all the markers of being "a global teen." While the three examples pertain to the lives of three children all residing in Norway and born to Polish parents, their stories of (national) belonging and affinity are dissimilar, showcasing a range of identities that migrant children construct for themselves and narrate.

In order to explore when and how migrant children construct national and transnational identities, this chapter examines the stories shared by school-aged children with (a more or less pronounced but family-tied) Polish ethnic origin, as they speak about their dynamically changing identities while living with their families in Norway. Drawing on interviews with the children, we outline those dimensions of children's lives that relate to their subjective sense of belonging and articulations of identifications found on the national, transnational, and pan-national continuum (e.g., Purkayastha 2005; Somerville 2008; Veale and Donà 2014).

STUDYING MIGRANT CHILDREN'S EXPERIENCES— AN OVERVIEW

Broadly speaking, the theoretical framework employed is a response to a turn toward childhood studies (Prout and James 1990; Smart 2011, 100) and migration scholarship addressing the changes to the positionality of children in mobility (Hess and Shandy 2008; Orgocka 2012; Sime and Fox 2014a), which are supplemented by the Polish context of family and mobility nexus.

The focus and degree of scholarly reflection to migrant children are often tied to the disciplinary assumptions, under which "a migrant" may signify an adult (Dobson 2009, 355). In migration scholarship, it resulted in children being—similarly to women—overlooked as "tied leavers" who are "socially present but sociologically invisible" (Morokvasic 1983, 13–24; Devine 2009, 521), and prompted contemporary researchers to state that children's position was formerly equated with that of "luggage" (Orellana et al. 2001, 578). Current research pertaining to children "on the move" instead favors studies on child migrants and their agency (Hess and Shandy 2008, 765, 767) in the mobility processes (e.g., Purkayastha 2005; Somerville 2008; Ní Laoire et al. 2011; Sime and Fox 2014a). In a somewhat compensatory trend (e.g., Dobson 2009; Smart 2011, 100; Orgocka 2012, 2), it identifies an urgency to describe experiences of "growing up transnationally" from children's standpoints (De Lima, Whitehead, and Punch 2012; Sime and Fox 2014a, 2015). As a composite result of both the *childhood studies*, and a *transnational turn* in migration scholarship, the studies recognize that children's belonging is dynamically constructed. Therefore, children must be given a voice in the decision-making processes that directly affect them (Smart 2011, 101–102, 107). This approach complements earlier research proving that transnationally raised (now adult) children may benefit from diverse forms of bi-located social capital (Reynolds 2008). It also shows the positive effects of the maternal transnational "capital brokering" (mitigating the presumed disadvantages of ethnic minority backgrounds through networks, as well as language and competencies; see, e.g., Erel 2012), as well as engages in the debate on the effects of cultural and educational transnationalism (see, e.g., Hess and Shandy 2008; Ní Laoire et al. 2011; Tyrrell 2011; Ryan and Sales 2013).

In the latter, childhood studies-specific approach (e.g., Ensor and Goździak 2010, 3; Ní Laoire et al. 2011; Tyrrell et al. 2013; Sime and Fox 2014a, 2015), children's voices are seen as crucial for understanding the complex nature of European young people's belonging in the global era (Tyrrell et al. 2013). Caitríona Ní Laoire and colleagues, for instance, aimed to challenge the application of predetermined notions and the transgressed limitations of adult-centered mobility assumptions by employing active methods designed to highlight how children with Polish origin living in Ireland talked about their migrant trajectories (2011, 1–2). Reiterating that children's experiences vary from those of adults, it is vital to note that the negotiations and performances of identities in the destination countries are tangibly bound to both that new locale and the connections and affinities they have with the places that they (or their parents) come from (Ní Laoire et al. 2011, 7).

What sets the scene for the case of children of Polish origin is that Polish families of post-European Union accession largely follow the pattern of migrating in stages (or phases): from *pretransnational* (migration of one family member, separation) to *posttransnational* family. In addition, various scholars have argued that "Polish" global families are marked primarily by kinship-oriented transnational family practices (White 2011; Praszałowicz et al. 2013), and migration-decision processes are concerned with children's well-being (Ryan and Sales 2013). The scale, type, and consistency of belonging practices have so far been described from the adult family members' perspective (e.g., Pustułka 2014), but might similarly affect the sense of belonging among children and determine their alternative embeddedness: "exclusively there," "exclusively here," "here and there," or, even, in neither of the societies they are involved with, depending on a particular context.

It has been noted that children make more or less strategic but definitely reflective decisions about their sense of belonging(s), and in doing so creatively escape the essentialist "two cultures" trap (Adams and Kirova 2006; Ní Laoire et al. 2011). In this chapter, we wish to address the evident dearth of studies dedicated specifically to migrant

210 PAULA PUSTULKA ET AL.

children as agents within the intra-European Union post-2004 mobility, seeing children through the above lens—that is, as constantly navigating and negotiating fluid identities influenced by two (or more) national contexts and globalization. This allows for dynamically conceived research and analysis, conceptually useful for capturing lived realities, marked by attachments, performances, longings, and boundaries, extending beyond a simplistic view of ethnic/national identification (see Ní Laoire et al. 2011, 7–8) but nonetheless affected by (bi)national and global elements. In that sense, the analysis seeks to determine how identities are shaped or hybridized across the contexts of post-migration lives. The *rooting into place(s)* and *routes within mobilities* may point to interconnectedness and/or be indicative of what is known as multi-belonging (Ní Laoire et al. 2011, 8).

METHODOLOGICAL APPROACH

This study was conducted within the Transfam project dedicated to Polish migrant families in Norway.[1] The data comprise the preliminary findings from the *Children's Experiences of Growing up Transnationally* sub-study, which consisted of 50 interviews with children aged 6–13 living in Norway and born to at least one Polish parent.[2]

The approach relies on the arguments outlined by contemporary childhood studies' methodologies (e.g., Greene and Hill 2002; Dockett, Einarsdottir, and Perry 2011; Lambert, Glacken, and McCarron 2013). The qualitative technique of interviewing was tailored to reflect the call for children's spontaneous accounts and engaged participation (Mason and Danby 2011; Lambert et al. 2013), while meeting the standards of ethnical research conduct (e.g., obtaining parental and children's consent). The recruitment activities centered on visiting places frequented by Polish migrants (e.g., the Polish Saturday School in Oslo, School Consultation Point at the Polish Embassy, Caritas Infosenter, "Polsk Kino" film screenings, and the Holmenkollen Ski Festival) aided by subsequent snowball sampling. These strategies yielded a group of children from various backgrounds under the following recruitment criteria: children's age (6–13), residence in Oslo and its surroundings (up to 200 km radius), and an ability to communicate in Polish. A deliberately inclusive approach encompassed stories from children born in Poland and in Norway, children from ethnically homogeneous (Polish) as well as mixed-couple families that in addition represented a variety of family sizes, living arrangements (married/cohabitating/divorced parents), employment statuses (from professionals to laborers), and religious beliefs. Children also varied in regard to their length of stay in Norway (from several months to their whole lives).

The interviews with children (lasting from 20 minutes to almost 3 hours) yielded the core empiric material. Polish was the main language used by children during the interviews (with marginal usage of Norwegian and English). The language used and the fact of being interviewed by Polish researchers were examined as potential factors obscuring prompting the later discussed identification choices (Spyrou 2011), though it appears that children rather openly declared their belonging throughout the narratives. Active interview probing was paired with a task of drawing one's family for the younger children (6–9) and a sentence completion method test available in three language versions of the child's choice for the older children (9–13). Additional material was collected through a structured observation of children's rooms (see, e.g., Lambert et al. 2013).

All interviews were meticulously transcribed and analytical grids were used to combine material with field notes and findings from supplemental techniques. Coding procedures were used as an elementary data analysis process for breaking down, examining, comparing, conceptualizing, and categorizing text units of the interviews (Inowlocki 2000). The data analysis entailed narrowing the selected empirical evidence through a careful winnowing process, acknowledging that the researcher exercises a degree of judgment over the selection of data in crafting the vignettes and the profiles of the respondents (Wolcott 1994; Seidman 2013, 120–123). The ongoing data analysis comprises open and selective coding, in which interviews are initially treated as stand-alone cases, and are then subjected to cross-case comparisons.

MULTIPLE BELONGING AND RELATIONS

First and foremost, the children articulate their understanding of ethnic differences (Moinian 2009; Eriksen 2012) and they manage their own identifications, depending on their individual circumstances, surroundings, and the people they encounter. The children's awareness of difference is activated by socialization agents (family, school, peer groups), and signifies reflexivity in matters of their identifications and belonging. Notably, these aforementioned contexts entail socialization settings (Znaniecki 1973) of a different type—the private realm of home and family on one hand, and the "public" or institutional importance of schooling and peer groups on the other. Following the works of Ní Laoire et al. (2011), we assume that migrant children construct their identities in a relational and context-dependent way, as

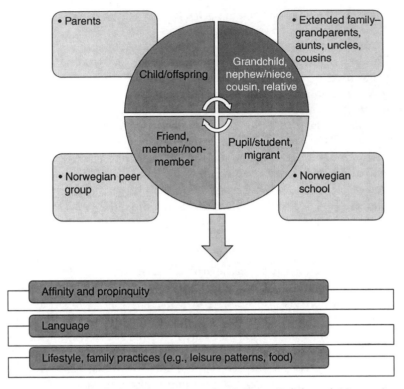

Figure 11.1 Multiple belongings and relations: Polish and Norwegian social contexts for children

illustrated by the model in Figure 11.1. Therefore, by examining *how*, *when*, and *why* children express and declare their belonging to either Poland or Norway, one can investigate everyday life factors—such as being in a temporally specific moment with certain people, as well as the presence of Polish/Norwegian elements (e.g., rituals, language skills) in family practices and within contact with the broader society (e.g., school, culture).

Affinity and Language—Polish Children in Norway or Young Norwegians of Polish Origin

While migration is often explained through national discourses in the narratives of adults, children have little awareness of Polish history as the nation's backbone. Instead, they largely associate "Poland" and understand being "Polish" through the relationships they have with their grandparents and cousins left behind. Despite the spatial separation, Aneta (nine), who lives in Bekkestua, has an emotional and close relationship with her grandmother who remains in Poland, evident in the fact that whenever she gets "sad or angry," she texts her:

> Always on a Saturday, every Saturday...when I call and our favourite TV programme *Win a Million* [a Polish game show] is on then and we always watch it together and speak to each other over the phone...And sometimes, when I should be sleeping but can't fall asleep I pretend that my grandma is there with me, [like during my visits to Poland].

For our respondents, grandparents have become "friends" who, unlike their busy parents, have the time they can invest in togetherness, which is often aligned with the transmission of "Polishness." The grandparents tell stories and legends, teach Polish history, correct the children when they speak Polish incorrectly, sign them up for Polish courses and summer camps, and foster relationships with other Polish kin. In that sense, they reinforce a national narrative that could otherwise be lost.

Although we particularly focus on the role of the grandparents, other kin and non-blood-related friends of the child are equally important:

> I don't have [siblings] but my Polish aunt [mother's sister] has a baby, who, well, now, she is almost big now and she is like a sister to me. We spend a lot of time together but only when I am at my aunt's place in Poland. (Karolina, eight)

When returning to her country of residence from a visit to Poland, Paulina (nine) has a sense of loss, saying that she would like to live there, be close to her grandmother and family, and that "her heart breaks" when she leaves for Norway:

> I would like to live in Poland because that would mean I would live close to my grandma and I would understand more at school. Whenever I visit Poland, I don't have the heart to leave for Norway. [When talking with her Norwegian friend at school about Poland] I speak a lot about how Poland is, talk about my grandma, and how things look like there, for instance that she has a dog, has 9 children, what she looks like, and what I do when I am there.

Oliwier (11) still regrets not being able to visit his grandmother and great-grandmother, who presumably do not travel abroad, and expresses a certain longing for connection, which causes an ambivalence about his life between two countries:

R: Do you like it here?
O: Hmm, very much so.
S: And what do you like best?
O: That here you can [do much], [it's a] big country. But just a little bit, yes, just somewhat I was also sad when I had to leave Poland...
S: And do you stay in touch with people in Poland?...
O: For me [Skype] is okay but ideally I like to see the other person...Not through a computer but "live", in person. I mean Skype also works but I don't want to speak on Skype too much. I can't talk to anyone—I only have one person in the contacts. And that's my mum's contact. I was going to ask my friends [in Poland]—one was going to give me [his Skype details], he was going to give it to me, but then he forgot his password and now I don't have it anymore.

For some children, the ties to Poland are somewhat incidental and relationally driven: Poland is (or becomes narratively) important mostly because certain significant others (i.e., kin) live there. As one might expect, the children's narratives often lack defined meanings of state, nationhood, or even local communities, but describe rather the local curiosities, differing holidays, and the like. It appears that parents cultivate this relational kind of more tangible bond with "nation" through family, as in children's accounts visits to Poland mostly comprise family practices—visits, celebrations, (care) obligations, and leisure activities. One of many examples for Poland being equated with family meetings can be seen in eight-year-old Klaudia's story:

> I like, like Poland very much. This is our tradition that we go to Poland [on holidays]. It is a family trip to my grandma and granddad...We are there for some time and then we come back...For me and Beata [sister], Poland is a second home, just not for the everyday...as that is more Norway. But it would be very sad without [going to] Poland.

Despite the persistence of transnationalism in families evidenced by, for example, an annual holiday in Poland, it should be noted that children's relationship to Poland is incidental in the sense of the particularity and "special" nature of the events connected to Polishness, such as rare rituals (e.g., attending the Polish First Communion ceremony) or contact with a given relative only once per year during the summer.

Consequently, the everyday life of the nuclear family is tied to Norway, even if we bear in mind that "children's identity formation is influenced by at least two distinct, and sometimes contradicting, cultural systems: the home culture and the school culture" (Adams and Kirova 2006, 8), too. For this reason, it is valid to assume that relationally constructed belonging to Poland will be declared by the children for as long as family bonds remain strong, especially since identity work is just as much directed at entering the society, belonging to the community, and being in coherence with social groups significant for the individuals.

The possible "belonging" constructions are always relational but must also take into account the temporal and life-course perspectives of children's development, as growing up and being a teenager generally has consequences in the form of weakened family bonds and a growing importance of the local Norwegian peer group, as well as global youth culture, which often transgresses national labels. In accordance with seeing identity as a process of evolving, one can see how the sense of belonging to Poland and the declaration of being a Pole may at a certain stage of life become "nested" (Medrano and Gutiérrez 2001), while the Norwegian sociocultural context leads to the creation of (additional) relationships (of differing strength and form) with Norwegian (national or localized) belonging, as well as possible emergence of other forms of Polishness or global ("citizen of the world") belonging. A fluid understanding allows for a multi-faceted composition of context-dependent feelings of belonging on a socio-temporal level.

Focusing on the subsequent component of national belonging and identities as closely associated with networks (Reynolds 2008; White 2011), it is crucial to acknowledge peer groups just as much as families. Karolina, even at the young age of eight, believes that being primarily in Norway means that this is where most of her closest friends are:

> I had friends in Poland—one girl and one boy. We used to play together, but now I can't find [and meet] them…When I go to Poland [these days] I live mostly with my Polish grandma. We sometimes bake a cake together…and generally do some cooking. And also sometimes I draw, watch the birds that come to eat the seeds…I would rather live here in Norway because this is where I have many friends. And here I spend the most time.

Interestingly, one can observe a feeling of loneliness that stems from the lack of a peer group in Poland: as much as family bonds with adults signify emotional propinquity, they increasingly become insufficient when there are no Polish peers in children's lives. Thus, while their pathways are likely to be marked by ambiguity at times, the children also often find a balance between different types of bonds in both countries, which are relationally created across borders. This is pinpointed by 12-year-old Dawid, who expressed acceptance and approval of his binational belonging and, when asked about friends, said:

> A lot are in Poland and a lot in Norway. I am friends with most of my [classmates], mostly with boys from Norway...I generally feel good in both countries.

So, at the same time, interactions with members of various groups serve as an important context of social comparisons (Giddens 1991) and requisition processes of self-positioning that determine how children frame their identity and sense of belonging (Kiuru 2008, 9; Ní Laoire et al. 2011, 73) and multicultural competencies within the context of global orders (Giddens 1991). Examining the processes of verbal self-labeling remains a crucial method for understanding the sense of belonging (Becker 1963), also among children, and in our analysis it corresponds well with the elements occurring in the model. Originating from the associations that one has about one's membership in different groups, self-labeling operates in the context of multiple choices, as a selection of "belongings" allows for a formulation of (subjective) identity and opinions about others (Becker 1963, 9). During interactions with others, the children not only negotiate their social positions and create bonds with others, but also need to dynamically redefine their status and inevitably make choices about their identities within a transnational realm (Ní Laoire et al. 2011, 155):

> Me, I am, well...Some people don't even know that I am from Poland when I talk to Norwegians...I like Norway also because many Polish people live here, and I like sport—the people [who I exercise with] are really great...I really like my life. (Marta, nine)

Among our respondents, self-positioning has predominantly been done in relation to Norwegian society, and included an evaluative component of whether or not they feel like they "fit in" (see also Ní Laoire et al. 2011, 156). Children often found it strange that they are Norwegian but can speak Polish. As such, language should be seen as one of the key factors that children understand as something that distinguishes them from their peers. Importantly, it is not necessarily knowing the language, but more its usage—both at home and in the public sphere—that determines the feeling of belonging to the two milieus. As children's everyday lives predominantly take place in Norway, they spend their days speaking Norwegian at school. At the same time, fluency in another language is a reason for pondering one's possible otherness and, as a consequence—"Polishness," as Igor (seven) expresses:

> I am not learning Norwegian. I know all the words already. I learnt it in kindergarten. I was not taught, it happened normally just so. I went online and learnt. I don't need to any more. I have taught myself. I am Polish, I am Polish, I am like... I am Norwegian. I can speak Polish— very strange, very, very strange.

As good observers of norms, values, and behaviors, children are capable of comparing and contrasting the elements that they attribute to the different national contexts of the sending and receiving societies, even though they are sometimes initially surprised or even confused by the realization of their unique positionality in the society they live in. Twelve-year-old Wojtek described these clashes of national discourses in a quote that illustrates not only the significance of ethnicity, but also the role of parental creative re-narrating of a rather negatively framed "us versus them" model of national/ethnic differences contingent on stories collected among other Poles who encounter cultural heterogeneity in the West[3] (see, e.g., Praszałowicz 2010, 49–51; D'Angelo and Ryan 2011, 254). It is valuable to take a look at the specific nature of Wojtek's narration—not only the meaning itself, but also the choice of wording, which suggests a Polish-Norwegian belonging with a strong connection to his parents' home country and ideals attached to those:

> Here in Norway children are interested in different things from me. They have their own different behaviors, different food. Different [sometimes] means same, but still they have their own. They have their national holiday on May 17th, it is therefore different...[Norwegians] have different rules. They believe that everyone should be friends... In Poland it is different: you have one best friend, one favorite friend. There's no requirement for everyone to play with everyone else, like here in Norwegian school [where teachers] say that this is how it must be. They [Norwegian peers] talk about things differently. They ask how much your dad makes, and how much your mum does... Norway is a very rich country. I understand that this is a very rich country, and that it is good that there are not only poor countries but also rich countries. Even though—come on!—talking about money in school is too much... This is what I think, but well, my mum now says that children

in Poland are also changing...But luckily my parents raised me well enough not to ask you how much money your father makes.

Notably, talking about Norway and Norwegians for Wojtek equals the use of the "they" pronoun, which stands in stark contrast with his language referring to Poland ("us") and, additionally, his story contained the usually absent reference to Poland as a society that is one's "own," something guided by somehow familiar rules, not only in family life:

> I am happy to go to Poland, as I can just go into a shop and say "I want this and that, a Tymbark [famous Polish food company] juice and some crisps". I feel like this is more my country, I can speak my language, can talk in my own national language to people. Here in Norway there are also nice people, yes, but I think that in Poland it is nicer. It is home, [at home] in the local community gardens many people know each other, because they are nice to each other. Simply put, in Poland I feel more like I am home than here.

For Wojtek, the opportunity to use Polish (which he considers his mother tongue) is significant, similarly to other occurrences rooted in daily life, such as buying a favorite Polish product (juice) and knowing the people in his neighborhood.

Keeping the various influences in mind, it is possible to explain why identities and belongings must be seen as dynamic, flexible, and subject to change, as they always somewhat depend on adults in respect to the affordability of journeys to Poland, grandparents' access to technologies (Internet, Skype), or presence of intra-family conflicts that may prevent children from "discovering" their Polishness.

Everyday Lives, Cultural Scripts, and "Obviousness"—Behaviors, Food, and Leisure

Following the arguments broadly outlined above, we further specifically argue that, particularly in the case of children, national identity is reproduced in what Michael Billig calls the "banality of the everyday" (1995, 6). Robert Foster (1999) delineates this from national identity in the political and patriotic sense, underlining the fact that identity practices are shaped by consumption patterns and everyday choices. This remains one of the easily identifiable areas of similarities and differences in identity-centered work:

> For them [Norwegians] a soup means something like tomato soup, or simply water with some add-on flavor, throw in some sausages and

carrots—here you go—that is "a soup". Or spaghetti—it [is] pasta with ketchup. And children normally eat it. My sisters eat it. I look at her and she said [she was having] ketchup with noodles, and I just glanced at her and said I would rather throw up and eat that rather than [her dish]. Or maybe not even then would I have eaten that. (Kasia, 13)

This example of culinary practices, as part of consumption practices discussed above, reflect the broader scholarship on "feeding the family" as a means of cultural transfer and caring, which is gaining interest in the Polish context. Both Agnieszka Bielewska (2013) and Izabella Main (2013) recently illustrated how migrants express Polishness through choosing Polish food, and they also discussed the importance of scheduling family meals in a certain way reflecting Polish customs. This kind of nostalgia for certain products and dishes as well as celebrating holidays primarily through food resurfaced in the stories of children:

Norway can become a bit boring. I am really missing my grandma's apple pie, Polish milk and also the yoghurts, Kubuś [Polish juice brand], as well as many, many things. That is why I like to take a ferry to Poland—it takes a lot of time but then you are allowed [i.e., unlike on the plane] to take a lot of milk with you. (Adrian, 10)

Many issues may be at play here, as children develop their own specific culinary and consumer preferences (e.g., the aforementioned Kubuś and Tymbark brands of juice are specifically targeted at children), but they may also evoke the broader family narrative about ways of preserving cultural identity practice that takes place in daily life abroad. These practices are often primarily associated with the grandparents' or "home" country, but they should be understood as forms of "displaying family"[4] (Finch 2007, 65–67), usually openly expressed toward both fellow conationals and other people who families happen to interact with. This is a form of demonstrating the elements of culture and identity that a migrant considers important, valuable, or distinctive. When they come into contact with different cultures, children notice, analyze, and describe a variety of situations, statements, practices, or ideas, and in doing so perform interpretations of cultural codes (see Rapaille 2007). The children were prone to displaying their cultural belonging and often wanted to proudly familiarize their "foreign" friends with Poland through food products:

[The Norwegians ask me at school] if, for example, we have different sweets, different candy. Because yes, there are many, many kinds in Poland that do not even sell, people do not buy so much of it..., while in Norway there are not many sweets, not many kinds, so they sell them out quick. So for example, Norwegians would really like to have all this candy, right? They only have one shop—for example Sandvika. However, there you can also find sweets that are originally from Poland. For example, Wedel [old and famous Polish chocolatier] sweets are there, things from Poland and other countries. For instance you see...mayonnaise that is called Kielecki [an adjective for something from the Polish town of Kielce and also an established brand of condiments]—you then know that this is a Polish product. Recently a friend of mine showed it to me at her home [but] she did not know it was from Poland...I think she would not have bought it had she known it was Polish...This one time I brought some Polish sweets to school—just so that the others could taste them, and they immediately asked me how much they were. And they were cheap, because they were from Poland, and they told me how expensive these sweets would have been to buy in Norway.

Alongside the culinary practices, lifestyle, leisure, and consumer choices factor into strengthening or decreasing one's sense of belonging to either the sending or the receiving country. The leisure patterns and modes of spending holidays "like the Norwegians do" were often conceived of as something facilitating belonging, as was the fulfillment of the more materialistic cravings (i.e., possessing particular electronic devices or a specific brand of items of clothing) under this strategy. The alternative choice pertained to being proud of one's uniqueness, which has taken the form of teaching school friends some Polish vocabulary, describing Polish customs and traditions, or debating famous Polish sportsmen:

> Sometimes I talk to my friends from school about Poland, especially when Kamil Stoch [Polish Olympic ski jumping champion] was in Norway. Also about Marit Bjørgen, Justyna Kowalczyk [among the world's top female cross-country skiing competitors]. So I talk about Kowalczyk and then I start speaking about Poland. The same goes for tennis and Agnieszka Radwańska [Polish female tennis player]. (Marta, nine)

Finally, while the elements of national culture might be promoted by migrant children's grandparents via intergenerational value transfer, and the Norwegian way of life supplies the backbone of daily life, Henry Jenkins (2006) argues that communication technologies facilitate the extra-generational youth mass culture transmission of styles and fashions, and teenagers from distant localities copy American youths, who simultaneously draw on these "foreign" inspirations. In a rapid cultural exchange, similarities belong to the area of leisure patterns and the likeliness of a degree of homogeneity when geographically (and culturally) separated youths of similar ages are likely to play the very same computer game or hum the same English pop song. Let us hear from Oliwier (11):

> O: My mum does not like to play on the computer but I really do.
> R: What games do you play?
> O: The Lego games. One I have already completed...And sometimes my [Norwegian] friend asks [online] "Where are you, you Pole?" Just for fun, not in a serious manner but just jokingly when she is trying to find me in the [online] game. Because we have this one very popular computer game.
> R: Which game is that?
> O: Minecraft.

Indeed, the child respondents in this study uniformly referred to the Minecraft computer game, specific Lego block sets, and particular characters from what Jenkins (2006, 155) has called pop-cosmopolitanism and can be seen as yet another shape of belonging—a "citizen of the world" ideal of hybridity, which replaces hierarchical ethnic/national discourses.

CLOSING REMARKS

Alongside hybridization, our findings foreground Steph Lawler's (2008) claims on identities as produced and embedded in social relationships, which are flexibly adapted to situational daily life practices. Belonging should therefore be addressed through the contextual lens—not an inherent, stable, and individual trait, but rather as something that children (just like adults; Lawler 2008) construct and dynamically negotiate with others. Importantly, children's identities are not only influenced by geographic or national spaces but also equally determined by temporality—the moment of time and the passing of time cause children's self-labels dynamically shift. In this way, identity is not something we have, but something we do, and is a cursively constructed category that can serve a variety of purposes (Potter and Wetherell 1987), as Beata's (13) words express:

> I was told that I have been asking who I was since I was little. I would ask what I should say when someone asked me who I was. My mum would say: "If you want, you can say you are half-Polish and half-Norwegian, or that you are Norwegian but your mum is from Poland."

While numerous works propose to treat national cultures as "hybrids," mosaics of multiple elements rather than monoliths (e.g., García Canclini 1995), the arguably homogeneous Polish society fosters nation-building on the pillars of ethnicity and religion (Zielińska 2010), which plagues the research on Polish mobility. While Poland experiences some influx of migrants, the low numbers and visibility do not necessitate a debate on multiculturalism or diversity (Slany and Slusarczyk 2008). Conversely, we argue that our respondents exhibit hybridity (to a varying degree), further agreeing with Ingunn Eriksen's reading of Bhabha on the need to avoid the term "multicultural," because it hides "the fact that cultures exist on uneven ground, where one culture often occupies the center, while others are in peripheral positions" (Eriksen 2012, 27). For our respondents, the two national contexts of Poland and Norway were clearly registered and generally it was (with few exceptions) not uncommon for one identity to be foregrounded, or even for the two ethnic contexts to be in competition, though this occurred in specific situations when displaying one or other ethnic identity was somewhat unavoidable. Conversely, many children managed to fittingly navigate relational dimensions of their ethnic identities across their differing environments.

The notion of "hybrid" belonging used to understand children's identities in this study takes into consideration the fact that Polish and Norwegian accents or cultural aspects, values, and customs must neither be evenly placed nor similarly shaped across various stories of individuals. They instead depend on where and with whom they are inter-negotiated. As Carola Suárez-Orozco and Marcelo Qin-Hilliard suggest (2004, 2): "While human lives continue to be lived in local realities, these realities are increasingly being challenged and integrated into larger global networks and relationships." These processes are coupled with children growing up in nation-states that "continue to regroup in fundamental ways on supranational lines" (Suárez-Orozco and Qin-Hilliard 2004, 9) and experiencing further cultural changes that are rapidly altering young people's experiences of youth. The entanglement of the migration and globalization processes leads to the reframing of the earlier concepts of "culture shock" and "loss." After overcoming initial difficulties, children's identity formations are usually inherently marked by cultural hybridity and relational constructions of belonging (Inda and Rosaldo 2002, 13–14; Reynolds 2008) necessitated by "superdiversity" (Vertovec 2007).

Therefore, all dimensions of socialization should be acknowledged as important for the analyses of children's narrations pertaining to national identities and sense of belonging (see also Ní Laoire et al.

2011, 155–156), which must be examined in a holistic manner, rather than bound to a singular environment of family, school, or peer group, or even pop culture that are truly mutually entangled.

NOTES

1. The research leading to these results received funding from the Polish-Norwegian Research Programme operated by the National Centre for Research and Development under the Norwegian Financial Mechanism 2009–2014 in the framework of Project Contract No. Pol-Nor/197905/4/2013.

2. Significantly, these were largely conducted concurrently to interviews with parents done within a second sub-study of the TRANSFAM project. While we do not discuss the findings from parental interviews in this chapter, it is important to acknowledge the particular undergird of intrafamilial multi-perspective and the validity that these interviews ensured during the complementary data analysis.

3. Polish national identity remains built on the notions of universal unity pertaining to race/ethnicity and religion (Katarzyna Zielińska, "W poszukiwaniu nowej wspólnoty? Feministki o narodzie, obywatelstwie i demokracji," in *Ponad granicami: Kobiety, migracje, obywatelstwo*, ed. Marta Warat and Agnieszka Małek [Kraków: Wydawnictwo Uniwersytetu Jagiellońskiego, 2010]). The macro-level data, which portrays social reality and affects the perceptions of homogeneity, shows that 98.6 percent of the Polish population is White-European, with 97.7 percent ethnic Poles (NSP 2011). During the 2011 census, only 1.44 percent among the 39 million residents stated that they are descendants of a single ancestry other than Polish. Ninety-eight percent of the inhabitants declare Polish as their first language (Eurobarometr 2012) and 87.5 percent of the population is Roman Catholic (NSP 2011). Regardless of high out-migration, the influx of foreigners to Poland is relatively low, estimated at around 100,000 (UdSC).

4. Drawing on H. G. David Morgan's (*Family Connections: An Introduction to Family Studies* [Cambridge: Polity Press, 1996]; and *Rethinking Family Practices* [Basingstoke: Palgrave Macmillan, 2011]) scholarship that centralizes family activities as the main scholarly research for defining what family is, Finch similarly focuses on what families do, and what sorts of meanings they assign to the various things they do. She defines "displaying family" as "the process by which individuals, and groups of individuals, convey to each other and to relevant audiences that certain of their actions do constitute 'doing family things' and thereby confirm that these relationships are 'family' relationships'" (Janet Finch, "Displaying Families," *Sociology* 41 (1) (2007): 67). In migration research, "displaying families" can be seen as an interface and interplay between family practices performed by the "majority" opposite ethnic minorities.

REFERENCES

Adams, Leah, and Anna Kirova. 2006 *Global Migration and Education: Schools, Children, and Families*. London: Routledge.

Becker, Howard S. 1963 *Outsiders: Studies in the Sociology of Deviance*. New York: Macmillan.

Bhabha, Homi. 2002. "Of mimicry and man: The ambivalence of colonial discourse." In *Race Critical Theories*, edited by Philomena Essed and David T. Goldberg. Malden, MA: Blackwell.

Bielewska, Agnieszka. 2013. "Kupowanie polskości—Tożsamość narodowa jako towar wśród polskiej migracji poakcesyjnej w Wielkiej Brytanii." In *Młoda polska emigracja w UE jako przedmiot badań psychologicznych, socjologicznych i kulturowych*, edited by Dorota Praszałowicz, Magdalena Łużniak-Piecha, and Joanna Kulpińska. http://www.euroemigranci.pl/dokumenty/pokonferencyjna/Bielewska.pdf. Accessed July 24, 2014.

Billig, Michael. 1995. *Banal Nationalism*. London: Sage.

D'Angelo, Alessio, and Louise Ryan. 2011. "Sites of socialization—Polish parents and children in London schools." *Studia Migracyjne—Przegląd Polonijny* 1: 237–258.

De Lima, Philomena, Ann Whitehead, and Samantha Punch. 2012 "Exploring children's experiences of migration: Movement and family relationships." CRFR Research Briefing, 61. https://www.era.lib.ed.ac.uk/bitstream/1842/6555/1/briefing%2061.pdf. Accessed December 10, 2013.

Devine, Dympna. 2009. "Mobilising capitals? Migrant children's negotiation of their everyday lives in the primary school." *British Journal of Sociology of Education* 30 (5): 521–535.

Dobson, Madeleine E. 2009. "Unpacking children in migration research." *Children's Geographies* 7 (3): 355–360.

Dockett, Sue, Johanna Einarsdottir, and Bob Perry. 2011. "Balancing methodologies and methods in researching with young children." In *Researching Young Children's Perspectives*, edited by Deborah Harcourt, Bob Perry, and Tim Waller, 68–83. New York: Routledge.

Ensor, Marisa O., and Elżbieta M. Goździak (eds.). 2010. *Children and Migration: At the Crossroads of Resiliency and Vulnerability*. New York: Palgrave Macmillan.

Erel, Umut. 2012. "Engendering transnational space: Migrant mothers as cultural currency speculators." *European Journal of Women's Studies* 19 (4): 460–474.

Eriksen, Ingunn M. 2012. "Young Norwegians belonging and becoming." PhD diss., Department of Culture Studies and Oriental Languages, Faculty of Humanities, University of Oslo.

Finch, Janet. 2007. "Displaying Families." *Sociology* 41 (1): 65–81.

Foster, Robert. 1999. "The commercial construction of 'new nations.'" *Journal of Material Culture* 4 (3): 263–282.

García Canclini, Nestor. 1995. *Hybrid Cultures: Strategies for Entering and Leaving Modernity.* Minneapolis: University of Minnesota Press.

Giddens, Anthony. 1991. *Modernity and Self-Identity: Self and Society in the Late Modern Age.* Stanford, CA: Stanford University Press.

Goulbourne, Harry, Tracey Reynolds, John Solomos, and Elisabetta Zontini. 2010. *Transnational Families: Ethnicities, Identities and Social Capital.* London: Routledge.

Greene, Sheila, and Malcolm Hill. 2002. "Conceptual, methodological and ethical issues in researching children's experience." In *Researching Children's Experience Approaches and Methods,* edited by Sheila Greene and Diane Hogan. London: Sage.

Hess, Julia M., and Dianna Shandy. 2008. "Kids at the crossroads: Global childhood and the state." *Anthropological Quarterly* 81 (4): 765–776.

Inda, Jonathan X., and Renato Rosaldo (eds.). 2002 *The Anthropology of Globalization.* Malden, MA: Wiley-Blackwell.

James, Allison, and Alan Prout,(eds.). 1990. *Constructing and Reconstructing Childhood.* London: Falmer.

Jenkins, Henry. 2006. "Pop cosmopolitanism: Mapping cultural flows in an age of media convergence." *Fans, Bloggers, and Gamers: Exploring Participatory Culture,* 152–172. New York: University Press.

Kiuru, Noona. 2008. "The role of adolescents' peer groups in the school context." *Jyväskylä Studies in Education, Psychology and Social Research* 331. http://julkaisut.jyu.fi/?id=978-951-39-3128-5. Accessed July 17, 2014.

Lambert, Veronica, Michele Glacken, and Mary McCarron. 2013. "Using a range of methods to access children's voices." *Journal of Research in Nursing* 18 (7): 601–616.

Lawler, Steph. 2008. *Identity: Sociological Perspective.* Cambridge: Polity.

Main, Izabella. 2013. "Zmiany praktyk kulinarnych wśród polskich emigrantek w Barcelonie i Berlinie." In *Młoda polska emigracja w UE jako przedmiot badań psychologicznych, socjologicznych i kulturowych,* edited by Dorota Praszałowicz, Magdalena Łużniak-Piecha, and Joanna Kulpińska. http://www.euroemigranci.pl/dokumenty/pokonferencyjna/Main.pdf. Accessed July 27, 2014.

Mason, Jan, and Susan J Danby. 2011. "Children as experts in their lives: Child inclusive research." *Child Indicators Research* 4: 185–189, doi:10.1007/s12187-011-9108-4.

Medrano, Juan Díez, and Paula Gutiérrez. 2001. "Nested identities: National and European identity in Spain." *Ethnic and Racial Studies* 24 (5): 753–778.

Moinian, Farzaneh. 2009. "I am just me: Children talking beyond ethnicity and cultural identities!" *Childhood* 16 (1): 31–48.

Morgan, David H. G. 2011. *Rethinking Family Practices.* Basingstoke: Palgrave Macmillan.

Morgan, David H. G. 1996. *Family Connections: An Introduction to Family Studies.* Cambridge: Polity Press.

226 ✦ PAULA PUSTULKA ET AL.

Ní Laoire, Caitríona, Allen White, Naomi Tyrrell, and Fina Carpena-Mendez. 2013. "Children's roles in transnational migration." In *Transnational Migration and Childhood*, edited by Naomi Tyrrell, Allen White, Caitríona Ní Laoire, and Fina Carpena Mendez, 1–12. Abingdon: Routledge.

Ní Laoire, Caitríona, Fina Carpena-Méndez, Naomi Tyrrell, and Allen White. 2011. *Childhood and Migration in Europe: Portraits of Mobility, Identity and Belonging in Contemporary Ireland*. UK: Ashgate.

Orellana, Marjorie F., Barrie Thorne, Anna Chee, and Wan Shun Eva Lam. 2001. "Transnational childhoods: The participation of children in processes of family migration." *Social Problems* 48 (4): 572–591.

Orgocka, Aida. 2012. "Vulnerable yet agentic: Independent child migrants and opportunity structures." *New Directions for Child and Adolescent Development* 136: doi: 10.1002/cad.20007.

Potter, Jonathan, and Margaret Wetherell. 1987. *Discourse and Social Psychology: Beyond Attitudes and Behaviour*. London: Sage.

Praszałowicz, Dorota. 2010. *Polacy w Berlinie: Strumienie migracyjne i społeczności imigracyjne*. Kraków: Księgarnia Akademicka.

Praszałowicz, Dorota, Małgorzata Irek, Agnieszka Małek, Paulina Napierała, Paulina Pustułka, and Joanna Pyłat. 2013. *Polskie szkolnictwo w Wielkiej Brytanii*. http://pau.krakow.pl/Polskie_szkolnictwo_UK/Polskie_szkolnictwo_UK_RAPORT.pdf. Accessed July 24, 2014.

Purkayastha, Bandana. 2005. *Negotiating Ethnicity: Second-Generation South Asian Americans Traverse a Transitional World*. New Brunswick: Rutgers University Press.

Pustułka, Paula. 2014. "Child-centred narratives of Polish migrant mothers: Cross-generational identity constructions abroad." *Migration Studies* 3: 151–170.

Rapaille, Clotaire. 2007. *The Culture Code: An Ingenious Way to Understand Why People around the World Live and Buy as They Do*. New York: Broadway Books.

Reynolds, Tracey. 2008. "Ties that bind: Families, social capital and Caribbean second generation return migration." *Sussex Centre for Migration Research Working Paper* no. 46.

Ryan, Louise, and Rosemary Sales. 2013. "Family migration: The role of children and education in family decision-making strategies of Polish migrants in London." *International Migration Review* 51 (2): 90–103.

Sargent, Jonathon, and Deborah Harcourt. 2012. *Doing Ethical Research with Children*. New York: Open University Press.

Seidman, Irving. 2013. *Interviewing as Qualitative Research: A Guide for Researchers in Education and the Social Sciences*. New York: Teachers College Press.

Sime, Daniela, and Rachael Fox. 2014a. "Migrant children, social capital and access to services post-migration: Transitions, negotiations and complex agencies." *Children & Society* doi: 10.1111/chso.12092.

POLISH CHILDREN IN NORWAY � 227

————. 2015. "Home abroad: Eastern European children's family and peer relationships after migration." *Childhood* 22 (3): 377–393. doi: 10.1177/0907568214543199.

Slany, Krystyna, and Magdalena Ślusarczyk. 2008. "Immigrants in Poland: Legal and socio-demographic situation." In *Migration and Mobility in an Enlarged Europe: A Gender Perspective*, edited by Sigrid Metz-Goeckel, Mirjana Morkvasic, and A. Senganata Münst, 281–301. Opladen and Farrington Hills: Barbara Budrich.

Smart, Carol. 2011. "Children's personal lives." In *Sociology of Personal Life*, edited by Vanessa May, 98–108. Basingstoke and New York: Palgrave Macmillan.

Somerville, Kara. 2008. "Transnational belonging among second generation youth: Identity in a globalized world." *Journal of Social Sciences, Special Issue on Youth and Migration* 10: 23–33.

Spyrou, Spyros. 2011. "The limits of children's voices: From authenticity to critical, reflexive representation." *Childhood* 18 (2): 151–165.

Suárez-Orozco, Carola, and Marcelo Suárez-Orozco. 2001. *Children of Immigration*. Cambridge, MA: Harvard University Press.

Suárez-Orozco, Marcelo, and Desiree B. Qin-Hilliard. *Globalization: Culture and Education in the New Millennium*. Berkeley, Los Angeles, and London: University of California Press.

Tyrrell, Naomi. 2011. "Children's agency in family migration." In *Everyday Ruptures: Children, Youth and Migration in Global Perspective*, edited by Cati Coe, Rachel R. Reynolds, Deborah A. Boehm, Julia Meredith Hess, and Heather Rae-Espinoza, 23–38. Nashville: Vanderbilt.

Tyrrell, Naomi, Allen White, Caitríona Ní Laoire, and Fina Carpena Mendez (eds.). 2013. *Transnational Migration and Childhood*. Abingdon: Routledge.

Veale, Angela, and Giorga Donà. 2014. *Child and Youth Migration: Mobility-in-Migration in an Era of Globalization*. Basingstoke, UK: Palgrave Macmillan.

Vertovec, Steven. 2007. "Super-diversity and its implications." *Ethnic and Racial Studies* 29 (6): 1024–1054.

White, Anne. 2011. *Polish Families and Migration since EU Accession*. Bristol: Policy Press.

Wolcott, Harry F. 1994. *Transforming Qualitative Data: Description, Analysis, and Interpretation*. London: Sage.

Zielińska, Katarzyna. 2010. "W poszukiwaniu nowej wspólnoty? Feministki o narodzie, obywatelstwie i demokracji." In *Ponad granicami: Kobiety, migracje, obywatelstwo*, edited by Marta Warat and Agnieszka Małek, 63–85. Kraków: Wydawnictwo Uniwersytetu Jagiellońskiego.

Znaniecki, Florian. 1963. *Socjologia wychowania*. T. I. Warszawa: PWN.

CHAPTER 12

Educating "Supermen" and "Superwomen": Global Citizenship Education

Tatjana Zimenkova

INTRODUCTION

The orientation toward global issues emerges as an integral part of educational practices and policies in many parts of the world. Often curricula and educational materials produce a harmonious picture of responsible citizens, easily switching between different loyalties and obligations and profiting from globalization processes. This picture is challenged by questions of nation-state interests, and citizens' responsibilities and loyalties. This chapter elaborates empirically on the questions of what modes of self-perceptions, loyalties, and responsibilities the Russian curricula and educational programs suggest to the learner with the depiction of global issues. The chapter differentiates between global learning as opposed to political global citizenship education. By reflecting on power in the analysis, I point to the roles ascribed to the learning citizens in the two different conceptions, articulate some questions those conceptions raise, and argue for global citizenship education as *political* education (Zimenkova 2012), a form of education addressing learners' *agency*, rights, and duties in a global context.

FRAMING THE ISSUE OF GLOBAL CITIZENSHIP

The very idea of citizenship is challenged in multiple ways by processes of globalization, transnationalization, and glocalization, as well as by the emergence of supranational political institutions (such as the European Union). Citizenship is no more an exclusive status of belonging to one nation-state (Kivisto and Faist 2009). Processes of migration bring about the transnationalisation of citizenship, resulting in multiple belongings, (dis)empowerments, and loyalties of citizens (Koopmans 2005; Kivisto and Faist 2007; Faist and Gerdes 2009; Pfaff-Czarnecka 2011). Global economic and ecological processes erode (or enlarge) borders of phenomena, challenging the life of citizens, and create new responsibilities, possibilities, and necessities of political influence, and result in new forms of ecological, economical, technological, and global citizenships (Falk 1994; Sáiz 2005) and those notions of citizenship that embrace nonhumans (Donaldson and Kymlicka 2011). At the same time, these notions bring about a range of citizen participation practices that are *beyond* conventional participation forms open exclusively to citizens of a certain nation-state (Norris 2011).

Global citizenship is both intuitively understandable and, if citizenship is seen as an (exclusive) office with rights and duties (Macket and Müller 2000, 16; Turner 2000a, 251), is difficult, if at all possible, to execute. Theories of citizenship and participation connect global citizenship to issues beyond national borders. Citizens should or would like to have influence on environmental, technological, and economic developments that result from globalization processes and call for transnational participation (see Falk 1994; Sáiz 2005). However, the concept of political citizen participation not bound to a nation-state reveals one of the fundamental theoretical tensions in our understanding of citizenship. Is citizenship the activity of a political subject (Barber 1984) or primarily a status granted by birth or naturalization? Processes of global migration have made this tension extremely relevant. Sometimes political participation in one's country of residence is impossible due to citizenship status, and active noncitizens are excluded from participation while citizens are disinterested in participating. The ethical considerations attached to the interrelatedness of the world might debilitate a citizen's actions due to the legal participation frameworks open to her.[1] For example, an active environmentalist might be moved to participate in political contexts due to her perception of global belonging and global responsibility but she might not have the rights of participation she *assumes* to have. In this case her desire to act is stronger than what political regulations of citizenship afford. Further on, her (political) actions might be motivated by a nonpolitical understanding of citizenship, connected not to power and insubordinations (Norris 2011, Gallagher 2008) but rather to a global *ethics* of interconnectedness of all living beings; thus, her activity is not a matter of *choice*, but the matter of impossibility of nonacting. Thus, political questions connected to global citizenship include the following: Who grants it? Who guarantees the (equal or universal) rights of global citizens? Who are these citizens (see, e.g., the issue of widening citizen rights to animals and nature [Turner 2000b])? Which responsibilities do (global) citizens have? And if they do have responsibilities and take on duties, who shall instruct them on how to fulfill them?

This chapter seeks to demarcate the differences between *global citizenship education* and *global learning*, demonstrating why the latter seems to be more compatible with the curricula that aim at educating a *nation's* citizen. Looking through the lenses of political theory and sociology, I demonstrate how the current challenges to the sovereignty of the nation-states (Held 2011, 165) are mirrored by the curricula and educational programs on global issues. By the means of curriculum analysis, I empirically describe (Oevermann 1979, 1993; Mayring 1997) the messages and modes of self-perception suggested to the learner and seek to depict conradictions (possibly) perceived by the learner that result from the twofold orientation toward global issues and national citizenship.

In this chapter I argue for global citizenship education as *political* education (Zimenkova 2012), which means a form of education that addresses learners' *agency*, rights, and duties in a global context. Global citizenship education as political education gives learners an idea of the powers at large in global processes and of their own power and powerlessness (Gallagher 2008) in light of global challenges. Global citizenship education addresses learners as capable of understanding the origins and interconnectedness of global problems and issues. These learners then can empower themselves to make political decisions and reflect on their own motivation, or lack thereof, as well as on opportunities for acting. The analysis below also demonstrates possibilities, challenges, and limits of global citizenship education as *political* education.

Certainly, the range of theoretical thought on global citizenship cannot be adequately presented here. The focus is rather on a few aspects of these theoretical considerations that are relevant to the challenges and (im)possibilities of global citizenship *education*. Using the example of Russia, this chapter focuses on challenges that national education policies (curricula) and practice (programs) face due to the globalization processes and the ways they respond to the complex and, at least for a nation-state, ambiguous task to educate *global* citizens. The Russian example was chosen because the education system very rarely frames the multicultural or cosmopolite discourse within the educational system (Zimenkova 2014, 210) if one compares it to the educational systems working strongly with conceptions of multiculturalism and cosmopolitanism (Mitchell 2003, 391ff.). Looking at the Russian example makes it possible to consider specific dimensions of global citizenship education as a challenge for a *nation-state* without involving a philosophical discourse on cosmopolitism but rather by detecting empirically whether elements of the cosmopolite discourse are traceable within the educational system in question (Nussbaum 1996; Heater 2004; Delanty 2006). The Russian case offers less challenge to identify these dimensions since the cosmopolite discourse does not trace over them. Despite the weak development of a cosmopolite educational discourse, *global issues* are articulated within Russian political and civic education, just as they are articulated in educational systems of other countries (e.g., Germany, France, Turkey, Bulgaria, and other countries; see Schissler and Soysal 2005). However, the presentation of global issues are challenging within educational systems with an explicit *nation-state goal setting* just as they are challenging within those educational systems that work intensively with discourses on multiculturalism and cosmopolitanism in education (Nussbaum 1996; Mitchell 2007).

The idea of global citizenship is accompanied by dilemmas that are essential to teaching and learning about global issues. Through the consideration of only two of the many dilemmas presented by global citizenship, as summarized by Nigel Dower (2002), it becomes visible how different actors in the education system might have different goals with respect to education about global issues or global citizenship. The dilemmas identified by Dower (2002) are, among others:

> Ethical or institutional? (a) World citizenship is an essentially ethical conception about what people ought morally to do. (b) World citizenship is an essentially institutional conception about membership of institutions of a specifically global kind.... Challenge to national citizenship? (a) World citizenship challenges national citizenship/loyalty. (b) World citizenship does not challenge national citizenship/loyalty but complements it. (30, 38)

With these two dilemmas in mind, one could ask: Who educates young citizens about global issues? What are the educational agendas? Should learners be motivated to act as global citizens? Which responsibilities, self-perceptions, and conceptions of citizenship might arise through different types of global learning? And, finally and centrally, are *global learning* and *education for global citizenship* complimentary, contradictory, or interchangeable concepts? And if their relations are unclear to the actors promoting educational policies and practices and to educators, what does this mean for learners?

CITIZENS: POLITICALLY OR ETHICALLY ACTING

The political, economic, environmental, and social developments of the world are seemingly mirrored by curricula and conceptions, seeking to educate global citizens or to help (young) people orienting themselves in a globalized world. Those responsible for educational policies and practices, and educational materials on global issues, often produce, at least on the surface, a rather harmonious picture of responsible citizens. These citizens are constructed as easily switching between different identities, feel comfortable despite varying loyalties, and fulfill their obligations while contributing to ideals of freedom, inclusion, cohesion, equality, and environmental protection as they profit from mobility and the educational opportunities of globalization processes (a picture Martha Nussbaum would probably support as long as the priorities of cosmopolite thinking are guaranteed: cf. Nussbaum 1996, 10). Even the neoliberal turn in policies and practices of multicultural or cosmopolitan education in many countries directs education toward an "ethical self" who maintains a global openness and takes as its premise the *accessibility* of global goods for everyone, given adequate education. Critiques of the neoliberal subject are many, such as Katharyne Mitchell (2003, 296, 399) who terms the neoliberal "ethical self" as the "superior footsoldier of global capitalism."

However, the harmonious picture of the global citizen in educational materials is challenged by some basic questions and tensions inherent to educational systems, not to mention within ideas of educators and consequently learners. Some of these questions are what are the limitations of global citizenship education within a national setting? How do educational conceptions, which suggest that citizen actions are unconstrained to the learner, cope with existing limitations of global actions, or those of political (e.g., citizenship rights) or economic nature (e.g., visa and labor market regulations)? Which aspects of global issues might be incompatible with the educational interests of the nation-state? Do educational approaches within the supranational settings (e.g., the European Union) make education about global issues easier or perhaps more complicated? Where should global citizens, according to different educational approaches, place their loyalty? And do conflicts emerge out of citizens' different loyalties and attachments? Are there differences between educating about global issues and educating global citizens (Davies 2006)?

Global citizenship education as part of the curriculum is prevalent in the appearance of global topics within compulsory subjects, such as politics, history, ecology, and economics. *Global learning* is a broader phenomenon addressing global issues in an educational context and whether or not they require any action on the part of citizens. It *informs* learners about the challenges and problems of global contexts and suggests frameworks for action. Global learning can address global political participation, but does not necessarily do so; it can as well be based, for example, on global ethics. It might as well address and educate toward global *action*, without reflecting on political *powers* involved in them or on the (dis)empowerment of an acting citizen. As an example, both types of education (*global citizenship education* and *global learning*) might address the same charity actions, the first one would, however, provide the political reflection on why the situation, causing the necessity of the charity action, appeared (e.g., a postcolonial perspective critical of power relations) and demonstrate possible ways of using citizens' power in order to influence the situation. The second type would rather offer experiences of poverty in different contexts and would appeal to the ethical responsibility of a learner as a human being. Within this chapter I examine different aspects of these two types of educational processes and frame some challenges concerning *political citizenship issues* within global education.

What I address as *global learning* is partly close to cosmopolitan education; however, the impressive work on conceptualizations of cosmopolitanism and cosmopolitan education done by many researchers so far describes much broader phenomena than global learning or global citizenship education as described in this chapter. The very *notion* of cosmopolitanism and cosmopolitan openness already considers the engagement beyond the borders and limitations of the nation-state (citizenship) as a given condition (e.g., Linklater 1998; Skrbiš and Woodward 2011, 61ff.), and is based on theories of globalization and global political participation (Kivisto and Faist 2007; Martell 2007; Robinson 2007). This chapter starts one step before the emergence of cosmopolite thought in educational contexts and in learners. It focuses on a *nation state's* challenges in educating global citizens (the relevancy of this aspect is underlined by exciting observations, such as Mitchell's [2003, 399] description of patriotic elements emerging from multicultural education). In the context of nation-state curricula on citizenship, the orientation toward global citizenship is not (yet) a self-evident idea. I state this with the qualification of understanding global citizenship differently to the "strategic cosmopolitanism" referred to by Mitchell (2003, 2007, 4) or the neoliberal concept of Lifelong Learning designed to improve the economic productivity of the individual in the context of a flexible labor market (cf. Fragoso and Guimaraes 2010, 18ff.[2]). However, even these concepts engage with self-responsibility of the economic citizen to orient herself in the global economy and to learn to profit from it (and through this maintain economic power of her home country). Yet the *political loyalties* do not go beyond (and definitely do not develop contrary to) those of a nation-state citizen.

RESEARCH METHODOLOGY

I analyze the Russian general federal curricula, the federal standards for social science subjects (social science, economics and law, history, and geography—in effect until 2010[3]) as well as the general standards of education[4] (in effect after 2012; see curricula list below) with the help of a combination of inductive and deductive category building (Reinhoffer 2005). The method of sequential analysis (Oevermann 1979, 1993; Wernet 2000) was combined with qualitative content analysis (Mayring 1997; Jensen 2000).

First of all, I examined the curricula with the help of qualitative content analysis (Mayring 1997). I identified through this method topics such as international relations, history of international relations, globalization, place of Russia in the world, multicultural relations, international legislation, and so on. In this analysis I included all parts of the curricula dealing with any affairs that required consideration beyond one nation-state as well as those where the sovereignty of the given nation-state was mentioned explicitly. Second, I analyzed the entire text of the given blocks of each curriculum with the help of sequential analysis, a sociolinguistic method reconstructing the latent meaning structures of the text (Oevermann 1979, 1993; Wernet 2000). This form of analysis engages with the basic meaning structures of the texts and reconstructs the messages the text provides to the reader. In order to aid the language analysis I introduce some contextual knowledge, such as the current political situation, school structure, and so on (for a more detailed description of method application, see Zimenkova 2008).

I used sequential analysis in order to describe which dimensions are central for addressing the global issues in the curricula. The open method of sequential analysis was essential in order to detect possible different dimensions of global issues addressed within one sequence of a curriculum. For instance, the Federal standards for upper school geography address, among others, the following goals for geography learning:

> Learning basic termini in geography, gaining knowledge about geographical specifics of nature, population and economy, industry and agriculture of different territories; learning about Russia in its whole geographical diversity and integrity; about the environment, the ways of maintaining its sustainability and rational usage...[to] raise love towards one's own locality, one's region and one's country; educating towards mutual understanding with other peoples; education towards ecological culture and careful handling of the environment. (MinObrNauki RF 2004e, 1[5])

This sequence addresses different aspects: not only emotional attachment to locality, emotional attachment to the country as connected to the other dimensions of emotional attachment, and multicultural understanding, but also national complexity and consolidation as well as ecological consciousness and culture. Analysis has shown that some of these aspects also play an important role in other curricula and some do not. After completing sequential analysis of all curricula sequences, categories of the detected dimensions, comprising subcategories, were built and put together in overreaching categories (Mayring 1997; see the list of the categories provided in the notes).

Besides category building, the sequential analysis has shown another important dimension of the curricula: the reconstruction of the implicit structures of the text that demonstrated the modes of self-perception as suggested to the learner. These modes, described with the help of positioning theory (Bora and Hausendorf 2006), are essential for the argument toward the articulation of messages and roles suggested or assigned to the learner by the curricula.

A CHALLENGING COMBINATION OF GLOBAL IDENTITY AND NATIONAL ATTACHMENT

Despite an educational reform in the Russian Federation in 2010 seeking to bring in more standardization into school education and elaborating on skills and competences of the learner (MinObrNauki RF 2011b),[6] neither the central topics relevant to global education nor their focus changed significantly. This can be seen by comparing pre-reform curricula (see list of curricula under references) and the so-called *subject orientation programs* (e.g., Kuznecov et al. 2010 a,b,c), which are consultative documents issued by the publishing house close to the Ministry of Education, *Prosveshenije*, which serves the overall planning of scholastic subjects for all school levels.

Below the thematic blocks, subjects and foci that address global issues in Russian curricula, as they were detected by the analysis, are listed. Some of the subcategories are listed in more than one over-reaching category. One of the interesting results of my analysis, despite some unsurprising subject-related differentiation, is the interconnection of subjects in relation to environmental culture, responsibility, and patriotism. Economic, political, and environmental changes connected to globalization are addressed in the curricula either *not at all* or from the vantage point of Russia as a global *economic* actor. Hence, even when global issues are addressed in the curricula, they remain strongly oriented toward the nation-state[7] and address learners as *Russian* citizens.

The thematic blocks that refer to global issues, retrieved from an analysis of Russian curricula for civics and law and humanities as well as from educational standards for elementary and secondary schools, can be summarized thematically,[8] as in Table 12.1.

Within these thematic blocks different modes of self-perceptions ("positionings" as termed by Bora and Hausendorf 2006) in regard to global issues could be identified with the help of sequential analysis. Those relevant to the *nation-state,* or to positioning of learners as *national* citizens, are me as a citizen of a global player country,

- me as a Russian citizen, knowing Russia's scope and role in solving global problems,
- me as a possible part of international conflicts,
- me as a citizen of a multiethnic, multicultural country/setting, and
- me as a member of civic, ethnic, cultural, (multi-)confessional society as a result of history.

In these positionings the learner is called upon to understand, at least on this level, her activities in a global context as a *Russian citizen.* Her reference is given as the nation-state (not a locality); she is made aware of the (military) conflicts, economic disparities, and environmental problems in the world. She is positioned as needing to have a strong attachment to her country. Her country is constructed as responsible to intervene in the world's problems and to try to solve

Table 12.1   Thematic summary of curriculum analysis

1. Legal components of global issues

1.1. International protection of human rights

1.2. International law under conditions of war and military conflicts, protection of war victims

1.3. Bodies of international law

1.4. Ecological legislation (violations of ecological norms, rights, and responsibilities)

1.5. *Competences:* Being aware of human rights and their international protection, knowing international legislation

2. Civics, culture, geography

2.1. International, intercultural, interreligious, and interethnic relations

2.2. Environmental culture

2.3. Russia in the world. Russia's position among other countries. Characteristics of economic, political, and cultural relations in Russia

2.4. *Competences:* Experience relations with people of other nationalities, be able to interrelate in a constructive manner with people from different cultures who hold different values, be able to share environmental culture, [development of] self-perception as a member of a civic, ethno-cultural, multi-confessional society that has emerged historically, be able to use knowledge on historical development of social norms and cultures in international communication, and be tolerant toward representatives of other cultures and nations

2.5. *Competences from general curriculum standards:* Understand global problems of modernity, maintain world peace

2.6. *Competences curriculum for elementary school:* Understand the unity of the nature, basics of ecological literacy, patriotism, tolerance, and ethical behavior in the world of nature and people

3. Ecology and the environment

3.1. Geo-ecological problems

3.2. Environmental situation in the modern world (imperative question: how to save nature)

3.3. Environmental legislation (violations of environmental norms, rights, and responsibilities)

3.4. Environmental culture

3.5. Basics of environmental literacy

3.6. *Competences general upper school curriculum:* Know main scientific theories about global climate change; evaluate the effects of climate change for different regions and countries. *Competences:* Learners should have their own position on the subject

4. Patriotism

4.1. Russia's participation in the formation of the global international legal system. Russia and the challenges of globalization

4.2. Self-perception as a member of a civic, ethno-cultural, multi-confessional society that has emerged historically

4.3. Educating toward love for one's own locality, region, and country; mutual understanding with other peoples, environmental culture, and respect for the environment

Continued

Table 12.1 Continued

4.4. Educating toward common global values in the context of Russian citizens identity formation

4.5. Russia's efforts to take up a deserved[9] place in world society

4.6. Russia's capacities for solving global problems of humankind

5. Global political issues

5.1. World economy, Russia's participation in world trade

5.2. Global politics and Russia's role in them

5.3. Russia's place in world society; Russia's capacities for solving global problems of humankind

6. Economics: Trade, global issues, national interests

6.1. International trade, state politics in the area of international trade, global economic problems

6.2. Specifics of Russia's current economy

6.3. *Competences*: Name global economic problems, globalization of world economy (both in combination with knowledge of Russia's economic system), name examples of mutually profitable international trade

7. Theory and history

7.1. Development of new ideologies (incl. development of the constitutional state), emergence of youth, pacifist, environmental, and feminist movements, problems of political terrorism

7.2. The emergence of world society and the basis of international legislation. The UN, the end of colonialism and the formation of the "third world," the beginning of European integration processes, the European Union, problems of the national sovereignty in a global world

7.3. Globalization and emergence of a global space of information, the contradictions of globalization

Source: Own research.

them. However, this responsibility originates from Russia's role as a global player, not from historical responsibilities. Thus, Russia's motivation for solving global problems is not a matter of *compensation*, but simply the present-day responsibility of those in power. As the orientation program for secondary schools puts it in its description of learner competencies: "The student is capable of explaining Russia's capacities for solving the current global problems of humankind" (Savinov 2011, 88).

If we take the definition of *global citizenship education* or *global learning* given above, we cannot consider the curricula just described to be examples of *political global citizenship education*, because political global citizenship education would address learner agency, rights, and duties in a global context, and would give learners an idea of the powers at large in global processes and of their own power and powerlessness in terms of these processes (Gallagher 2008). The curricula and programs analyzed provide learners with the image of belonging to a strong global player that knows how to solve problems. Young citizens are therefore called upon to support national attempts to solve global problems. They are not called upon to reflect on the powers at large or on their own ideas, power, and powerlessness with respect to global issues.

Citizenship education is a potent instrument for developing loyalties, and is used mostly with the goal of educating functioning rather than critically engaged citizens (see Hedtke 2012; Hedtke and Zimenkova 2012). Nation-states can hardly be expected to develop politically active citizens who are ready to choose between different loyalties. However, this point is only part of the explanation why particular ways are used to address global issues in national curricula. Another possible explanation draws from the debate on the development, opportunities, and limits of global citizenship, which requires global political institutions and new forms of participation and attachment (see, e.g., Davidson 2000; Kivisto and Faist 2007). So who should educate global citizens and for which not-yet-settled forms of global participation should they be prepared?

EDUCATING SUPERWOMAN AND SUPERMAN: THE ETHICAL RESPONSIBILITY OF THE INDIVIDUAL LEARNER

Confusingly for learners, attachment to the nation-state is only *one* of two important components central to global learning and global education in Russia. Despite the nation-state orientation, which is not very surprising within the framework of national education, there is an implicit consensus—or as Antonio Nóvoa (2002) would probably call it, a "planet speak" of global learning—in the curricula, policies, and teaching materials. This grand narrative of global learning comprises ethical components: teaching people to live together, share the same resources, care for the same natural environment, understand themselves as part of a bigger setting, support the idea of sustainability, and take on responsibility for future generations. For example, the Russian orientation program for general upper school education addresses global topics in a very Russia-centered way, while it turns away from nation-state attachment when, out of the blue, learners are asked questions such as "how can nature be preserved?" (Savinov 2011, 258). Learners are thus confronted with questions such as am

I supposed to save nature as a *Russian* citizen? As a world citizen? As a human being?

However, global issues in curricula are not addressed solely from the vantage point of the nation-state, rather curricula switch between national and global perspectives. The most interesting aspect of the global perspective is that learners are consistently addressed as *individually* responsible for solving global problems. For example, we can observe that despite patriotic and national biases, the Russian curricula and state-approved teaching programs work with a global concept of ethics. The sequential analysis of the curricula and education programs identified the following modes of self-perception. The learner is encouraged to see herself as

- a global person and keeper of world peace;
- a holder of legal rights, capable of acting internationally;
- someone who protects the environment and upholds international environmental legislation;
- someone who knows how to act sustainably; and
- someone who possesses knowledge on the historical development of social norms and cultures, can participate in international communication, and is tolerant toward representatives of other cultures and nations.

These modes of self-perceptions or self-positionings (Bora and Hausendorf 2006) address the power of the individual learner to improve world conditions. Although legislation and legal rights are mentioned, implying a legal and political framework for individual actions, the focus is more on what I would call *ethical* rather than *political* participation, and hence the curricula analyzed cannot be seen of those providing global citizenship education as *political* education. The role of the citizen as defined here does not include critical reflection, and does not necessarily involve reflection on powers, but provides a ready-made framework of action for ethical world citizens *without* considering the possibility of action beyond national borders limited by legal frameworks of citizenship.

This kind of learner instruction, taking place from a specific position of power (derived from national belonging) and of powerful individuals, is likely to result in *confusion for* citizens. Learning is divided into two main agendas, such as to be part of a global player country with influence and the power to solve global problems, and to act *individually* to confront complex global issues. This global individual responsibility does not, however, relieve the learner from her national attachment; instead it makes this attachment implicit. The learner is supposed to act *because* she is a part of a certain political entity, but on an individual basis and seemingly without that country's support. These phenomena can also be observed in many other countries, making the tendencies delineated here generalizable (cf. Schissler and Soysal 2005).[10]

Learners are addressed as active citizens, loyal to the nation-state and acting on global issues out of *moral and individual* obligation, which supports notions drawn upon in the idea of development aid and leads to the reproduction of (post)colonial thinking (see Andreotti 2006). The helper narratives (Hussey and Curnow 2013) might be seen as a consequence of this kind of implicit nation-state attachment and nation-state power talk, which was detected in the curricula and programs analyzed. The learner is called to act individually while facing global issues; simultaneously the *powerful-global-player* narrative, describing the learner's country of citizenship, does not open up the framework for discussing the consequences and origins of this very state power (Gallagher 2008). The learner is not called to reflect on the interconnectedness of global problems and issues as those are *not* to be *solved* through the power-weakness, helper-helped relationships, but rather *resulting* from imbalances of powers (cf. Hussey and Curnow 2013). Rather, the combination of belonging to a global player and being individually responsible cannot but result in the motivation to *help* those "disempowered" without elaborating on *why* those considered to be in need of help are disempowered and *who* disempowers them. Learners' self-understanding as political subjects is not a part of this kind of approach to education about global issues. Addressing learners' *actions* strongly, the approach excludes critical reflection on necessity and suggested forms of such actions.

National curricula do not aim to produce citizens able to *detach* themselves from national citizenship loyalty. At the same time it produces "ethical global helpers" who perceive their global responsibility primarily on economic (Mitchell 2007) and environmental terms. The superficial commonality of the two approaches—addressing learners as *national citizens* and as *globally responsible ethical people*— and their differentiation can be rather confusing in a learning setting. Is the learner a part of a strong global player country capable of improving living conditions across the globe? Or is the learner herself responsible for maintaining peace, saving the environment, and helping other countries to overcome global economic disparities? Each of the perspectives can as well be used to shift the responsibility: an ethical individual might expect the strong nation to act, and the citizens might see global action as ethical, not citizens' responsibility. The very idea of responsibility might even disappear between these two approaches, giving a person and perhaps the nation a comfortable feeling that no action is required on their behalf.

GLOBALIZATION PROCESSES AND LEARNER REALITIES: MAIN CHALLENGES FOR THE EDUCATIONAL SETTINGS

Turning back to the definitions of *global learning* and *global citizenship education* suggested in this chapter, one can say that the former cannot be considered education for political global citizenship as soon as it instrumentalizes the learner. If learning suggests *ready-made* evaluations of global processes, *predefines* learners' self-perceptions as placed within the world, and develops means of global participation, instead of providing the learner with the capacity to make these evaluations for *herself*, and decide, whether, why, and how she wants to act on global issues, it cannot be considered *a political education* (Zimenkova 2012). But is this only a matter of definition? And for whom is it a problem?

First, positioning the learner as a helper who should participate in development aid activities creates a divided image of a world. The learner belongs here to those in power, responsible discretely for solving the problems of and for the *others*. Moreover, this image suggests hierarchies of participation and action. It deprives "those in need of help" of political participation. The learner is positioned as the strong and active person, the *other*—whoever they are—as passive recipients. This hierarchical picture of the winners and losers of globalization processes[11] cannot but exclude all learners who are directly or indirectly caught up on the nonprofitable side of globalization processes (Solano-Campos 2014). Hence, let me turn back here to the first question posed at the beginning of the chapter: How far and *how* are challenges to the nation-state sovereignty (Held 2011) visible in the analyzed approaches toward global education? As I have shown in my analysis of the *global-player* and *power* discourse, state sovereignty is not threatened as individual actions are necessarily preluded and heightened by the state power narrative.

Second, without addressing power, contradictions, and (unsolvable) conflicts, global education creates a simplified view of the world that conceals democratic dissatisfactions (Sack 2012) and hence creates a world in which buying a fair trade T-shirt (and thus consuming) is a sufficient action for improving working conditions in the producing countries and hence an effective way to contribute to the reduction of global disparities. Thinking of the question of loyalties (Nussbaum 1996), as addressed by the curricula analyzed, and of the conflicting messages to the learner emerging out of citizens' different loyalties and attachments, aid and helper narratives successfully disguise these contradictions. In other words, as far as conflicts are not explicated and the modes of problem solution from the position of power are suggested to the learner, the *conflicts of loyalties* do not appear. In nonpolitical global learning, instead, of a form of *compatibility* between loyalties to nation-state and the globe is suggested. In this sense this learning approach *simulates* a nonconflicting form of cosmopolitanism.

Appealing to a morally ideal and assumedly harmonious picture is only, at first glance, the easiest way to approach difficult global topics in a learning situation. One of the examples reported by my student in teachers' instruction is her experience with a teaching unit on coltan mining. This unit was meant to reflect on the workers' living conditions and on the contradiction between the necessity of mining for the workers' families, the health dangers of coltan mining, and the deforestation of the region. Instead of controversially discussing the issues, students (sixth grade) presented posters on a charity activity that suggested sending old cell phones to Africa, so that coltan mining and deforesting would no longer be necessary and "sweet gorilla babies" would be saved. It was not possible for the teacher student to bring the class back to a discussion of the conflicts between the shortage of workplaces, poverty, working conditions, environmental protection, and consumption. The class was glad to have found a "happy-end" solution: everybody has new phones and feels good because they have saved the forest. This anecdotal situation is an example of the effects of the harmonizing, nonpolitical helper discourse described above in the curricula analysis.

Reflection on both types of global education, one *with a political citizenship component* and one *without*, could help teachers and learners to frame the teaching material, curricula, and discussions, and reflect on the choices they make between comfortable and cozy solutions and uncomfortable discussions on power and political agency. The question of whether the teaching materials, concepts, and curricula address the *contradicting interests* active in global issues can help to decide whether a unit/material/curriculum is to be understood as political global citizenship education or nonpolitical global learning. It is not enough to demonstrate to the learner different interests within global issues if, at the same time, the learner has been placed by the curriculum on one side of the hierarchy (we as a global power, we as helpers). Learners must be empowered to know which powers have which expectations on *them as citizens*, and be enabled to make decisions on their own.

CONCLUSION

The curricula analyzed suggest very different answers to mine earlier to the question of what kind of global (citizenship) identities are promoted through Russian education. In the Russian curricula the notion of the "global ethical self" (Mitchell 2003, 399) is placed at the front, with a strong (and seemingly nonconflicting) attachment to the nation-state. Despite the fact that there are also elements of the global ecological citizen (Van Steenbergen 1994) and the global reformer (Falk 1994), these elements are *subordinated* to the loyalty and self-conception of a *nation-state citizen*.

Global citizenship education can be introduced in both types of global education (from the position of the nation-state and from the position of individual responsibility), demonstrated in this chapter. In the first type, it can help the learner to reflect on her attachment to her country within global processes and empower her to be compliant or incompliant with global political actions (Gallagher 2008). In the second type, it can support students not only to act, but also to ask why they act the way they do. How do they position themselves in the global system? Do they contribute to the division of the world through their actions? Are they capable of thinking up other actions? Who really profits from their actions? *Global citizenship education* with politics could help learners to understand which actors are trying to place their responsibility for global issues on learners, and why.

Is educating global citizens possible at all, given the notion of the essentiality of curricula for *national* socialization (cf. Paasi 1996)? The article demonstrated on the basis of empirical analysis the inherent contradiction between education of *global* and *national* citizens. Still it is a fact that most of the national education curricula do touch upon questions of global citizen's responsibilities. The advance of globalization, as well as environmental and technological developments, increases the need for globally thinking citizens in all nations. Citizens who are ready to support or even *promote* unpopular political decisions and make sacrifices for fellow-world-citizens are needed to solve the current global situations and problems. And hence, even *nation-states* need them, for the unpopular political decisions, for example, in favor of environment, agreed upon on a supranational level, are being put into force within single nation-states and affect nation-states citizens. And if nation-states want globally thinking political subjects, they need only allow them to appear.

ACKNOWLEDGMENT

I am very thankful to Zsuzsa Millei and Robert Imre for their intensive editing work and support, giving me essential ideas for designing this text; Martina Barsuhn for her sensitivity to the topic; and Katrin Alida Müller for her support in final corrections.

NOTES

1. For many centuries and in different contexts women were excluded from (full) citizenship. This chapter consistently uses the female form when speaking about citizens of all genders as a contribution to reflections on the history of female citizenship.
2. Comparable developments are described for Asian education by S. Han, "The lifelong learning ecosystem in Korea: Evolution of learning capitalism?," *International Journal of Lifelong Education* 27 (5) (2008).
3. In the year 2010, a new federal educational standard was introduced (MinObrNauki RF 2010). The new legislation on education (Federal Law on Education in Russian Federation, standart.edu.ru/attachment.aspx?id=546) went into effect on December 26, 2012.
4. The federal standards of education of the Russian Federation for all school forms can be found under http://минобрнауки.рф/%D0%B 4%D0%BE%D0%BA%D1%83%D0%BC%D0%B5%D0%BD%D1%82% D1%8B/543 in effect since 2010, accessed on June 5, 2014.
5. All translations of Russian curricula done by the author.
6. For more on Russian educational reforms and meanings of standards and standardization in educational discourse, see, for example, E. Minina, "Educational standards reform in Russia: Why doesn't the telephone ring?," *InterDisciplines* 5 (2) (2014).
7. However, in the context of *cultural* topics curricula switch to addressing a learner as a world citizen in her ethical responsibility and almost esoteric connection to the nature.
8. Due to the limited space I cannot include references to all curricula corresponding to each of the categories. Interested readers may request them by email.
9. All the contents refer to the texts of the curricula and not to the author's opinion.
10. I am very thankful to my colleague Margarita Jeliazkova, who supported me in a brief analysis of the twelfth-grade Bulgarian curriculum, "The world and the person" (Uchebna programa po sviat i lichnost za XII klas, http://www.see-educoop.net/education_in/ pdf/prog_svet-bul-blg-t06.pdf, accessed July 4, 2014).

11. And this problem would not be solved even through the introduction of the narrative of collective responsibility in postcolonial states.

REFERENCES

Adams, M., and J. Raisborough. 2008. "What can sociology say about fair trade? Class reflexivity and ethical consumption." *Sociology* 42: 1165–1182.

Andreotti, V. 2006. "Soft versus critical global citizenship education." *Policy & Practice: A Development Education Review* 3 (Autumn): 40–51.

Banks, J. A. 2009. "Multicultural education: Dimensions and paradigms." In *The Routledge International Companion to Multicultural Education*, edited by James A. Banks, 7–23. New York and London: Routledge.

Bora, A., and H. Hausendorf. 2006. "Communicating citizenship and social positioning: Theoretical concepts." In *Analysing Citizenship Talk*, edited by A. Bora and H. Hausendorf, 23–49. Amsterdam and Philadelphia, PA: John Benjamins.

Davidson, A. 2000. "Democracy, class and citizenship in a globalizing world." In *Citizenship and Democracy in a Global Era*, edited by Andrew Vandenberg, 110–120. New York: St. Martin's Press.

Davies, L. 2006. "Global citizenship: Abstraction or framework for action?" *Educational Review* 58 (1): 5–25.

Delanty, G. 2006. "The cosmopolitan imagination: Critical cosmopolitanism and social theory." *The British Journal of Sociology* 57: 25–47.

Donaldson, S., and W. Kymlicka. 2011. *Zoopolis: A Political Theory of Animal Rights*. Oxford: Oxford University Press.

Dower, N. 2002. "Global citizenship: Yes or no?" In *Global Citizenship. A Critical Reader*, edited by N. Dower and J. Williams, 30–40. Edingburgh: Edingburgh University Press.

Faist, T., and J. Gerdes. 2009. "Doppelte Staatsbürgerschaft: Loyalitäten und Zugehörigkeiten." *Terra cognita: Schweizerische Zeitschrift zu Integration und Migration* 15: 52–57.

Falk, R. 1994. "The making of global citizenship." In *The Conditions of Citizenship*, edited by B. van Steenbergen, 127–140. London, Thousand Oaks, CA, and New Delhi: Sage.

Fragoso, A., and P. Guimaraes. 2010. "Is there still a place for social emancipation in public policies? Envisioning the future of adult education in Portugal." *European Journal for Research on the Education and Learning of Adults* 1 (1–2): 17–31.

Gallagher, M. 2008. "Foucault, power and participation." *International Journal of Childrens' Rights* 16: 395–406.

Glaesser, J., and B. Cooper. 2011. "Selectivity and flexibility in the German secondary school system: A configurational analysis of recent data from the German socio-economic panel." *European Sociological Review* 27 (5): 570–585.

Golmohamad, M. 2009. "Education for world citizenship: Beyond national allegiance." *Educational Philosophy and Theory* 41: 466–486.

Han, S. 2008. "The lifelong learning ecosystem in Korea: Evolution of learning capitalism?" *International Journal of Lifelong Education* 27 (5): 21–28.

Heater, D. 2004. *World Citizenship: Cosmopolitan Thinking and Its Opponents.* London: Bloomsbury Academic.

Hedtke, R. 2012. "Who is afraid of non-conformist youth? The right to dissent and to not participate." In *Education for Civic and Political Participation: A Critical Approach,* edited by R. Hedtke and T. Zimenkova, 54–78. London and New York: Routledge.

Hedtke, R., and T. Zimenkova (eds.). 2012. *Education for Civic and Political Participation: A Critical Approach.* London and New York: Routledge.

Held, D. 2011. "Cosmopolitanism, democracy and the global order." In *The Ashgate Research Companion to Cosmopolitanism,* edited by Maria Rovisco and Magdalena, 163–177. Ashgate and Farnham: Nowicka.

———. 2002. "Law of states, law of people". *Legal Theory* 8: 1–44.

Hussey, I., and J. Curnow. 2013. "Fair trade, neocolonial developmentalism, and recialized power relations." *Interface: A Journal for and about Social Movements* 5 (1): 40–68.

Jensen, O. 2000. "Zur gemeinsamen Verfertigung von Text in der Forschungssituation." *Forum: Qualitative Sozialforschung/Forum: Qualitative Social Research* 1 (2): Art. 11. http://nbn-resolving.de/urn:nbn:de:0114-fqs0002112. Accessed July 15, 2014.

Kivisto, P., and T. Faist. 2009. "The boundaries of citizenship: Dual, nested and global." In *Politics of Globalization,* edited by S. Dasgupta and J. N. Pieterse, 356–376. New Delhi: Sage.

Kivisto, P., and T. Faist. 2007. *Citizenship: Discourse, Theory and Transnational Prospects.* Oxford: Blackwell.

Koopmans, R., P. Statham, M. Guigni, and F. Passy. 2005. "Migrants between transnationalism and national citizenship." In *Contested Citizenship: Immigration and Cultural Diversity in Europe,* edited by R. Koopmans, P. Statham, M. Guigni, and F. Passy, 107–145. Minneapolis: University of Minnesota Press.

Linklater, A. 1998. "Cosmopolitan citizenship." *Citizenship Studies* 2 (1): 23–41.

Mackert, J., and H.-P. Müller. 2000. "Der soziologische Gehalt moderner Staatsbürgerschaft: Probleme und Perspektiven eines umkämpften Konzeptes." In *Citizenship: Soziologie der Staatsbürgerschaft,* edited by J. Mackert and H.-P. Müller, 9–42. Wiesbaden: Westdeutscher Verlag.

Martell, L. 2007. "The third wave in globalization theory." *International Studies Review* 9: 173–196.

Mayring, P. 1983/1997. *Qualitative Inhaltsanalyse: Grundlagen und Techniken.* Weinheim: Deutscher Studien Verlag.

Minina, E. 2014. "Educational standards reform in Russia: Why doesn't the telephone ring?" *InterDisciplines* 5 (2).

Mitchell, K. 2007. "Geographies of identity: The intimate cosmopolitan." *Progress in Human Geography* 31 (5): 706–720.

———. 2003. "Educating the national citizen in neoliberal times: From the multicultural self to the strategic cosmopolitan." *Transactions of the Institute of British Geographers* NS 28: 387–403.

Nikel, J., and A. Reid. 2006. "Environmental education in three German-speaking countries: Tensions and challenges for research and development." *Environmental Education Research* 12 (1): 129–148.

Norris, P. (ed.). 2011. *Democratic Deficit: Critical Citizens Revisited.* New York: Cambridge University Press.

Nóvoa, A. 2002. "Ways of thinking about education in Europe." In *Fabricating Europe. The Formation of an Education Space*, edited by A. Nóvoa and M. Lawn, 131–155. Dordrecht: Kluwer Academic.

Nussbaum, M. 1996. "Patriotism and cosmopolitanism." *Boston Review* 19 (5): 3–16.

Oevermann, U. 1993. "Die objektive Hermeneutik als unverzichtbare methodologische Grundlage für die Analyse von Subjektivität." In *Wirklichkeit im Deutungsprozess: Verstehen und Methoden in den Kultur- und Sozialwissenschaften*, 106–189. Frankfurt am Main: Suhrkamp.

Oevermann, U., T. Allert, E. Konau, and J. Krambeck. 1979. "Die Methodologie einer 'objektiven Hermeneutik' und ihre allgemeine forschungslogische Bedeutung in den Sozialwissenschaften." In *Inter-pretative Verfahren in den Sozial- und Textwissenschaften*, edited by H.-G. Soeffner, 352–434. Stuttgart: Metzler.

Paasi, A. 1996. *Territories, Boundaries and Consciousness: The Changing Geographies of the Finnish-Russian Border.* London: John Wiley.

Pfaff-Czarnecka, J. 2011. "From 'identity' to 'belonging' in social research: Plurality, social boundaries, and the politics of the self." In *Ethnicity, Citizenship and Belonging: Practices, Theory and Spatial Dimensions*, edited by S. Albiez, N. Castro, L. Jüssen, and E. Youkhana, 199–219. Madrid: Iberoamericana.

Reinhoffer, B. 2005. "Lehrkräfte geben Auskunft über ihren Unterricht: Ein systematischer Vorschlag zur deduktiven und induktiven Kategorienbildung in der Unterrichtsforschung." In *Die Praxis der Qualitativen Inhaltsanalyse*, edited by P. Mayring and M. Gläser-Zikuda, 123–141. Weinheim und Basel: Beltz.

Robinson, W. 2007. "Theories of globalization." In *The Blackwell Companion to Globalization*, edited by G. Ritzer, 125–143. Oxford: Blackwell.

Sack, D. 2012. "Dealing with dissatisfaction: Role, skills and meta-competencies of participatory citizenship education." In *Education for Civic and Political Participation: A Critical Approach*, edited by R. Hedtke and T. Zimenkova, 13–35. London and New York: Routledge.

Saiz, A. V. 2005. "Globalisation, cosmopolitanism and ecological citizenship." *Environmental Politics* 14 (2): 163–178.

Schissler, H., and Y. N. Soysal (eds.). 2005. *The Nation, Europe, and the World: Textbooks and Curricula in Transition.* New York: Berghahn Books.

Seybol, H., and W. Rieß. 2006. "Research in environmental education and education for sustainable development in Germany: The state of the art." *Environmental Education Research* 12 (1): 47–63.

Skrbiš, Z., and I. Woodward. 2011. "Cosmopolitan openness". In *The Ashgate Research Companion to Cosmopolitanism*, edited by M. Rovisco and M. Nowicka, 53–68. Ashgate: Farnham.

Solano-Campos, A. 2014. "Refugee children saying and doing citizenship: Global-local tensions and common civic spaces in an international school in the United States." *Citizenship Teaching and Learning* 9 (2): 135–156.

Turner, B. 2000a. "Grundzüge einer Theorie der Staatsbürgerschaft." In *Citizenship: Soziologie der Staatsbürgerschaft*, edited by J. Mackert and H.-P. Müller, 229–263. Wiesbaden: Westdeutscher Verlag.

———. 2000b. "Outline of theory of human rights." In *Citizenship and Social Theory*, edited by B. Turner, 162–190. London: Sage.

Van Steenbergen, B. 1994. "Towards a global ecological citizen." In *The Conditions of Citizenship*, edited by B. van Steenbergen, 141–152. London, Thousand Oaks, CA, and New Dehli: Sage.

Wernet, A. 2000. *Einführung in die Interpretationstechnik der objektiven Hermeneutik*. Opladen: Leske + Budrich.

Zimenkova, T. 2012. "Active citizenship as harmonious co-existense? About the political in participatory education." In *Education for Civic and Political Participations: A Critical Approach*, edited by R. Hedtke and T. Zimenkova, 36–53. London and New York: Routledge.

———. 2008. "Citizenship through faith and feelings: Defining citizenship in citizenship education: An exemplary textbook analysis." *Journal of Social Science Education* 9 (1): 81–111.

RUSSIAN CURRICULA AND PROGRAMS

Federal Standards in Effect until 2010 (all accessed on July 9, 2014)

MinObrNauki RF. 2004a. "Federal standards for high school advanced level in geography." In *Federal'nyj komponent gosudarstvennogo standarta obshhego obrazovanija. Chast' I. Nachal'noe obshhee obrazovanie.* Osnovnoe obshhee obrazovanie, Moscow: Ministerstvo obrazovanija Rossijskoj Federacii. http://window.edu.ru/resource/293/39293/files/46.pdf

MinObrNauki RF. 2004b. "Federal standards for high school advanced level in history." In *Federal'nyj komponent gosudarstvennogo standarta obshhego obrazovanija. Chast' I. Nachal'noe obshhee obrazovanie.* Osnovnoe obshhee obrazovanie, Moscow: Ministerstvo obrazovanija Rossijskoj Federacii. http://www.school.edu.ru/dok_edu.asp?ob_no=14415

MinObrNauki RF. 2004c. "Federal standards for high school in law (advanced level)." In *Federal'nyj komponent gosudarstvennogo standarta obshhego obrazovanija. Chast' I. Nachal'noe obshhee obrazovanie.* Osnovnoe

obshhee obrazovanie, Moscow: Ministerstvo obrazovanija Rossijskoj Federacii. http://window.edu.ru/resource/291/39291/files/44.pdf
MinObrNauki RF. 2004d. "Federal standards for high school in law (basic level)." *In Federal'nyj komponent gosudarstvennogo standarta obshhego obrazovanija. Chast' I. Nachal'noe obshhee obrazovanie.* Osnovnoe obshhee obrazovanie, Moscow: Ministerstvo obrazovanija Rossijskoj Federacii. http://www.school.edu.ru/dok_edu.asp?ob_no=14423
MinObrNauki RF. 2004e. "Federal standards for upper school geography." In *Federal'nyj komponent gosudarstvennogo standarta obshhego obrazovanija. Chast' I. Nachal'noe obshhee obrazovanie.* Osnovnoe obshhee obrazovanie, Moscow: Ministerstvo obrazovanija Rossijskoj Federacii. http://www.school.edu.ru/dok_edu.asp?ob_no=14400
MinObrNauki RF. 2004f. "Federal standards for upper school in civic education (including law and economics)." In *Federal'nyj komponent gosudarstvennogo standarta obshhego obrazovanija. Chast' I. Nachal'noe obshhee obrazovanie.* Osnovnoe obshhee obrazovanie, Moscow: Ministerstvo obrazovanija Rossijskoj Federacii. http://www.school.edu. asp?ob_no=14416
MinObrNauki RF. 2004g. "Federal standards for upper school in civic education (including law and economics), advanced level." In *Federal'nyj komponent gosudarstven-nogo standarta obshhego obrazovanija. Chast' I. Nachal'noe obshhee obrazovanie.* Osnovnoe obshhee obrazovanie, Moscow: Ministerstvo obrazovanija Rossijskoj Federacii. http://www. school.edu.ru/dok_edu.asp?ob_no=14417
MinObrNauki RF. 2004h. "Federal standards for upper school in history." In *Federal'nyj komponent gosudarstvennogo standarta obshhego obrazovanija. Chast' I. Nachal'noe obshhee obrazovanie.* Osnovnoe obshhee obrazovanie, Moscow: Ministerstvo obrazovanija Rossijskoj Federacii. http://www.school.edu.ru/dok_edu.asp?ob_no=14396

Federal Standards in Effect since 2012

MinObrNauki RF. 2011a. Federal'nyj gosudarstvennyj obrazovatel'nyj standart nachal'nogo obshhego obrazovanija (Federal State Educational Standard for General Education). Accessed June 5, 2014. http://минобрнауки.рф/%D0%B4%D0%BE%D0%BA%D1%83%D0%BC%D0%B5%D0%BD%D1%82%D1%8B/922/%D1%84%D0%B0%D0%B9%D0%BB/748/%D0%A4%D0%93%D0%9E%D0%A1_%D0%9D%D0%9E%D0%9E.pdf
MinObrNauki RF. 2011b. Federal'nyj gosudarstvennyj obrazovatel'nyj standart obshhego obrazovanija (Federal State Educational Standard for General Education). Accessed July 5, 2014. http://минобрнауки.рф/%D0%B4%D0%BE%D0%BA%D1%83%D0%BC%D0%B5%D0%BD%D1%82D1%8B/938/%D1%84%D0%B0%D0%B9%D0%BB/749/10.12.17-%D0%9F%D1%80%D0%B8%D0%BA%D0%B0%D0%B7_1897.pdf

Subject Orientation Programs Corresponding to the Federal Standards in Effect since 2012

Kuznecov, A. A., M. V. Ryzhakov, and A. M. Kondakov. 2010a. *Primernye programmy po- uchebnym predmetam. Geografija. 6–9 klassy.* Moscow: Prosveshhenie.

Kuznecov, A. A., M. V. Ryzhakov, and A. M. Kondakov. 2010b. *Primernye programmy po- uchebnym predmetam. Obshhestvoznanie.* Moscow: Prosveshhenie.

Kuznecov, A. A., M. V. Ryzhakov, and A. M. Kondakov. 2010c. *Primernye programmy os-novnogo obshhego obrazovanija. Istorija. 5–9 klassy.* Moscow: Prosveshhenie.

Savinov, E.S. (ed.). 2011. *Primernaja osnovnaja obrazovatel'naja programma obrazovatel'-nogo uchrezhdenija. Osnovnaja shkola.* Moscow: Prosveshhenie. http://standart.edu.ru/catalog.aspx?CatalogId=6400. Accessed June 6, 2014.

CONTRIBUTORS

Bree Akesson is currently assistant professor of Social Work at Wilfrid Laurier University. Her program of research focuses broadly on international child protection issues, ranging from micro-level understandings of the experiences of families affected by war to macro-level studies on child protection systems strengthening. She is currently conducting research with Syrian refugees in Jordan, Lebanon, and Turkey.
Email: bakesson@wlu.ca

Lucy Hopkins is a lecturer in children and family studies at Edith Cowan University, Perth, Australia. She works on "global" childhoods and issues of ethics and subjectivity in discourses of childhood, discourses of "whiteness," and post-structuralist and feminist theories. She is currently undertaking research in Bhutan on childhood, education, and poverty.
Email: lucy.hopkins@ecu.edu.au

Robert Imre is senior lecturer in politics and international relations at The University of Newcastle, Australia. His research interests concern the intersection of social media and the construction of the self, and political radicalization. He has published in a variety of international academic journals. He is currently working on a research project in Finland.
Email: Robert.Imre@newcastle.edu.au

Mikko Joronen holds a PhD in political geography and is currently working as a postdoctoral researcher at the University of Tampere, School of Management. His publications consist of themes around ontology, globalization, neoliberalism, political power, and geographical theory. He is currently working with questions of governmentality and politics of exception in relation to Israel's occupation of Palestinian territories.
Email: mikko.joronen@uta.fi

Trish Lunt teaches children's literature analysis and criticism at Deakin University, Melbourne, at undergraduate and postgraduate

levels. She is completing a PhD that considers spatialities of the national and the notional in contemporary Australian picture books featuring asylum seekers and migrants. She has previously published in *Papers: Explorations into Children's Literature*.
Email: trish.lunt@deakin.edu.au

Marguerita Magennis is a member of the British Psychological Society, an ABA Therapist, and lecturer in the area of early childhood, pedagogy, and psychology. She is currently lecturing in Portobello Institute, Dublin, in conjunction with London Metropolitan University and Mary Immaculate College, Limerick, where she is completing the final year of her PhD in Education.
Email: marguerita06@gmail.com

Esther Miedema is a lecturer/researcher affiliated to the programme group Governance and Inclusive Development at the Amsterdam Institute for Social Science Research (AISSR) of the University of Amsterdam. Her main interests lie in the ways in which understandings of gender, cultural identity, and the global intersect and shape sexuality and HIV- and AIDS-related education.
Email: e.a.j.miedema@uva.nl

Zsuzsa Millei is a research fellow at SPARG, University of Tampere, Finland, and senior lecturer at The University of Newcastle, Australia. Her interdisciplinary research considers child politics, including policies for children, and children as subjects of politics and as political agents. Her current project explores how children make their place in a transnational world.
Email: Zsuzsa.Millei@uta.fi

Paula Pustulka earned a PhD in Sociology from Bangor University, the United Kingdom (2014), with a doctoral study dedicated to Polish migrant mothers parenting in the United Kingdom and Germany. She holds a researcher post at the Institute of Sociology of the Jagiellonian University. Her scholarly interests include migration/family nexus and qualitative research methodologies.
Email: paulapustulka@gmail.com

Alistair Ross is also an emeritus professor at London Metropolitan University (United Kingdom), and also hold a personal Jean Monnet European Commission Chair in Citizenship Education. His interests are in equality issues in education and young people's social and political understanding: his most recent book is

Constructions of Identities by Young New Europeans: Kaleidoscopic Selves (2014).
Email: a.ross@londonmet.ac.uk

Magdalena Ślusarczyk holds a PhD in Sociology and Bachelor of Arts in German Studies (2002). She is assistant professor in the Department of Population Studies at the Institute of Sociology of the Jagiellonian University. Her extensive research track record and academic publications covers the topics of migration, family, and educational systems.
Email: magdalena.slusarczyk@uj.edu.pl

Prasanna Srinivasan is currently working as a lecturer at Monash University. Her key research focus in the past and the present has been around respectful engagement with cultural diversity. With the use of postcolonial and critical race theories, she particularly problematizes the role of "whiteness" in colonizing and silencing cultures, especially in Australia.
Email: prasanna.srini@monash.edu

Stella Strzemecka is a PhD candidate in Sociology in the Department of Population Studies at the Institute of Sociology of the Jagiellonian University. She is currently preparing a thesis on the children of Polish immigrants growing up in Norway. Her research interests comprise childhood, migration, and virtual space.
Email: stella.strzemecka@gmail.com

Miaowei Weng is assistant professor of Spanish at Southern Connecticut State University, with a specialization in Contemporary Spanish literature and culture from a transnational perspective. Her research interests include wartime childhood memories in post-dictatorial societies, China image in Spanish writings, and the politicization of art. She has published articles in English, Spanish, and Chinese, in journals such as *Arizona Journal of Hispanic Cultural Studies* and *Journal of PLA Art Academy*. She is currently working on her manuscript on "Franco's Children" in post-dictatorial Spanish literature and cinema.
Email: Wengm2@southernct.edu

Tatjana Zimenkova is professor for diversity in teacher's training and education research at the Centre for Teacher Training at TU Dortmund University (Germany). Her research interests are citizenship education, theories of democracy and participation, diversity, and minority learners. She holds a PhD from Bielefeld University.

She is guest editor of *The Journal of Social Science Education* and has recently coedited a volume on *Education for Civic and Political Participation: A Critical Approach.*
Email: tatiana.zimenkova@tu-dortmund.de

INDEX

CPSIA information can be obtained at www.ICGtesting.com
Printed in the USA
LVOW10*1206170316

479593LV00010B/179/P